W9-BZT-700

Prefixes

ante	before	post	after
ab	away from	pre	before
ad	toward	re	back, again
ex	out of	sub	under
in	into		

Abbreviations

b.i.d.	bis in die	twice a day
t.i.d.	ter in die	three times a day
i.e.	id est	that is
e.g.	exempli gratia	for example
A.M.	ante meridiem	before noon
P.M.	post meridiem	after noon
P.S.	post scriptum	written after
N.B.	nota bene	note well

Sayings for Life

Birth	Lux sit.	Let there be light.
Graduation from kindergarten	Volo lodiculam.	I want my blankie.
Graduation from college	Homo sapientissimus.	Most wise man.
Bear market	Sic transit gloria mundi.	Thus goes the glory of the world.
Bull market	Fortuna sequatur.	Let fortune follow.
Marriage	Nuptias non concubitus, sed consensus facit.	Not cohabitation but consensus makes a marriage.
Divorce	Res tuas tibi habeto!	Take your things and go!
Death	Requiescat in pace.	Rest in peace.

Roman Numerals

I	one	X	ten	XIX	nineteen
II	two	XI	eleven	XX	twenty
III	three	XII	twelve	XL	forty
IV	four	XIII	thirteen	L	fifty
V	five	XIV	fourteen	XC	ninety
VI	six	XV	fifteen	C	one hundred
VII	seven	XVI	sixteen	D	five hundred
VIII	eight	XVII	seventeen	M	one thousand
IX	nine	XVIII	eighteen		

alpha
books

Fifty Common Latin Words

ab	away/from	legere	to read
ad	toward	loqui	to speak
ager	field	magnus	great
albus	white	malus	bad
amare	to love	mater	mother
ambulare	to walk	natare	to swim
amicus	friend	natus	born
animus	mind	nomen	name
annus	year	omnis	all
aqua	water	optimus	best
audire	to hear	pater	father
bonus	good	pax	peace
capere	to take	qui	who
currere	to run	regina	queen
deus	god	res	thing
ducere	to lead	rex	king
domus	house	ridere	to laugh
est	is	salvere	to be well
ex	out of	scribere	to write
facere	to do	semper	always
fides	faith	soror	sister
fortis	brave	sunt	are
frater	brother	terra	land
ire	to go	trans	across
laudare	to praise	valere	to be well
legere	to read	via	road
loqui	to speak	volo	to want

How to Say ...

Hello!	Salve!
Good bye!	Vale!
Go.	I (ite).
How are you?	Quid agis?
Pretty well.	Satis bene.
Please.	Quaeso.
Thank you.	Tibi gratias ago.
Excuse me.	Mihi ignosce.
Madam	Domina
Mister	Domine
Let's talk Latin.	Latine colloquamur.
Where's the bathroom?	Ubi est latrina?

THE **COMPLETE IDIOT'S GUIDE**® TO

Learning Latin

by Natalie Harwood

alpha books

A Pearson Education Company

Publisher
Marie Butler-Knight

Product Manager
Phil Kitchel

Managing Editor
Cari Luna

Senior Acquisitions Editor
Renee Wilmeth

Development Editor
Michael Koch

Production Editor
Christy Wagner

Copy Editor
Amy Borrelli

Illustrator
Jody P. Schaeffer

Cover Designers
Mike Freeland
Kevin Spear

Book Designers
Scott Cook and Amy Adams of DesignLab

Indexer
Chris Barrick

Layout/Proofreading
Svetlana Dominguez
Jeannette McKay

Contents at a Glance

Contents

Foreword

The Complete Idiot's Guide to Learning Latin is a new and fresh approach to a subject of practically unlimited possibilities. While producing a substantial survey of grammar and vocabulary in an amusing and attractive format, Natalie Harwood has liberated Latin from its narrow focus on a handful of ancient authors and texts. This guide introduces the reader to the whole range that Latin has occupied in Western civilization—from antique myths to modern medicine and law, from generals and emperors to comebacks and mottoes, from love poetry and drinking songs to hymns and Christmas carols. Natalie Harwood shows the pervasiveness of Latin in the Western world, a pervasiveness that continues in the twenty-first century in the numerous professional vocabularies that depend on Latin.

Although all the major components of Latin syntax and morphology are included, they are usually followed by a "But hey! Forget all that! All you really need to remember is ..." Ms. Harwood's many years of experience teaching Latin show in her deft presentation, in an accessible and fun manner, of one of the most feared topics in the curriculum. Various sidebars give clever mnemonics for vocabulary, brief historical and cultural sketches, study tips, and "Hysteria's Herstory"—accounts of famous Roman women to balance the picture of the mostly male history. All this supplementary material has been chosen carefully to integrate the grammar and vocabulary with the study of Roman and medieval culture. From the beginning to the end, Natalie Harwood's exuberant sense of humor makes the whole enterprise a delight.

Answers to all exercises and Latin translations are given in a key so readers can work through the text by themselves and check their own work. A complete glossary of the 2,400 Latin words introduced in the text is complemented by an English–Latin glossary to help readers write their own compositions. There is something here for everyone—those who studied Latin years ago and would like to revisit the old friend, those who never studied Latin and thought they had missed their chance, and even for Latin teachers who are looking for fresh ideas and approaches to this rich subject.

The presentation moves sensibly from words to phrases to sentences to interesting selections from ancient and medieval authors that show how very modern the issues and problems that puzzled generations of Latin writers are. Authors of selections include Terence, Caesar, Cicero, Vitruvius, Pliny, the Vulgate, Augustine, and many more.

If you thought Latin was a dead language that required more effort than it could be worth—*Tolle! Lege!* (Take! Read!). *The Complete Idiot's Guide to Learning Latin* was written for you!

Stephen A. Nimis
Professor of Classics
Miami University, Oxford, Ohio

Introduction

Latin, a dead language? Doctors use Latin—*vertebra, fibula, humerus, patella.* Lawyers use Latin—*nolo contendere, habeas corpus, res iudicata, subpoena.* Architects use Latin—*tympanum, basilica, post, lintel.* You use Latin when you buy a car—*Nova, Fiat, Maxima*—when you write a research paper—*ibid, idem, et al.*—when you exchange money—*annuit coeptis, e pluribus unum*—when you go to church—*mea culpa, pater noster*—or when you're just sitting around the house watching old movies like *Spartacus* or *Julius Caesar.*

Perhaps you want to know what the Latin actually means. Perhaps you want to read the words of Caesar, Cicero, and other writers from 2,000 years ago. Perhaps you are in Latin I class and are wondering how to ace it. Perhaps you are an advanced Latin student but were sleeping when everyone else learned the relative pronouns.

In any case, reading this book will help you review or learn from scratch the language that is basic to all the Romance languages. In the process you will learn history, improve your vocabulary, freshen up your English grammar, and maybe even have a little fun.

This Is Not *(Shudder)* a Latin Textbook!

This book is based on the premise that you can learn a language as an adult by imitating how you learned a language as a child. If you were a fairly normal child, you began speaking English one word at a time. Like most children, you did not come out with complete sentences at the age of 12 months. And you certainly did not learn English by reciting grammar rules or memorizing lists of words.

So you approach learning Latin the same way. You start with single words, then combinations, then phrases, clauses, sentences, and finally paragraphs. I have tried to include words that have useful derivatives, words that you can use at work, in the boardroom, or at a boxing match (*Quite a pugilist!*).

I've tried to group words in interesting ways, rather than simply alphabetically. Nouns are listed as living things, places, and inanimate things. Verbs are grouped into very physical, slightly active, and couch-potato states of being.

How to Use This Book

In broad strokes, here's what you will find in this book:

Part 1, "Frequently Asked Questions," gives you common rationalizations for not knowing Latin. The history of Latin is explained and simple pronunciation guides help you speak Latin correctly. Finally, I give you plenty of reasons for learning Latin, just in case you have a dimwitted friend who laughs at you for reading this book. Remember, *stulti Latinam linguam rident* ("fools laugh at the Latin language").

Part 2, "What's in a Word?" starts you off with handy nouns you can use everyday. You learn about number, gender, and case, and you get lots of practice. Then you learn verbs (so your nouns can do something), objects, and then adjectives so you can describe your nouns. After a few more necessities like pronouns and time and place words—and lots of practice—you are ready to move on.

Part 3, "Expressing Yourself in Latin," expands your capabilities with infinitive phrases, prepositional phrases, and the notorious ablative absolute. Then I have you jump into relative clauses, purpose, and result clauses. The last two chapters of this part simply put to work all the previous lessons and give you a chance to review your English grammar. Remember complex, compound, and simple sentences?

Part 4, "Reading Latin—Selections from Ancient Authors," gives you, at last, some original Latin. Selections from Pliny, Cicero, Julius Caesar, Terence, and Vitruvius will get you started reading authentic Latin and learning something about people who lived 2,000 years ago. The selections include advice on architects and contracts, descriptions of animals such as elephants and oysters, a street scene, a dinner scene, and reactions to an unhappy marriage.

Part 5, "Coping with Latin in the Modern World," explores the Latin words and expressions that people working in the everyday world today experience. The historical background is explained and the actual meaning of some of the Latin words will leave you saying, "I always wondered what that really meant!" Lawyers, scientists, doctors, and even stay-at-home moms will find this section relevant.

Finally, the appendixes include vocabulary lists, grammatical summaries, answer keys, and an assortment of real-life Latin exams that will enable you to test your skills and knowledge.

If you are learning Latin from scratch, start with Chapter 1 and work through Parts 1 through 3. You can refer to Part 5 at your leisure, for those chapters do not require much grammatical know-how. You'll need to do Parts 1 through 3, however, before tackling the real Latin in Part 4.

Perhaps you know some Latin—you got through Latin II and then wimped out for French or Spanish in high school—and just want to freshen up your memory. Start at the beginning. However, because people have different amounts of Latin expertise, you may be able to skip the first declension nouns, for example, or just skim over the present tense. Most students begin to bog down in the third declension, and many leave the arena when faced with relative clauses and the subjunctive mood. This book should guide you through the rough spots with ease. Use the grammatical index to look up those irregular adjectives or the subjunctive mood that stumped you 30 years ago.

Extras (a Latin Word That Means "Outside the Usual")

In addition to Latin vocabulary, grammatical explanations, impressive polysyllabic additions to your vocabulary, practice exercises, and Latin selections, you will find even more information by reading these sidebars:

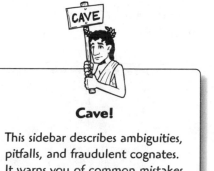

Cave!

This sidebar describes ambiguities, pitfalls, and fraudulent cognates. It warns you of common mistakes that many Latin students make and ways to avoid them.

Tene Memoria

This sidebar reminds you to memorize a few important details. It also refreshes your memory of important points from previous chapters.

Grammar Guru

This sidebar explains basic grammatical facts and gives mnemonic devices to help you remember those facts.

Did You Know?

Here you can find interesting information about the lives of Romans 2,000 years ago. It includes social history, military history, biographical notes on famous Romans, and interesting facts about animals and natural history.

Hysteria's Herstory

Read this sidebar to learn more about gender-specific historical tidbits. Hitherto unknown facts and deeds of famous and not-so-famous women of the Roman world are highlighted in these boxes.

And if this weren't enough, you'll also find plenty of exercises and short review tests throughout this book to help you evaluate your knowledge each step along the way. You won't be composing Ciceronian orations or Vergilian epic poetry by the time you're finished with this book, but you can expect to be able to read simple, real Latin, and understand much more of the Latin you'll encounter in the modern world.

Dedication

To my mother, who always believed I would write a book.

To my children and grandchildren, who continually shape my life in wonderful ways.

To my sister, who calls me from New York.

To my brother and sister-in-law, for their great sense of humor.

To Miss Dorothy Rounds, who would have wanted to be known for publishing *An Index to Festschriften*. For me, however, she will always be the dedicated Arlington High School Latin teacher who had a dress with sleeves like bat wings and who fell into the wastebasket while reading from *Apollonius Rhodius*.

Acknowledgments

I would like to give special thanks to the students and faculty at Talawanda High School in Oxford, Ohio, for their patience and information.

Special Thanks to the Technical Reviewer

The Complete Idiot's Guide to Learning Latin was reviewed by an expert who double-checked the accuracy of what you'll learn here, to help us ensure that this book gives you everything you need to know about learning Latin. Special thanks are extended to Mary Vandivier.

Trademarks

All terms mentioned in this book that are known to be or are suspected of being trademarks or service marks have been appropriately capitalized. Alpha Books and Pearson Education cannot attest to the accuracy of this information. Use of a term in this book should not be regarded as affecting the validity of any trademark or service mark.

Part 1
Frequently Asked Questions

When you carry this book in public, three things will happen to you. First, people will look at you quizzically as if you were an idiot.

"Latin?" they will say. "Don't you know it's a dead language?"

Second, they will then try to show their erudition by spouting forth the little Latin they know, probably mangled irreparably from misuse since their high school days. Then they will say, "It's Greek to me."

Finally, they will launch into their favorite story about their Latin teacher, how she fell into the wastebasket or stood on a chair imitating Cicero.

Be prepared! Semper paratus!

Chapter 1

Why Learn Latin?

In This Chapter

➤ Latin—the bad boy of foreign languages

➤ Latin increases your English vocabulary

➤ Latin helps you learn about history

➤ You can pronounce Latin

➤ Latin words you already know

> Latin is a language
> Dead as it can be.
> First it killed the Romans
> And now it's killing me!

This age-old witticism is a good example of Latin's bad press. Why does everyone roll his or her eyes, groan, and grimace when you mention that you want to learn Latin? Inevitably they will repeat the word in disbelief and peer at you as if you have lost your mind. Latin? Why on earth?

Latin—the Bad Boy of Foreign Languages

Latin is so hard! Take French or Spanish! High school students perpetuate the myth that Latin is difficult to learn. But the truth is that learning Latin does not have to be arduous. Look at these words: *elephantus, dictator, navigator, Europa, Italia, intellegentia, gloria*. Are you having trouble translating those?

Latin is much easier than Japanese or Chinese. It has cultural and historical foundations that easily transfer to English. *Senator? Architectus?* What's so hard about that?

The first step in learning Latin is to rid yourself of the mind-set that Latin will be difficult. Attitude is everything. Latin will be a breeze.

Your Latin Teacher Was Tough

Latin teachers may seem a little rigid. After all, they may have learned the language in a convent, and rules are rules. Latin teachers are well aware that they are teaching a language that has not changed in a thousand years and so, by gosh, neither will they.

Your Latin teacher may have discouraged you by assigning homework and giving tests. She probably made you memorize word endings. This book will do none of that. You are your own teacher.

Dead but Not Forgotten

Languages, like people, have lives. Languages are born, grow, change, and exist to help people communicate. They live useful lives, spreading culture, making distinctions, and expressing emotions. Sometimes, like people, the language dies and—if nothing has been written—becomes extinct. When the culture disappears—as with the Romans—but the language has been preserved, then the language is simply dead—gone, but not forgotten.

So why learn a dead language? English, still alive and kicking, changes all the time. Compare, for example, the language of Chaucer—*forsworn, hath*—and today—*Internet, rap*. Latin, the dead language, will not change because no one is using it every day to communicate. This is why science uses Latin. A genus name will be internationally understood and won't change over time.

Latin is old and classic. So people use it to give prestige to a name—Super Bowl XIX, the Maxima.

But the most important reason for learning Latin is so anyone from the twentieth century can read the words and, therefore, minds and hearts of men and women who lived in the first century. Reading Latin authors brings history to life and perpetuates the miracle of a civilization that started on the shores of the Mediterranean Sea. Best of all, reading Latin reminds us that for 2,000 years—and we hope for 2,000 more to come—women get mad at their husbands, people keep fish as pets, and human beings are still trying to catch an elephant.

It is true that Latin is an inflected language. There are different endings for different purposes. German is inflected, too, and you don't see people crying about German being so difficult. The problem is that Latin textbooks give you all the endings at once. Memorize the first declension. Learn the perfect personal endings. I will let the endings fend for themselves or just worm their way into your consciousness. And the ones that are hardly ever used, I'll just ignore.

Alumneye or Alumnee?

How do teachers know how to pronounce Latin? Obviously they have no direct recordings of Romans hanging out in the Forum discussing the latest model of chariots. But scholars have extrapolated from written evidence—poetry, prose, and dialogue from plays—and they do have a reasonable idea of how Latin sounded. Luckily for you, most of the letters are exactly like English. The exceptions include

a as in *father*

e as in *bed;* with long mark *ē*, as in *late*

i as in *bit;* with long mark *ī*, as in *knee*

o as in *often;* with long mark *ō*, as in *dope*

ae as in *bye*

au as in *now*

ei as in *hey*

v as in *wine*

c and *g* always hard, as in *car* and *game*

j as in *yes*

There are more rules, of course, but these will get you started. Pronunciation guides can be found in the front of any Latin dictionary if you're really into this sort of thing.

Two final questions: Who cares if I'm pronouncing correctly? And what about *alumni* and *alumnae?*

No Roman is around to give you a dirty look if you mispronounce a Latin word. But consistency is the key here. When you read, you often say the word, if not aloud, then mentally. Good readers hear as well as see the words. Beginning readers often move their lips as they read, perhaps sounding out the words.

As you are learning Latin, you'll want to say as well as read the words, and consistency of the sounds will make the remembering easier.

One of the biggest problems facing Latin students today is that many words have become English: *senator, dictator, alumnus, alumna.* Do you use the English or the Latin pronunciation? My solution is to use the anglicized pronunciation when the word has become an English word. To put it another way, if the word is in the English dictionary, follow the dictionary's phonetic spelling. So *alumni* becomes *alumneye* and *alumnae, alumnee,* using the English pronunciation.

If, on the other hand, you are standing around with a bunch of Latin students and you are all speaking Latin, then, of course, you would say, *Alumnee bonee sunt* ("Men who have graduated from this university are good").

Latin Words You Already Know

Since so many of the words in the English language come to us from Greek or Latin, you will see the resemblance of many Latin words to their English counterparts. Except for pronouncing *v*'s like *w*'s and *c*'s like *k*'s, Latin even sounds like the English. However, Romans tended to accent toward the end of the word, while English speakers, always eager and impetuous, tend to accent the first syllable they come to. Thus we say *INdustry,* while the Latin is *inDUStria, VICtory* as opposed to *vicTORia.*

Here is a list of Latin words you already know:

Latin	English	Pronunciation
calamitas	calamity	*kah-LAH-mih-tahs*
causa	cause	*COW-sah*
clamor	clamor, noise	*KLAH-more*
cura	cure, care	*COO-rah*
discordia	discord	*dis-COR-dee-ah*
elephantus	elephant	*ell-eh-FAHN-toos*
est	is	*ehst*
Europa	Europe	*yoor-OH-pah*
forma	form	*FOR-mah*
fungus	mushroom	*FUN-gus*
gloria	glory	*GLOH-ree-ah*
hippopotamus	hippopotamus	*hip-poh-POT-ah-moos*
industria	industry	*in-DUS-tree-ah*
intellegentia	intelligence	*in-tel-leg-EN-tee-ah*
Italia	Italy	*ee-TAHL-ee-ah*
nobilis	noble	*noh-BIHL-is*
palma	palm	*PAHL-mah*
populus	people	*POP-yoo-lus*

Latin	English	Pronunciation
Roma	Rome	*ROW-mah*
senator	senator	*SEN-ah-tor*
victoria	victory	*wick-TOR-ee-ah*
villa	villa, house	*WEEL-ah*
violentia	violence	*wee-oh-LENS-ee-ah*

Did You Know?

A Roman *villa* was any house in the country. The *villa rustica* was often a working farm, with separate quarters for the farm workers, animals, tools, wagons, and winepresses. The owner would have a house slightly apart from the smells and sounds of the farm. The wealthy Roman often had several vacation homes called *villae,* which would be situated in the mountains or near the sea. Pliny, a well-to-do Roman writer, describes one of his retreats in a letter which has come down to us. His luxury condo had over 30 rooms, including porticos, walkways, sunrooms, exercise rooms, bedrooms, towers, and courtyards. Complete with a full-time staff of slaves, this retreat would rival any four-star resort of today.

The Latin language does not have definite and indefinite articles, so Romans did not have to worry about whether to say *a* or *an,* and they never had to bother about that silly little word that clutters up our English sentences, *the.* So when you translate, you have to put the articles in wherever you feel comfortable. For example, *Elephantus nobilis est* is not "Elephant is noble," but "An elephant is noble" or "The elephant is noble," either one being correct and true, depending on the context.

The other little quirk about Latin is that more often than not the word order is different from English. Usually in Latin the verb is near the end of the sentence. For example, if you want to say "Rome is in Italy" in Latin, you'd say, *Roma in Italia est,* not *Roma est in Italia.*

Cave!

Watch out for small changes in spelling. "Intelligence" is a good example. Knowing the Latin *inteLEGentia* might cause you to misspell "inteLIGence." For the most part, Latin will help you remember your English spelling. But sometimes it can lead you astray.

Hysteria's Herstory

The word *hysteria* is from the Greek *hystera,* meaning "womb." The illness that manifests itself in violent movements of the arms and legs and wild, exaggerated facial expressions was thought to be caused by movements of the womb, and, therefore, affected women only. This unfortunate fallacy persists to this day when it is said that women become hysterical, while men are merely excited.

In many Latin textbooks you will find the diacritical mark, the macron, used frequently over vowels. The long mark, as it is also called, alters the pronunciation and can affect the quantity of the syllable in poetry. There are also many texts, however, when the macron is not used, and then you are left without your crutch. So with the exception of the list earlier in this chapter, this book is not using the macron, and you will be better off in the long run. Learn to stand on your own two feet, diacritically speaking.

The Least You Need to Know

➤ Latin has an unjustified bad reputation.

➤ You won't have to memorize long lists of incomprehensible endings when learning Latin using this book.

➤ Many Latin words look exactly like English.

➤ Speaking Latin is a breeze.

➤ Your Latin teacher tried her best.

Chapter 2

What Exactly Is Latin?

In This Chapter

➤ Digging up Indo-European roots

➤ The rise and fall of Rome in one paragraph

➤ Late Latin

➤ More Latin words you already know

Latin has its roots in the Proto-Indo-European language spoken by the inhabitants of Latium (the central part of what is now Italy) from at least the eighth century B.C.E.

Latin became the language of Roman literature, which started with translations from the Greek and swiftly became the vehicle of original Roman poetry, prose, and drama. Livius Andronicus was the first to translate the *Odyssey* into Latin around 200 B.C.E. Plautus was an early playwright, famous for *Aulularia, The Pot of Gold,* and other comedies. Cicero has left us many speeches, letters, and essays, among which are his famous *On Friendship* and *Old Age.* Julius Caesar wrote *The Gallic Wars,* a classic in every second-year Latin class. Vergil, of course, wrote *The Aeneid,* an oft-quoted epic poem on the glories of Rome. Horace and Juvenal wrote poetry and satires, and Ovid and Catullus are famous for their works on the art of love. The influence of these authors survived the Dark Ages and Middle Ages and flourished during the Renaissance, and their ideas and works are found in every aspect of western civilization.

Digging Up Your Indo-European Roots

Isn't English a Germanic language? Father—*Vater?* Mother—*Mutter?* Book—*Buch?* Why is it that so many words come from Latin?

First, the Romans occupied Europe, including part of Germany and the British Isles, for 500 years. During that time, much of Roman culture, including language, was assimilated by the native population.

Indo-European and Proto-Indo-European languages.

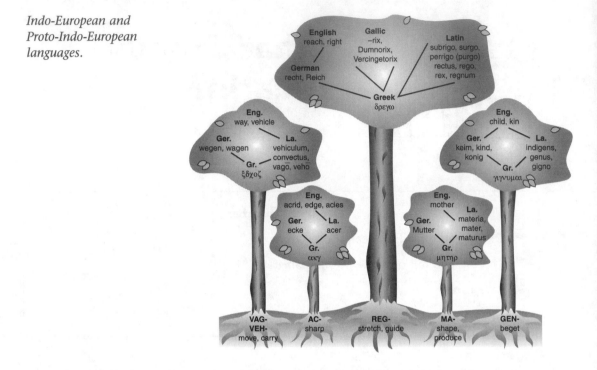

Second, English, Latin, and German spring from the same parent language—Indo-European. Scholars believe that many thousands of years ago there was one language, probably in Eastern Europe, called Proto-Indo-European. Based on linguistic evidence, this language is the mother of Sanskrit, Hindi, Persian, Pashto, Lithuanian, Latvian, Russian, Polish, Serbo-Croatian, Armenian, Albanian, Greek, all Celtic languages, Latin, Italian, French, Spanish, Portuguese, Romanian, German, English, Dutch, and the Scandinavian languages. The earliest written Indo-European language is Hittite dating from the seventeenth century B.C.E. Samples from other early languages such as Sanskrit and Greek show that all Indo-European languages were highly inflected (having different endings for different grammatical purposes) and were conjugated (having verb forms to show person, number, voice, mood, and tense).

A Brief History of Rome

Latin is the language of the Latins, whose king, Latinus, welcomed Aeneas, the mythical hero and partly divine refugee from the Trojan War. With the help of Lavinia, Latinus's daughter, they founded the Latin family. Romulus, one of their descendants, established a city and named it Rome after himself. Rome added suburbs, cities, and countries and eventually deposed its king and became a republic lasting roughly 500 years. Augustus took over and Rome became an empire for another 500 years. Then it got so fat that it burst into two sections and self-destructed.

Did You Know?

The traditional date for the founding of Rome is 753 B.C.E., although the area was inhabited long before that date. Probably Rome was formed from a number of small villages grouped around the ancient city of Alba Longa, later destroyed by Tullus Hostilius and never rebuilt. He got his just reward, however, when he was killed by a lethal combination of fire, lightning, a flammable house, and many enemies both mortal and divine.

Late Latin

Even after the fall of Rome in the sixth century, Latin continued to be spoken. When the Christian Church rose in stature in the Dark Ages, its adoption of Latin as the official language assured its eternal life. Late Latin, also known as Medieval Latin or Church Latin, is the language of the European monasteries, cathedrals, and schools of the sixth to the sixteenth centuries. Late Latin includes all the new vocabulary necessary for the functioning of the Church. Late Latin has also come down to us in the drinking songs of the Goliards, the wandering scholar-poets of the twelfth and thirteenth centuries. I've included some examples of these in Chapter 23, "Live! From Ancient Rome!"

More Latin Words You Already Know

The following words vary in grammatical type from nouns to adjectives to proper nouns; the English derivative comes to us almost untouched:

Latin	English	Pronunciation
architectus	architect	*ahr-kee-TEC-tus*
consul	consul	*KOHN-sool*
Ephesus	Ephesus	*eh-FEE-soos*

continues

continued

Latin	English	Pronunciation
humanus	human	*hoo-MAH-noos*
inferior	inferior	*een-FEER-ee-or*
magistratus	magistrate	*mah-gees-TRA-toos*
orator	orator	*OH-rah-tor*
privatus	private	*pree-WAH-toos*
publicus	public	*POO-bli-coos*
silentium	silence	*see-LEN-tee-um*
superior	superior	*soo-PEER-ee-or*
toga	toga	*TOW-gah*
troglodyta	troglodyte	*troh-glow-DIH-tah*
vasum	vase	*WAH-sum*

Hysteria's Herstory

There are many Latin words for work that men do—*consul, senator, dictator, architectus*—but the work of women has been largely ignored in both language textbooks and history. Women of all classes worked at varied occupations. Lower-class women were handmaidens, attendants, hairdressers, fishmongers, and bath attendants. Upper-class women usually oversaw the household activities. They were also businesswomen, weavers, and poets.

Although there were many Roman women poets, the name of only one has survived to our time—Sulpicia, circa 15 B.C.E. She wrote love poetry of which 40 lines from six poems are extant. She probably remained single all her life and lived with her patron, Messalla. Her poetry, addressed to her lover, Cerinthus, is remarkably open and fervid. Here is an excerpt:

> *Tandem venit amor, qualem texisse pudori quam nudasse alicui sit mihi, Fama, magis.*
>
> "At last love has come, of such quality that to cover it would be more shameful than to lay it bare."

Some words that are identical in Latin and English have acquired connotations that would be quite foreign to a Roman. *Toga,* for example, a very short word for a very long garment, has come to be associated with wild fraternity parties. However, the original toga represented a personality just the opposite of the party animal. Beginning as a rectangular blanket wrapped around the body for warmth, it developed a certain style all its own.

Usually the toga was five to six feet long and made of heavy, unbleached wool. Draped over one shoulder, the toga was slung under the arm and then positioned over the other shoulder and held up by gravity (*gravitas*), and that's one reason why the Romans were so dignified and serious. Over the years the toga's decoration developed from the plain purple stripe of the *toga praetexta* to fringes and edging of later emperors.

Cave!

Ladies! Don't go to a toga party in a toga! Only men wore togas. Women wore a dress, *stola,* and over it a plain length of material, draped as a stole, a *palla.*

Practice Makes Perfect

Read the following sentences aloud, then use the pattern to ask questions to a friend or your boss:

1. Esne (*ess-nay*) consul?   Are you a consul?
2. Esne hippopotamus?   Are you a hippopotamus?
3. Esne troglodyta?   _____
4. Esne orator?   _____
5. Esne senator?   _____
6. Esne architectus?   _____
7. Esne elephantus?   _____
8. Esne fungus?   _____

The Least You Need to Know

➤ Latin, German, and English are Indo-European languages.

➤ The word *Latin* comes from the names of a tribe, an area, and a king from central Italy, all of which begin with *L*.

➤ Rome grew from a one-horse town to an empire and then collapsed.

➤ Latin used in the Middle Ages is called Late Latin.

Part 2

What's in a Word?

A single word can smile, laugh, cry, yell, and whisper. It can sneer, humiliate, or praise. We start our learning Latin with single words, many of which you know already. Superior.

Some Latin words will be very similar to another language such as mater *(Mutter, German),* bonus *(bon, French), or* aqua *(agua, Spanish). Single words can denote more than single subjects, such as men, women, ideas. Finally, derivatives from these single words will add color and excitement to your vocabulary—your mashed potatoes are margaritaceous!*

LET'S FIND OUT.

People, Places, and Things

Words are powerful communicators. Edgar Allan Poe's raven drove a man to insanity with one word—"Nevermore!" Single words can command ("jump"), describe ("beautiful"), exclaim ("wow!"), or make a statement ("cool"). Put two words together and you compound the meaning, like "bulldog" and "featherbrain." Words can also bore you to death like "antidisestablishmentarianism."

The Romans used single words to make a point, many of which are still with us. Cicero said, "*O tempora, o mores*," bewailing the lack of morals in then-modern times (65 B.C.E.). Julius Caesar's immortal words "*Veni, vidi, vici*" recall his world-famous military victories.

So let's start learning Latin with single words, many of which will ultimately appear in the Latin selections in Part 4, "Reading Latin—Selections from Ancient Authors," when you begin to read longer selections of real Latin. This first list that follows names people, places, or things.

I am including simple and not-so-simple derivatives to help you remember the Latin word and its meaning.

RETINEO

Grammar Guru

Remember parts of speech?
These are classifications of words
according to their function or
meaning. A noun is a person,
place, or thing.

First-Declension Feminine Nouns

The first grammarians back in ancient times started
out so logically. Group together all the nouns ending
in *a* and call them feminine, and since it's always ladies
first, call these nouns the first declension. So far, so good.

Living Things and Their Parts

All nouns first appear in the nominative case ending
in vocabulary lists. The nominative case shows the
subject of a sentence. It is also used for the predicate
noun, placed after a linking verb in English. The genitive case is always second and is translated *of* or *'s*.

Nominative	Genitive	Meaning	Derivative
amica (*ah-MEE-kah*)	amicae (*ah-MEE-keye*)	girlfriend	amicable
beta (*BEH-tah*)	betae (*BEH-teye*)	beet	betaine
cauda (*KOW-dah*)	caudae (*KOW-deye*)	tail	caudal
dea (*DEH-ah*)	deae (*DEH-eye*)	goddess	deify
femina (*FEM-in-ah*)	feminae (*FEM-in-eye*)	woman	feminine
filia (*FEE-lee-ah*)	filiae (*FEE-lee-eye*)	daughter	filicide
hecyra (heh-KEH-rah)	hecyrae (heh-KEH-reye)	mother-in-law	—
helvella (*hel-WELL-ah*)	helvellae (*hel-WELL-eye*)	potherb	helvella
herba (*HEHR-bah*)	herbae (*HEHR-beye*)	grass	herbicide
hospita (*HOHS-pih-tah*)	hospitae (*HOHS-pih-teye*)	guest	hospice
malva (*MAHL-wah*)	malvae (*MAHL-weye*)	mallow	marshmallow

Nominative	Genitive	Meaning	Derivative
muraena (*moor-EYE-nah*)	muraenae (*moor-EYE-neye*)	eel	moray eel
ostrea (*OHS-treh-ah*)	ostreae (*OHS-treh-eye*)	oyster	oyster
perna (*PEHR-nah*)	pernae (*PEHR-neye*)	ham, thigh	pernio
puella (*poo-EHL-ah*)	puellae (*poo-EHL-eye*)	girl	—
turba (*TUR-bah*)	turbae (*TUR-beye*)	crowd	turbulent

When you come to the *coda* in your musical composition, remember it comes from the Latin, *cauda*. And while you are standing in line at the bakery waiting to buy that last loaf of marble rye, you can entertain the people in the queue by reminding them that *queue* comes from *cauda*.

Remember your grandmother complaining about having chilblains? Another name for that redness of toes and pains in the legs associated with chilly weather is *pernio*, derived from the Latin and Sanskrit word that means "leg, thigh, especially of a hog used for food." A bit of a stretch there, I'll admit.

Betaine refers to a salt contained in beet juice. It's edible, unlike a beta ray or radiation particle.

The *mallow* is a pinkish, purplish plant. The roots produce a sticky substance used in, of all things, the marshmallow!

Finally, beware the *moray*, described as brightly colored, often savage, voracious eel with narrow jaws and strong, knifelike teeth. Nice aquarium pet.

Places and Inanimate Things

Remember that even though the following words are places and things, in Latin they are considered grammatically feminine.

Nominative	Genitive	Meaning	Derivative
aqua (*AII-kwah*)	aquae (*AII-kweye*)	water	aquatic
cena (*KAY-nah*)	cenae (*KAY-neye*)	dinner	cenacle
concha (*KOHN-kah*)	conchae (*KOHN-keye*)	shell	conch

continues

continued

Nominative	Genitive	Meaning	Derivative
epistula (*eh-PISS-too-lah*)	epistulae (*eh-PISS-too-leye*)	letter	epistle
impensa (*im-PEHN-sah*)	impensae (*im-PEHN-seye*)	cost	impending
insula (*EEN-soo-lah*)	insulae (*EEN-soo-leye*)	island	insulate
margarita (*mahr-gahr-EE-tah*)	margaritae (*mahr-gahr-EE-eye*)	pearl	margaritaceous
mensa (*MEHN-sah*)	mensae (*MEHN-seye*)	table	mensa
pecunia (*peh-KOON-ee-ah*)	pecuniae (*peh-KOON-ee-eye*)	money	pecuniary
piscina (*piss-KEE-nah*)	piscinae (*piss-KEE-neye*)	fishpond	piscine
poena (*POI-nah*)	poenae (*POI-neye*)	penalty	penal
terra (*TEHR-rah*)	terrae (*TEHR-reye*)	land	terrarium
vita (*WEE-tah*)	vitae (*WEE-teye*)	life	vital

A *cenacle*, by the way, is from the Latin *cena* and denotes the room where the Last Supper took place. It has also come to mean a religious retreat house. Feel free to use *margaritaceous* at your next dinner party. You can apply it to the boiled onions or your dinner partner's teeth. It means *pearly white.*

And it's not all right to call your Aunt Martha *piscine* (*PEYE-seen*) even thought she breathes through her mouth and tends to roll her eyes like a tuna.

Hysteria's Herstory

Cornelia, wife of Sempronius Gracchus and mother of two political reformers, was famous for her virtuous conduct and devotion to her family. Once she was visiting with another Roman matron who was showing off her pearls and precious gems. "Where are your jew-els?" asked the woman curiously. Proudly, Cornelia brought forth her two small sons and in a statement about as old as Adam said, "These are my jewels."

The Case of the Life of an Oyster

To review, Latin words are always listed with the first word in the nominative case, *ostrea,* and the second form in the genitive case, *ostreae.* The nominative case is used for the subject of a sentence, and the genitive case is used to show possession. In English we use the *'s* or the preposition *of.* So *ostrea, ostreae,* would translate, "the oyster, of the oyster." Latin has no words for *the* or *a* or *an,* so you can throw them in whenever you wish.

Practice Makes Perfect 1

Say aloud and translate:

1. Vita ostreae _____
2. Amica puellae _____
3. Aqua Romae _____
4. Cena herbae _____
5. Filia deae _____
6. Gloria causae _____
7. Industria insulae _____

Now try translating into Latin:

1. The grass of Rome _____
2. Life of the girl _____
3. The table of the caveman _____
4. The pearl of the oyster _____
5. A woman of the fishpond _____

Second-Declension Masculine and Neuter Nouns

The letter after the genitive case in the vocabulary list designates the gender. Most words for women are feminine, most words for men are masculine. The *n.* designates neuter, which is the Latin word for *neither.* So why in the world is *world* masculine? No one knows for sure. You can be sure, however, that all Latin words will have gender, sensible or not.

Living Things and Their Parts—Masculine Nouns

The following list includes masculine nouns. Bring them to your next party and be the *vita convivii* with such witticisms as "I have been otiose all week" or "The verbosity of a funambulist is elephantine."

Nominative	Genitive	Meaning	Derivative
coquus (*KOH-kwuhs*)	coqui (*KOH-kwee*)	cook	cook
deus (*DEH-uhs*)	dei (*DEH-ee*)	god	deify
filius (*FEE-lee-uhs*)	fili (*FEE-lee*)	son	filial
funambulus (*foo-NAM-boo-luhs*)	funambuli (*foo-NAM-boo-lee*)	tightrope walker	funambulist
Graecus (*GREYE-koos*)	Graeci (*GREYE-kee*)	a Greek	Greek
lautus (*LOW-tuhs*)	lauti (*LOW-tee*)	gourmet, gentleman	lavish
nasus (*NAH-suhs*)	nasi (*NAH-see*)	nose	nasal
nervus (*NEHR-wuhs*)	nervi (*NEHR-wee*)	nerve	nerve
populus (*POHP-yoo-luhs*)	populi (*POHP-yoo-ee*)	people	popular
vir (*WHEER*)	viri (*WHEER-ee*)	man	virile

Lautus comes from the Latin *lavo* (*lavare*), "to wash." Additional meanings are "nicely turned out" and "sumptuous." So *gourmet,* in this context, means more of someone enjoying life to the fullest, rather than one who is an epicurean expert.

Of course, it may be difficult to enjoy life if you are *nasicorn,* that is, bearing a horn on the nose. The rhinocerous is a nasicorn animal. Unfortunately, so is Uncle Edwin.

Places and Things—Masculine Nouns

These places and things are grammatically masculine in Latin and, therefore, end in *us* in the nominative and *i* in the genitive singular.

Nominative	Genitive	Meaning	Derivative
animus (*AHN-ee-muhs*)	animi (*AHN-ee-mee*)	mind	animated
lectus (*LEHK-toos*)	lecti (*LEHK-tee*)	bed	lectisternium
locus (*LOH-kuhs*)	loci (*LOH-kee*)	place	local

Nominative	Genitive	Meaning	Derivative
modus (*MOH-duhs*)	modi (*MOH-dee*)	way	mode
mundus (*MOON-duhs*)	mundi (*MOON-dee*)	world	mundane
nodus (*NOH-duhs*)	nodi (*NOH-dee*)	knot	node
nucleus (*NOO-kleh-us*)	nuclei (*NOO-kleh-aye*)	kernel	nucleus
versiculus (*wehr-SIK-coo-luhs*)	versiculi (*wehr-SIK-coo-lee*)	single line	versicule

A *lectisternium* is a special celebration, mostly in Greek and Roman times, where the couches are laid out for the gods and food is spread for their enjoyment. I suppose if they fail to show up for the party, you are entitled to eat 'til you drop. While dining on the food of the gods, you might recite a *versicule,* a short poem.

Places and Things—Neuter Nouns

Finally, let's learn about things that are neuter in both English and Latin. Note that neuter nouns end in *um* in the nominative and *i* in the genetive singular.

Nominative	Genitive	Meaning	Derivative
aedificium (*eye-dih-FIHC-ee-uhm*)	aedifici (*eye-dih-FIHC-ee*)	building	edifice
aurum (*OW-ruhm*)	auri (*OW-ree*)	gold	aureate
consilium (*kohn-SIHL-ee-uhm*)	consili (*kohn-SIHL-ee-ee*)	plan	counsel
convivium (*kohn-WEE-wee-uhm*)	convivi (*kohn-WEE-wee-ee*)	party	convivial
decretum (*deh-KREH-tuhm*)	decreti (*deh-KREH-tee*)	judgment	decree
dictum (*DIK-tuhm*)	dicti (*DIK-tee*)	contract	dictum
ferrum (*FEHR-ruhm*)	ferri (*FEHR-ee*)	iron, steel	ferrous
otium (*OH-tee-uhm*)	oti (*OH-tee*)	leisure	otiose
prandium (*PRAHN-dee-uhm*)	prandi (*PRAHN-dee*)	dinner	prandial

continues

continued

Nominative	Genitive	Meaning	Derivative
pretium (*PREH-tee-uhm*)	preti (*PREH-tee*)	price	—
vasum (*WAH-suhm*)	vasi (*WAH-see*)	vase	vase
verbum (*WEHR-buhm*)	verbi (*WEHR-bee*)	word	verbosity

A *postprandial* belch used to be a good thing, a compliment to the chef.

Practice Makes Perfect 2

Be sure to read the Latin phrases aloud and then translate them to English:

1. Nervus funambuli _____
2. Vir silenti _____
3. Nasus elephanti _____
4. Otium populi _____
5. Vasum ferri _____
6. Modus mundi _____
7. Locus feminae _____
8. Concha betae _____
9. Hecyra muraenae _____
10. Victoria Graecae _____
11. Filius violentiae _____
12. Intellegentia animi _____
13. Prandium pernae _____

Now translate into Latin:

1. The price of land _____
2. Word of the penalty _____
3. The son of the gourmet _____
4. Single line of the letter _____
5. A guest of the Greek _____
6. The cost of the toga _____
7. The word of god _____
8. A house of gold _____

A Quick Summary

By now you can see that feminine nouns end in *a* in the nominative and *ae* in the genitive. Masculine nouns end in *us* or *r* in the nominative and *i* in the genitive. Neuter nouns end in *um* in the nominative and *i* in the genitive. Remember, the genitive can be translated *'s* or *of*.

Did You Know?

Nero's famous House of Gold, *Domus Aurei*, was so named for its lavish walls overlaid with gold, precious jewels and mother-of-pearl. The main dining room was a rotunda that revolved with the vault of heaven itself. The ceiling featured sliding panels that opened up to shower the guests with perfume and flowers.

Mouse, Mice; House, Hice? Plurals

In English, we have separate forms for plurals—boy and boys, man and men—so it really isn't any inconvenience to do the same in Latin. We can't keep talking about just one elephant and one tail, supposing you see one elephant with *two* tails. If you haven't been drinking, you may want to write it in Latin.

Mouses?

Here are some plurals you will see and their translations:

aedificia	buildings
betae	beets
caudae	tails
dei	gods
filii	sons
loci	places
nervi	nerves
poenae	punishments
vasa	vases
verba	words

25

Here are the plural endings for the first- and second-declension nouns, masculine, feminine, and neuter:

	Masculine	Feminine	Neuter
Nominative	*i*	*ae*	*a*
Genitive	*orum*	*arum*	*orum*

Practice Makes Perfect 3

Translate the following expressions:

1. Nodi virorum   _____
2. Nervi ferri   _____
3. Nuclei ostrearum   _____
4. Modus oti   _____
5. Piscinae balneorum   _____
6. Caudae hippopotamorum   _____
7. Silentium Romae   _____
8. Amica dei   _____
9. Viae Romae   _____
10. Industria funambulisti   _____

Here's the ultimate test! Translate these into Latin:

1. Vases of the goddesses   _____
2. Dinners of men   _____
3. The places of sons   _____
4. The life of the party   _____
5. The couch of the guest   _____
6. Money of the farm   _____
7. Shells of oysters   _____
8. Plan of the contract   _____

Declensions—It's All Downhill from Here!

Try filling in the blanks with all the endings you have learned so far.

	Masculine Singular/Plural	Feminine Singular/Plural	Neuter Singular/Plural
Nominative			
Genitive			

Notice the patterns. Nouns with the genitive ending in *ae* are usually feminine. They are said to be in the first declension. Nouns with the genitive ending in *i* are masculine or neuter and in the second declension.

Don't be put off by the word *declension*. Somebody in the distant past thought of all these pesky endings as falling down from the nominative—hence *declining*, and therefore *declension*. It's really just a way of bunching certain words together that have certain similar characteristics. Just think of declension as family. So nouns with *ae* in the genitive belong to the Smith family and the nouns with *i* in the genitive belong to the Gotti's.

Word Order—the Oyster Elephant's or the Elephant's Oyster?

The Romans were famous for their sense of order. They organized and recorded their legal code. They arranged their legions in admirable straight lines and could set up a camp for 6,000 legionaries in a different place every night. They had a strict order of political offices so one could rise to power according to protocol. But when it came to language, the Romans lost it. They depended on case endings to designate how a word was used in a sentence, not word order, and if you forgot your second-declension genitive plural, you didn't know who belonged to what! English, of course, counts on word order to give meaning to a phrase or sentence. There is a mountain of difference between "The man ate the oyster" and "The oyster ate the man."

Cave!

How can you tell the difference between the nominative plural and the genitive singular of some words? They appear to have the same ending. Compare *viri* ("men") and *viri* ("of the man"). Use your common sense and make an educated guess. For example, *Viae Romae* would not make sense translated "Romes of the Road."

Tene Memoria

Remember to learn the gender and the nominative and genitive forms for each noun. Be sure to pronounce them correctly as you memorize—*ostre-ah, ostre-eye, mod-us, mod-ee.*

So watch out for those endings—*ostrea viri* and *viri ostrea* mean the same thing in Latin. "The man's oyster" and "the oyster man's" just don't equate.

Did You Know?

Apicius, a Roman chef of the first century, considered oysters a staple of any gourmand's diet and once had fresh oysters trucked (so to speak) to the Emperor Trajan in Parthia, a journey of many days. His recipe for oyster stew: chopped small fresh oysters, ovaries of sea urchins, almonds, and shellfish liquid. Boil together and enjoy!

And ... Conjunctions!

Conjunctions are used to join words (see Chapter 5, "Let's Have Some Action!" for a full explanation of the term "word") and come in two varieties. *Coordinating* conjunctions are used to join words and phrases of equal importance. The other type, *subordinating* conjunctions, are used for joining clauses and phrases and will be covered in Part 3, "Expressing Yourself in Latin." For now let's use the following conjunctions:

Latin	Pronunciation	Meaning
aut	*owt*	either
autem	*OW-tem*	moreover, on the other hand
et	*eht*	and
etiam	*EH-tee-ahm*	also
que	*kway*	and
sed	*sehd*	but
sicut	*SEE-kut*	just as, as
et ... et		both ... and
aut ... aut		either ... or
non modo ... sed etiam		not only ... but also

Practice Makes Perfect 4

Say these aloud and then translate them:

1. Perna et ova   _____
2. Feminae virique   _____
3. Publicus et privatus   _____
4. Ostreae sed non elephanti   _____
5. Elephanti sed etiam hippopotami   _____
6. Coquus et funambulus   _____
7. Palmae et margaritae   _____
8. Aut aqua aut helvella   _____
9. Senatus Populusque Romanus   _____
10. Non modo betae sed etiam malva   _____

The Least You Need to Know

➤ A noun is a person, place, or thing.

➤ Latin nouns are presented in two forms—nominative and genitive.

➤ Latin nouns have gender.

➤ Latin nouns have separate forms for singular and plural.

➤ The genitive form is translated *of* or *'s*.

➤ Conjunctions join words and phrases.

➤ Elephants have only one tail.

Chapter 4

What's in a Name?
More Nouns

In This Chapter

➤ Third-declension words

➤ The Roman family and *patria potestas*

➤ Fourth- and fifth-declension words

➤ Roman names for men and those other people

With this chapter, you will have more than enough nouns to read the Latin selections in Part 4, "Reading Latin—Selections from Ancient Authors." Try to get comfortable with declensions: the third, the fourth, and the fifth are added here. You should be familiar with the nominative and genitive cases by now. They are basic to vocabulary skills and you'll be using them for the rest of your Latin reading life. However, don't get the idea that Romans spoke only one or two words naming person, places, or things. We'll get to the other parts of speech soon.

Third-Declension Nouns

If you think of declensions as families, the first declension is a group of mostly girls and all blondes—feminine nouns with nominative case ending *a*. The second declension is a group of all boys and a few oddballs, and they all have crew cuts—masculine and neuter nouns with nominative case endings *us* or *um*. The third declension is as different as the crowd at Macy's parade. The nouns, unfortunately, have all three genders and many different nominative forms. What makes them related is the genitive singular, *is*.

As in vocabulary lists in previous chapters, we start with living things and their parts. Note that the entire family is here, as well as ancestors and family pets.

Nominative	Genitive	Gender	Meaning	Derivative
adiutrix (*ahd-JOO-triks*)	adiutricis (*ahd-joo-TRIK-is*)	f.	helper	adjutant
anser	anseris	m./f.	goose	anserine
apis	apis	m./f.	bee	apiary
arbor	arboris	f.	tree	arboretum
Caesar (*KEYE-sahr*)	Caesaris (*keye-SAHR-is*)	m.	Caesar	czar
caro	carnis/caronis	f.	meat	carnal
clunis	clunis	f.	buttock	—
comes (*KOH-mayss*)	comitis (*KOH-mih-tihs*)	m./f.	companion	comity
crus	cruris	n.	leg	crural
dens	dentis	m.	tooth	dental
dictator	dictatoris	m.	dictator	dictator
dux	ducis	m.	leader	ducal
femur	femoris	n.	thigh	femoral
frater	fratris	m.	brother	fraternity
gladiator	gladiatoris	m.	gladiator	gladiator
homo	hominis	m.	man	hominoid
maiores (*may-YOHR-ayss*)	maiorum (*may-YOHR-um*)	m. pl.	ancestors	major
mater	matris	f.	mother	maternal
mulier (*MOO-lee-yehr*)	mulieris (*moo-lee-YEHR-iss*)	f.	woman	muliebral
pater	patris	m.	father	patricide
pes	pedis	m.	foot	pedal
pisces (*PIHS-kayss*)	piscis (*PIHS-kiss*)	m./f.	fish	pisciculture
poples	poplitis	m.	behind the knee, hamstring	popliteal
pugil	pugilis	m.	fighter	pugilist
soror	sororis	f.	sister	sorority
urinator	urinatoris	m.	diver	urinant
uxor	uxoris	f.	wife	uxoricide

You will remember some third-declension words from previous chapters. *Caesar,* for example, is a third-declension noun with the genitive, *Caesaris.* Most nouns ending in *tor,* such as *navigator, dictator,* and *gladiator,* have the ending *oris* in genitive and are masculine, third declension.

Some of these words will be easy to remember; most people know when they have stumbled into an *apiary* (buzzing noises?) as opposed to an *arboretum* (leaves falling?).

Comity means civility or mutual courtesy, often used in a phrase such as *There was comity between nations.* This word is not seen much, however, because of its proximity to *comedy,* causing ridicule, or *committee,* which might result in endless meetings going nowhere.

There isn't much point in complaining to your spouse, "Ow! I'm having crural pain!" because she will think you said *cruel* or *rural.* It will impress your masseuse, however.

Hominoid means *manlike,* which is the old-fashioned way of saying *humanlike,* which includes women, too.

Muliebral, relating to women, is probably related to the Latin *mollis,* meaning *soft, malleable.*

Hysteria's Herstory

Mulier comes from *mollis?* Whose cockamamie idea was that? In truth, female and the Latin *femina* originally come from the Sanskrit *dhayati* ("to suck"). Feminine is also related to *fecundus* meaning productive and fertile and ultimately Felix, the lucky, productive feline.

The following table shows more third-declension nouns. As with the first and second declensions, many of what we would consider neuter things have masculine or feminine gender and as such are referred to with the appropriate pronoun. So in Latin we would say: *The axe is large and she is imbedded in the tree.* More on this later when we get to pronouns.

Nominative	Genitive	Gender	Meaning	Derivative
aestimatio	aestimationis	f.	estimate	estimate
agmen	agminis	n.	line of battle	agminate

continues

continued

Nominative	Genitive	Gender	Meaning	Derivative
bipennis	bipennis	f.	axe	bipenniform
civitas	civitatis	f.	city, state	civic
condicio	condicionis	f.	condition	condition
fraus	fraudis	f.	mischief	fraud
honor	honoris	f.	honor	honor
inaures	inaurium	f. pl.	earrings	—
ius	iuris	n.	right	justice
lex	legis	f.	law	legal
merx	mercis	f.	merchandise	merchant
opus	operis	n.	work	opera
pars	partis	f.	part	part
pax	pacis	f.	peace	pacify
pernicitas	pernicitatis	f.	agility	pernicity
rete	retis	n.	net	reticule
rumor	rumoris	m.	rumor	rumor
sal	salis	m./n.	salt	saline
tempus	temporis	n.	time	temporal
varietas	varietatis	f.	variety	variety
vetustas	vetustatis	f.	old age	veteran

Agminate comes from the Latin *ago,* "to do or drive," and the suffix *men,* meaning things that do something. So *agminate,* like *congregate,* is a group of people who do something together. It is also a line of an army or a marching column. So impress your listeners with statements like *Why are those sheep agminated?* or *The stockbrokers are all agminated!* (not to be confused with *agitated*).

Tene Memoria

Remember that the second-declension neuter nominative ending is *um,* just like all the genitive plurals.

Bipenniform means having the shape of a double-edged axe and also related to *bipinnate,* the shape of a leaf.

Your popliteal (pronounced *pop-LIT-e-al*) space is the lozenge-shaped space at the back of the knee joint. This word will go as far as in the classic pick-up line *I couldn't help but admire your outstandingly beautiful popliteal space!* It may also get your face slapped.

Finally, you are thinking there has been a typo. *Urinator* means "diver"? Although there is a Latin word, *urina,* meaning "urine," the verb *urino* and the noun *urinator* mean "to plunge into water." In heraldry, a fish or water animal that is placed head down on a shield is called a *urinant.*

The Third Declension, the *I* of the Storm

Remember that this declension, which has more words than the others, is characterized by *i*. The genitive singular is always *is* and the genitive plural is *um* and sometimes *ium*. The nominative plural is *es*. The third declension is famous for its familial relations—ma, pa, bro, sis—and body parts—foot, mouth, buns, thigh, head, tooth, and others.

The Roman Family and *Patria Potestas*

The Roman family began with the ceremony of marriage. During the Republic there were three recognized marriages: *usus, confarreatio,* and *coemptio.*

Usus was simply cohabitation and not considered legal until a year had passed. The *coemptio* was a Roman holdover of the custom of purchasing a bride. During the ceremony each party pretended to buy each other with a piece of coin. This symbolized the wife becoming free from the authority of her father and coming under the protection of her husband. The *confarreatio* was the formal marriage ceremony in which a cake was used. Ten witnesses were required to be present and the ceremony was performed by a priest.

Did You Know?

The word *spurious*, meaning "not genuine, counterfeit" comes from a Latin name. The members of the Spurious family were aristocrats who lived in the first century B.C.E. They were darned proud of their name until a cloud came over it. It happened this way. When a mother had a child out of wedlock, a no-no even then, she had to record the child as *Sine Pater*, "without a father." This came to be abbreviated as *Sp*, which was also the abbreviation for the Spurious family. Uh-oh. The Spurious family name just quietly disappeared in the first century C.E.

In upper-class families, the wife was in charge of the slaves, who performed most of the domestic duties—cooking, cleaning, keeping the linens and clothes clean and orderly. The children were raised by the parents, who also saw to their education. Adoption of a poor relative was common. Early Romans like Cato the Censor taught their children themselves. Later Romans engaged private tutors, often Greek slaves to keep with the schooling. The husband was lord and master, *dominus,* over the family. He became owner of his wife's property at marriage. He had complete legal power over everyone and everything in his family. This *patria potestas* was, according to tradition, established by the first Roman king, Romulus, who allowed fathers to imprison, whip, throw into chains, sell into slavery, or kill their sons. Although reason seems to have prevailed over the years, and there were mostly sane, loving, caring fathers in Roman times, the ideology remained the same: Father knows best!

Fourth and Fifth Declension and "That's All, Folks"

The last two declensions are like your long-lost cousins from Alaska. There is a family resemblance, but they're not people you see very often. The fourth declension has *u*'s all over the place. The genitive is *us* and *uum;* the nominative plural is *us.* The fifth declension has about three words that are used often and is characterized by the only vowel left, *e.* The genitive singular is *ei,* the plural is *erum,* and the nominative plural is *es.*

Nominative	Genitive	Gender	Meaning	Derivative
actus	actus	m.	act	act
conventus	conventus	m.	coming together	convention
dies	diei	m.	day	diurnal
res	rei	f.	thing, matter	reify
strepitus	strepitus	m.	noise	strepitous
sumptus	sumptus	m.	cost	sumptuary
venatus	venatus	m.	hunting	venatic
vultus	vultus	m.	face, countenance	—

To *reify* is to make a concept or abstraction into a concrete thing. So if you're in a bar having a heated argument about existentialism and you hear "Would you like to step outside and reify this?" unless you are a renowned pugilist, head for the back door.

And beware of your spouse laying down the *sumptuary* law. It probably means your credit card balance is out of sight.

Here is a summary of the endings you've learned so far:

Declension	Nominative Singular	Nominative Plural	Genitive Singular	Genitive Plural
First	*a*	*ae*	*ae*	*arum*
Second	*us/r*	*i*	*i*	*orum*
Third	—	*es*	*is*	*um*
Fourth	*us*	*us*	*us*	*uum*
Fifth	*es*	*es*	*ei*	*erum*

Practice Makes Perfect 1

Read aloud and translate the following:

1. Actus fratris _____
2. Agmen elephantorum _____
3. Calamitas civitatis _____
4. Vetustas dictatoris _____
5. Comes feminae _____
6. Condicio pacis _____
7. Opus ostreae _____
8. Otium virorum _____
9. Pernicitas piscis _____
10. Dens oris _____

Now try translating these into Latin:

1. The helpers of Spartacus _____
2. The estimates of the architect _____
3. The time of life _____
4. The trees of Rome _____
5. Buns of steel _____
6. The hamstring of the man _____
7. Axes of wives _____
8. Affairs of state _____
9. Affairs of the leader _____
10. Price of meat _____

Names for Men and Those Other People

Some people have long names, like John Jacob Jingle Heimer Schmitt, and others, short, like Cher. Some names describe what you do, like Baker, Smith, or Farmer, while others describe where you live—Hill, Fields, or Woods—or whose child you are, like Johnson, Jackson, or Peterson.

The Roman upper-class male had three names. The first name, the *praenomen,* was his personal name. The second, the *nomen,* was the name of his clan. The third, the *cognomen,* was originally a nickname, but came to denote the particular family within the clan. So Marcus Tullius Cicero was called Marcus and belonged to the Tullian clan and the Cicero family, the originator of which probably had a nose like a chickpea. The famed Julius Caesar was called Gaius and belonged to the Julian clan and the Caesar side of the family, whose progenitor may have had a huge head of hair (not passed on to the notoriously balding Julius).

Cave!

Be sure to read names carefully. There is a generation of difference between G. Julius Caesar and L. Julius Caesar (father of G.), who died rather ingloriously while putting on his shoes.

Roman boys were always named for their father or adopted father, as was the case with Pliny. Gaius Plinius Secundus, known as Pliny the Elder, was the scholar and natural historian who died while investigating the eruption of Mt. Vesuvius. His adopted son, Gaius Plinius Caecilius Secundus, known as Pliny the Younger, was actually the son of L. Caecilius, Pliny's wife's brother. The younger Pliny declined an invitation to go near the eruption on that fateful day in A.D. 79, saying that he preferred to stay home and read. See? It pays to study.

Very often a second cognomen was added to a man's name to commemorate a special event or victory in his life. Publius Cornelius Scipio Africanus was so named for his triumph over Hannibal in Africa.

A girl was named for her father. So Julia is the daughter of Julius, Marcia of Marcus, Lucia of Lucius, and Antonia of Antonius. If ill fortune plagued her house and another girl was born, she would be named Julia Secunda or, heaven forbid, Julia Tertia. Sometimes sisters were called Julia Major and Julia Minor. The girl's formal name would include the father's name in the genitive case: Julia, filia Gai Juli Caesaris.

Slaves had only one name, often denoting their place of origin. So Syrus was from Syria, Germanicus from Germany, and Phyrgia from Phyrgia. They, too, took the name of their master in the genitive case.

Hysteria's Herstory

We may not have had our own names, but the one name we did have sure stuck! Women have come down to us through history, in spite of men being the only historians for hundreds of years—Cleopatra, Sappho, Lucretia, and Zenobia, just to name a few.

Practice Makes Perfect 2

Fill in the correct endings.

Declension	Nominative		Genitive	
	Singular	Plural	Singular	Plural
First				
Second				
Third				
Fourth				
Fifth				

Now see how you do translating the following:

1. Res vitae _____
2. Pedes pugilium _____
3. Rete gladiatoris _____
4. Vasum salis _____
5. Silentium agnorum _____
6. Sumptus temporis _____
7. Turba urinantium _____
8. Uxor Caesaris _____
9. Ius maiorum _____
10. Pretium mercedis _____

Now translate into Latin:

1. Women of the house _____
2. The noise of the streets _____
3. A convention of companions _____
4. Leg of lamb _____
5. Leaders of the world _____
6. Expectations of the crowd _____
7. A woman's thigh _____
8. The mischief of the brother of the wife _____
9. The earrings of the eel _____
10. Laws of the people _____

By now you have figured out that some words will have similar endings (*i, ae*) yet be in different cases (nominative, genitive). Let's see how much you remember. Check the appropriate box or boxes:

Latin Word	Nominative Singular	Nominative Plural	Genitive Singular	Genitive Plural
gloriae	❏	❏	❏	❏
Caesaris	❏	❏	❏	❏
alumni	❏	❏	❏	❏
alumna	❏	❏	❏	❏
ostreae	❏	❏	❏	❏
pacis	❏	❏	❏	❏
res	❏	❏	❏	❏
rete	❏	❏	❏	❏
uxor	❏	❏	❏	❏
ferri	❏	❏	❏	❏
strepitus	❏	❏	❏	❏
sumptuum	❏	❏	❏	❏
comitium	❏	❏	❏	❏
viri	❏	❏	❏	❏
silenti	❏	❏	❏	❏
pacum	❏	❏	❏	❏

The Least You Need to Know

➤ The third declension has many different endings in the nominative forms.

➤ The most important third-declension ending is the genitive singular, *is*.

➤ Roman men had three names.

➤ Roman women had no name of their own.

➤ The fourth and fifth declensions have *u*'s and *e*'s.

➤ Never use the pick-up line "I can't help but admire your popliteal space."

Chapter 5

Let's Have Some Action!

In This Chapter

➤ Active, sedentary, and couch potato verbs

➤ Conjugations

➤ It's happening now: the present tense

➤ To be or not to be able

➤ Your goose is cooked ... or is it doing the cooking?

It's time for some action. Nouns—persons, places, and things—must do something to make a sentence come to life. So in this chapter our cavemen will jump and the oysters will swim. We also learn passive verbs, where something is done to the subject. Elephants are jumped on by the cavemen, oysters are captured by the divers, and your goose is cooked. Verbs make your world exciting.

Words to Be Memorized

The following lists consist of verbs—action words or words describing a state of being. Latin verbs are universally listed in dictionaries beginning with the first person singular, present tense form, then the present infinitive, the perfect active, and finally the perfect passive participle.

But hey! Forget all that! In these lists the third-person singular will follow the first-person present and then the third-person plural. For example, the first listing would translate, "I knock down, he knocks down, they knock down." The traditional forms can be found in the vocabulary at the end of the book.

Notice that if the first word ends in *io,* the third person plural form is *iunt* rather than *unt.*

Really Active Verbs

This list of verbs describes all physical actions, ranging from mild (grab a beer) to violent (knock down a tree).

First Singular	Third Singular	Third Plural	Meaning	Derivative
accido	accidit	accidunt	cut down	accident
affligo	affligit	affligunt	knock down, damage	afflict
apprehendo	apprehendit	apprehendunt	grab	apprehend
cado	cadit	cadunt	fall	cadence
caedo	caedit	caedunt	kill, cut	matricide
capio	capit	capiunt	take, capture	captive
clamo	clamat	clamant	shout	clamor
concido	concidit	concidunt	fall	coincidence
convolo	convolat	convolant	fly about	volatile
coquo	coquit	coquunt	cook	cook
decido	decidit	decidunt	fall down	deciduous
desilio	desilit	desiliunt	jump down	saltate
procumbo	procumbit	procumbunt	fall down	recumbent
pugno	pugnat	pugnant	fight	pugnacious
stipo	stipat	stipant	press, plant	stipe
subruo	subruit	subruunt	uproot	rush

Just a few explanations. *Desilio* comes from the Latin *salto,* which means "to jump or dance." So you can yell at your kids "Don't saltate on the bed!" and by the time you have explained what it means, they will have stopped.

From *stipo* comes *stiff* and *stipe,* which is a short stalk or stem.

Cubo means "to lie down or recline," and for a Roman this meant climbing on his couch and planting his arm in a pillow and leaning on it. So *cubitum* came to mean "elbow." From there it came to mean a sharp bend resembling the elbow, and after adding a few sides and sticking them all together, we get—*voilà!*—a cube.

There are two potentially confusing verbs. *Cado* means "to fall," while *caedo* means "to cut." The confusion comes when the verb forms are compounds, the base words with a prefix. Both *cado* and *caedo* change to *cido* in compounds. So *accido* can mean "fall toward" and "cut toward." Same problem with *decido*, which can mean "fall down or cut down." So how do you tell the difference? Well, if your sentence includes a woodsman with an axe and a tree, *decido* is probably "cut down." If, on the other hand, your sentence is about a person chewing gum and walking at the same time, *decido* will probably be "fall down."

Tene Memoria

Remember that if the first-person singular (the first word in the vocabulary listing) ends in *io*, then the third-person plural will end in *iunt*.

Slightly More Sedentary Verbs

The following verbs describe actions to be done with minimal effort. Burying a body might be the exception, requiring some time and strength. However, burying your head in the sand takes minimal effort, especially if you're an ostrich.

First Singular	Third Singular	Third Plural	Meaning	Derivative
abhorreo	abhorret	abhorrent	shrink back	abhor
admoneo	admonet	admonent	warn	admonish
antecedo	antecedit	antecedunt	surpass	antecedent
appello	appellat	appellant	call, name	appellation
applico	applicat	applicant	apply, attach	applicable
condio	condit	condiunt	season	condiment
consumo	consumit	consumunt	use up	consume
diffundo	diffundit	diffundunt	pour out	diffuse
exigo	exigit	exigunt	take out, demand	exigency
obruo	obruit	obruunt	bury, hide	rush
orno	ornat	ornant	decorate	ornate
peto	petit	petunt	beg, attack	petition
refero	refert	referunt	bring back	refer
relinquo	relinquit	relinquunt	leave	relic

Didn't you always wonder why ketchup was called a *condiment?* Well, now you know.

Be sure to use *exigencies*, accent on the first syllable, as a synonym for *needs, demands, requirements*. Somehow it sounds more urgent. "The exigencies of my job require longer vacations" will certainly impress your boss and result in another week at the beach.

Couch Potato Verbs

Here's my favorite list—words describing actions from the couch. I don't think the average Roman was much of a couch potato, or Latin would include words for clicking the remote or ordering out.

First Singular	Third Singular	Third Plural	Meaning	Derivative
dico	dicit	dicunt	speak, say	dictate
exsisto	exsistit	exsistunt	stand out, appear	exist
includo	includit	includunt	include	include
—	inquit	inquiunt	he/she says	—
obligo	obligat	obligant	obligate, earmark	obligate
placeo	placet	placent	be pleased	placid
possum	potest	possunt	be able	potent
praesto	praestat	praestant	be responsible	presto
quaeso	quaesit	quaesunt	ask	question
sum	est	sunt	be, is, are	is
volo	vult	volunt	want	voluntary

Conjugations, or the Perfect Marriage

Conjugation comes from the Latin and Sanskrit word, *iugum,* meaning "a yoke by which a plough or chariot is drawn." A device of the same shape was used to carry baskets or buckets of water. A *iugum* was used to humiliate conquered prisoners of war by forcing them to bend low and walk under the yoke.

So being yoked together with someone (forget the subjection and humiliation part) is a conjugation, and thus we talk about conjugal rights.

A conjugation joins the stem of the verb with the personal ending. In English, we use the personal pronouns *I, you, he, we, you,* and *they* to show who is doing the action.

Although Latin also has personal pronouns, they are used mostly to show emphasis. Instead, the personal ending is added directly to the verb. These endings are *o, s, t, mus, tis,* and *nt.*

RETINEO

Grammar Guru

The prefix *con* means "with"—condominium, ownership with; confide, trust with; conform, shape with; conjugal, yoked with (in the good sense, of course).

Singular		Plural	
coquo	I cook	coquimus	we cook
coquis	you cook	coquitis	you (all) cook
coquit	he, she cooks	coquunt	they cook

Now, more often than not you will have a subject—the goose, the elephant, love, marriage, agility, whatever. In that case, remember to have the verb ending agree with the subject in number, singular or plural, and person. So if the subject is *we the people*, you must use the first-person plural ending for the verb. If it's *you all*, you need …

But hey! Forget all that! Just remember *o* means "I," *t* means "he, she, or it," and *nt* means "they." We'll worry about agreeing with the other people later.

Did You Know?

Rome was governed by seven kings for the first 243 years of its existence. Romulus was the first and he killed his brother, carried off the Sabine women, and finally was carried to heaven in a cloud. Numa Pompilius prayed a lot. Tullus Hostilius, as his name implies, was hostile to the neighbors and carried on much war. He was the king to destroy the ancient city of Alba Longa and move to Rome, where he died when his house was struck by a bolt of lightning. Ancus Marcius built bridges and the seaport, Ostia. Lucius Tarquinius Priscus, the first of a series of Etruscan kings, gained the throne by fraud and was deservedly murdered. Servius Tullius enlarged the city of Rome and held the first census. His daughter, the ambitious and evil Tullia, goaded her husband to kill her father and take over. To add insult to injury, Tullia ran over her father's dead body with her cart. The seventh and final king was Tarquinius Superbus, but more on him later.

It's Happening Now!

So verbs show action or a state of being. Now that you can show *who* is doing the action, the next step is *when*. The present tense in English has three different forms:

➤ Simple present (*I cook*)

➤ Progressive present (*I am cooking*)

➤ Emphatic present (*I do cook*)

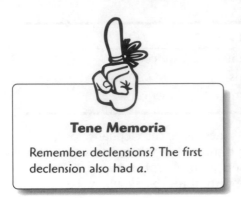

Tene Memoria

Remember declensions? The first declension also had *a*.

In Latin it's a little simpler. There is only one form of the present tense and it is formed by adding the personal endings to the present stem of the verb. Verbs of the first conjugation have present stem *a*—*amat* (he loves), *appellant* (they call), *convolat* (it flies about).

How do you know if the verb is in the first conjugation? You can look in the dictionary and look at the second word listed, the present infinitive. It should end in *re*, and if it's a first-conjugation verb it will end in *are*. So you will find *amo* and *amare*, *appello* and *appellare*, *volo* and *volare*.

The second-conjugation verb ends in *eo* and the infinitive ends in long *ere*—*habeo* and *habere*, *respondeo* and *respondere*, *admoneo* and *admonere*—and will have an *e* before the personal ending.

The third and fourth conjugations (there is no fifth, thank goodness!) end in *o* or *io* and have the infinitives of *ere* and *ire*. In the present tense they both have the same stem—*i* in the singular and *u* or *iu* in the plural.

But hey! Forget all that! I promised no long and complicated rules. Just look at the following words, and I'll bet you can translate them. Just remember the *o*, *t*, and *nt* thing.

Practice Makes Perfect 1

Translate and remember: If there is no noun subject, you'll have to provide a personal pronoun.

1. Stipant _____
2. Coquo _____
3. Funambuli antecedunt _____
4. Mensa concidit _____
5. Frater relinquit _____
6. Apprehendunt _____
7. Convolant _____
8. Exsistit _____
9. Pugno _____
10. Procumbunt _____

To Be or Not To Be Able

The verb *esse*, "to be," is irregular and, therefore, special. The complete present tense conjugation is …

Singular		Plural	
sum	I am	sumus	we are
es	you are	estis	you are
est	he, she it is	sunt	they are

These should be memorized because these forms are used as helping verbs for other tenses. The infinitive, *esse*, gives you the English *essence, essential, absence,* and *presence.*

Although the verb *to be* is often at the end of the sentence, sometimes it can be found at the beginning, and then it is translated as "there is" or "there are." So *Sunt ostreae* could be translated as …

➤ They are oysters.

➤ There are oysters.

➤ Oysters are.

A predicate noun is a word that follows a linking verb, most often the verb *to be*. In Latin, the predicate noun is in the nominative case because it renames the subject. In English we also use the nominative, or subjective, case after a linking verb. That's why you should say *It is I,* not *It is me*.

Because the verb usually comes near the end of the sentence in Latin, you cannot count on word order to indicate a predicate noun. Often the predicate noun is before the verb. For example:

Vir pugil est. ("The man is a boxer.")

Meus frater urinator est. ("My brother is a diver.")

Finally, the verb *possum*, "to be able," is conjugated very much like *sum:*

Singular		Plural	
possum	I am able	possumus	we are able
potes	you are able	potestis	you are able
potest	he is able	possunt	they are able

Practice Makes Perfect 2

Fill in the blanks with words from the following word pool. You should only have to use a word once, but it may not work out and, hey, it's an imperfect world.

1. _____ dux est.
2. Est _____ apium.
3. _____ est elephantus.
4. _____ sunt urinantes.
5. _____ cadunt.
6. _____ desiliunt.
7. _____ affligunt.
8. _____ petit.
9. _____ caedit.
10. _____ obruunt.

Word pool: Graecus, coquus, muraenae, dictatores, trogodytae, arbores, dux, ostreae, apis, funambulus.

Now try writing some Latin verbs. Remember that the personal pronoun is the ending of the verb. The first one is done for you.

1. I ask Peto. _____
2. He comes. _____
3. They fall down. _____
4. They wish. _____
5. He attaches. _____
6. They uproot. _____
7. I fall. _____
8. She brings back. _____
9. I season. _____
10. They are responsible. _____
11. We are able. _____

Hysteria's Herstory

This is a pathetic story, but it must be told. The youngest son of Tarquinius Superbus, the last king of Rome, was named *Sextus Tarquinius* and he was enamoured of Lucretia, the lovely wife of his cousin, Tarquinius Collatinus. Unable to control himself, he raped her one night, saying that if she did not submit, he would kill her and then place the body of a slain slave next to her in the bed and everyone would think that ....

So the next day Lucretia, a most noble and virtuous woman, called her husband and father to her, related the whole ugly story, took a knife, and stabbed herself to death rather than to live as a dishonored woman. Of course, this led to a general revolt among the friends of Collatinus and eventually Brutus, an ancestor of the "*Et tu, Brute*" Brutus, assassinated the hated king and thus began the Republic.

The Goose Is Cooked

We might as well tackle the active/passive voice problem right away, as the passive voice appears much more frequently in Latin than in English.

The passive voice is used when the subject is acted upon as opposed to doing the action. It is formed in English by using the verb *to be* and the *ed* form of the verb. The present passive uses the present tense of the verb *to be*—*I am loved, the goose is cooked, we are hunted.*

In Latin, it's much easier. You simply add an *r* to the *o* in the first person, and an *ur* to the *t* and *nt* of the third singular and plural.

But hey! Forget all that! Just look for the *r*'s.

So it's *capior*, "I am captured"; *appellantur,* "they are called"; and *coquitur,* "it is cooked."

Grammar Guru

The passive voice has a subject of the verb, but the subject is passive and not acting. So the goose is being cooked, as opposed to a very active goose that has gone to cooking school and is now doing the cooking.

Practice Makes Perfect 3

Translate the following:

1. Fungi diffunduntur. _____
2. Caesar dictator appellatur. _____
3. Relinquitur. _____
4. Dicitur. _____
5. Pecunia obligatur. _____
6. Nervus exigitur. _____
7. Villa ornatur. _____

Now try translating these short sentences into Latin:

1. The meat is consumed. _____
2. The work is produced. _____
3. The oyster is held. _____
4. Feet are planted. _____
5. Gold is buried. _____

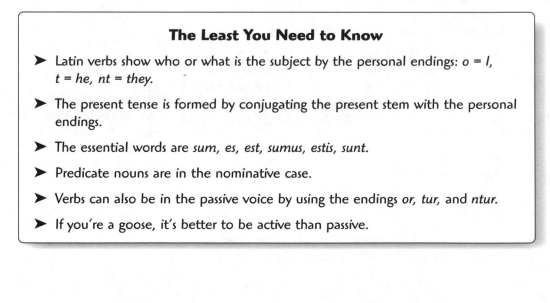

The Least You Need to Know

➤ Latin verbs show who or what is the subject by the personal endings: *o = I*, *t = he*, *nt = they*.

➤ The present tense is formed by conjugating the present stem with the personal endings.

➤ The essential words are *sum, es, est, sumus, estis, sunt*.

➤ Predicate nouns are in the nominative case.

➤ Verbs can also be in the passive voice by using the endings *or*, *tur*, and *ntur*.

➤ If you're a goose, it's better to be active than passive.

Chapter 6

Action Without an Ending—Verbals

In This Chapter

➤ To be or not to be: infinitives

➤ Seeing is believing: present participles

➤ Things that must be seen: passive perphrastic

➤ Reviewing verbals

A verbal is a verb form that is not used as a verb but as some other part of speech. So instead of being an action word, it can function as an adjective and describe a noun, or as a noun and be a person, place, or thing. Think of it as being similar to when you use a pencil, not to write with, but to prop up a window. It is no longer a pencil, even though it looks like a pencil. The pencil has become a window propper and functions like one.

Verbals are infinitives, participles, and gerunds.

To Be or Not To Be: Infinitives

Has your annoying neighbor ever gotten your ear at the annual barbecue and gone on and on, *ad infinitum* or *yadda, yadda, yadda,* about how to grow a better tomato?

Infinitive literally means "without an ending" and is the verb form that is translated in English with *to*. Also known as the second principle part, the infinitive form is always listed second in dictionaries and vocabulary lists. As mentioned in Chapter 5, "Let's

Cave!

Don't confuse the root *ferr*, meaning "iron," with the root *fer*, meaning "to bear or carry." Also, *mandare* ("to command") is quite different from *mandere* ("to chew"). Remember, the first conjugation has an *a* before the personal ending and the third conjugation has an *i*. So, it's *mandat* ("he entrusts") and *mandit* ("he chews").

Have Some Action!" the infinitive ending is an accurate way of classifying verbs in their conjugations: *are*, first; *ere*, second; *ere*, third; and *ire*, fourth.

The infinitive can be used as a noun: *To see is to believe*. The first infinitive is the subject of the sentence and, therefore, used as a noun. In the sentence *I like to eat* the infinitive is used as the direct object.

The infinitive is also used to complement or complete the meaning of another verb—*dicitur* ("it is said"), *videtur* ("it seems"), *licet* ("it is allowed"), *necesse est* ("it is necessary"), *potest* ("he is able"), and *vult* ("he wants") all can take a complementary infinitive.

First-Conjugation Verbs

The easiest group of verbs to remember and deal with are those whose infinitive ends in *are* and have an *a* before the personal ending. Here are some examples:

First Person Singular	Infinitive	Meaning	Derivative
amo	amare	to love	amour
do	dare	to give	donate
mando	mandare	to command	mandate
permuto	permutare	to exchange	permutation
supero	superare	to surpass	superior
sublevo	sublevare	to get up	levade
urino	urinare	to dive	urinant

Second-Conjugation Infinitives

Second-conjugation verbs have the first person singular, the first word in the dictionary listing, ending in *eo*. The infinitive ends in long *ere* and is pronounced *AY-reh*. The personal endings are preceded by an *e*, as you might expect—*doleo* (*DOH-leh-oh*) ("I am sad"), *dolere* (*doh-LAY-reh*) ("to be sad"), *dolet* ("he is sad"), *dolent* ("they are sad").

First Person Singular	Infinitive	Meaning	Derivative
abstineo	abstinere	to abstain	abstention
caveo	cavere	to be careful	caution
deleo	delere	to destroy	delete
doleo	dolere	to be sad	dolente

Third-Conjugation Infinitives

The third-conjugation infinitive ends in *ere* and is pronounced *eh-reh: agere* (*AH-geh-reh*), *mandere* (*MAHN-deh-reh*). The vowel before the personal endings is *i* or *u* in the third-person plural—*agit* ("he does"), *agunt* ("they do").

First Person Singular	Infinitive	Meaning	Derivative
ago	agere	to do	agent
consisto	consistere	to stop	consist
duco	ducere	to lead	ducal
erigo	erigere	to straighten	rigid
mando	mandere	to chew	mandible
pendo	pendere	to hang	pendant
perago	peragere	to do	act
vendo	vendere	to sell	vendor

Third io and Fourth-Conjugation Infinitives

This last category of verbs has the first word ending in *io*. While the third-conjugation verbs keep the infinitive *ere,* the fourth-conjugation infinitive is *ire*. However, the formation of the personal endings is similar; *it* for the third-conjugation singular and *iunt* for the third-conjugation plural—*audit* ("he hears"), *capit* ("he captures"), *audiunt* ("they hear"), *dormiunt* ("they sleep").

First Person Singular	Infinitive	Meaning	Derivative
accipio	accipere	to receive	accept
audio	audire	to hear	audio
dormio	dormire	to sleep	dormitory
fero (irregular)	ferre	to carry	ferry
sum (irregular)	esse	to be	essence

Tene Memoria

Remember that *per* is a Latin prefix meaning "perfection" or "completion." So the perfect tense shows completion, a *per-mutation* is a complete change and a *permanent* is completely yours until it grows out ... at least when it comes to hair.

Dolente is used in music to denote a sorrowful tone. The next time you are watching a movie and everybody around you are dabbing their eyes and sniffling, you can impress your friends by saying, "*Sotto voce, multo dolente!*"

When your boss loses 10 pounds, score a few points by saying, "Quite a *permutation!*"

And remember Roy Rogers and his wonder horse Trigger? When Trigger passed on, he was preserved in his famous forefeet-in-the-air stance, and now stands in the Roy Rogers Museum in a permanent and eternal *levade.*

Practice Makes Perfect 1

Say out loud and then translate:

1. Dormire   _____
2. Ferre   _____
3. Permutare   _____
4. Agere   _____
5. Superare   _____

Translate these into Latin:

1. To bring   _____
2. To straighten out   _____
3. To be   _____
4. To demand   _____
5. To get up   _____

And now some sentences:

1. Vult dormire.   _____
2. Videtur agere.   _____
3. Necesse est sublevare.   _____
4. Licet dare.   _____
5. Consistere est delere.   _____

Ready to translate into Latin?

1. He is able to command. _____
2. To change ... _____
3. To sleep is to overcome. _____
4. She seems to be ... _____
5. It is necessary to straighten up. _____

The present passive infinitive is formed by changing the final *e* of the active infinitive to an *i*, except for the third conjugation, which drops the entire infinitive ending *ere* and ends with an *i*. For example ...

amare ("to love") amari ("to be loved")

tenere ("to hold") teneri ("to be held")

ducere ("to lead") duci ("to be lead")

punire ("to punish") puniri ("to be punished")

Hysteria's Herstory

Carthage, the hated enemy of Rome and chief antagonist in the 100 years of the Punic Wars, was founded by Elissa, daughter of Belus, King of Tyre. After her husband was killed, she fled with some followers and founded the city in northern Africa. After a productive reign in which she enlarged the size of the original city and increased commerce, she was pressured into marrying Iarbas, a neighboring monarch. Unwilling to do this, she built a funeral pyre, ostensibly to honor her first husband, and before the eyes of all her people, climbed to the top and stabbed herself. The Roman Aeneas claims, of course, that she was driven to suicide by her unrequited love for him and his sneaky departure the night before. The people named her Dido, "valiant woman," and made her a goddess.

Seeing Is Believing

The present participle in English is the *ing* form of the verb. It can be used as a noun, as in *Seeing is believing,* or as an adjective, as in *seeing-eye dog.* Because it is used as a noun or adjective, the present participle has to belong to a declension, and the third declension adopted this hybrid into its family. Here are the present participle forms.

| | Masculine/Feminine | | Neuter | |
	Singular	Plural	Singular	Plural
Nominative	*ns*	*ntes*	*ns*	*ntia*
Genitive	*ntis*	*ntium*	*ntis*	*ntium*
Dative	*nti*	*ntibus*	*nti*	*ntibus*
Accusative	*ntem*	*ntes*	*ns*	*ntia*
Ablative	*nti*	*ntibus*	*nti*	*ntibus*

But hey! Forget all that! Just translate any verb with *ns* or *nt* in it as *ing.* Here's a short list of present participles:

First Person Singular	Infinitive	Present Participle	Meaning
audio	audire	audientes	listening
		audientibus	listening
doleo	dolere	dolens	suffering
perago	peragere	peragens	doing
pendo	pendere	pendens	hanging
urino	urinare	urinantes	diving

RETINEO

Grammar Guru

An adjective describes, limits, or specifies a quantity.

Especially in the plural, the present participle, while describing people, sometimes actually becomes the people and, therefore, sounds and acts like a noun. *Urinantes* ("divers") is really the present participle, "the diving ones." *Audientes* ("the listeners") translates as "those listening"; *spectantes* ("the spectators") becomes "those watching"; and *delentes* means "the destroying ones." Note that the ending *es* is for both men and women.

Practice Makes Perfect 2

Practice by translating the following expressions:

1. Urinantes pueri _____
2. Dolens femina _____
3. Pendens hortus _____
4. Peragentes _____
5. Audientibus _____

And now translate the following into Latin (nominative case):

1. The listeners _____
2. The active man _____
3. The suffering women _____
4. The diver _____
5. Those hanging _____

Things That Must Be Seen—
the Passive Periphrastic

Webster's unabridged dictionary has a 50-page *addenda,* things that must be added. Other words that come from the Latin are *corrigenda,* things that must be corrected, and *agenda,* things that must be done.

This wonderful Latin grammatical device, the passive periphrastic construction, consists of the future passive participle and some form of the verb "to be" and implies obligation. The endings for this participle are the same as the second and first declension.

But hey! Forget all that! Just remember *nd* and *est* means *must be ----ed.*

The same *nd* form, the future passive participle, can be used as a noun and be translated like the present participle, *ing.* This participle, called a gerund in English, has only four forms—genitive (*ndi*), dative (*ndo*), accusative (*ndum*), and ablative (*ndo*).

Cave!

Remember that when the verbal is the subject, it is usually in the infinitive form, not the present participle, as in English. For example, "Diving is good" translates as *Urinare bonum est.*

Practice Makes Perfect 3

Translate the following expressions into English:

1. Permutandum est. _____

2. Adicienda est. _____

3. Agendum est. _____

I'm sure you've got the idea. Now try some gerunds:

1. Vendendo _____

2. Ducenda _____

3. Cavendum _____

4. Sublevandi _____

Translate English into Latin:

1. Of suffering _____

2. Sleeping _____

3. It is the time for acting. (use genitive) _____

4. He changes completely for the purpose of selling. (use *ad* with accusative) _____

And now a few longer combinations:

1. Esse aut non esse. _____

2. Carthago delenda est. _____

3. Modus operandi. _____

4. Pendentes horti Babyloniae. _____

5. Volo sublevare et erigere. _____

Reviewing Verbals

In the following sentences, find the verbals and list them in the appropriate heading. The total number of each verbal form is indicated for you at the bottom of the list.

1. Ea sola dormire vult.

2. Hodie nivis consistere videtur.

3. Villas vendendo mangonicat.

4. Cum primum eam agere coepi, pugiles clamorem fecerunt.

5. Tempus agendi nunc mihi est.
6. Erat officium magistratuum auxilium semper dare.
7. Recipit opus quod curandum est.
8. Ad aestimationem adicienda est.
9. Ad perficiendum pecunia exigitur ex eius bonis.
10. Species arborum stantium reliquit.

Gerund	Infinitive	Present Participle	Periphrastic Participle
3	4	1	2

Did You Know?

During the First Punic War, when the Romans were fighting the Carthaginians for rights to Sicily and the Mediterranean Sea, Hasdrubal (brother of famous Hannibal) came face to face with Metellus, Roman general and consul. In the battle of Panormus, modern Palermo, Hasdrubal released a battle line of 140 elephants trained in fighting. They terrified the usually unflappable Roman legionaries until Metellus unveiled his anti-elephant device. He ordered the Roman archers to shoot arrows, dipped in flaming pitch, into the herd of elephants. The giant elephants (who seem to be afraid of mice *and* flaming arrows) turned tail and ran in a panic, trampling everything in front of them, including the Carthaginians.

The result was a victory for Metellus. He captured 20 of the African elephants and brought them to march in his triumphal procession through the streets of Rome, where they ended at the Circus Maximus and were slaughtered to the cheers of thousands. That's gratitude for you.

The Least You Need to Know

➤ Infinitives end in *re* and are translated as verbs with *to*.

➤ Present participles end in *ns* or *nt* and are translated as verb forms with *ing*.

➤ Gerunds and gerundives end in *nd* and are translated *ing*.

➤ The gerund and *est* implies obligation.

➤ This whole verbal thing is needlessly complicated and has no ending.

Chapter 7

The Good and the Bad— Adjectives and Accusatives

Adjectives are words that describe a noun. Adjectives are the writer's palette, used to fill in colors, size, shape, texture, or sounds. Adjectives make good writing come alive and give depth and dimension to the written picture. A beautiful woman is *curvaceous*, the sound of the saxophone is *mellifluous*.

Classical Latin authors, at least those whose works have survived and remain with us, were not as enamored with the adjective as we are today. Romans were practical, down-to-earth people, and we can thank them for clean-lined architecture and a system of codification of laws, but we can't thank them for exciting, vivid writing. Nevertheless, there are many Latin adjectives, used mostly to clarify, enumerate, or describe factually.

More Words You Know Already

The meanings of the following adjectives are fairly obvious. You will notice that some end in *us* while others end in *is*. Remember declensions in Chapters 3, "People, Places, and Things," and 4, "What's in a Name? More Nouns"? Words like *mundus, i,* m., are second declension, and others like *clunis, clunis,* m., are third declension. So, adjectives also come in two varieties. In the vocabulary lists, the genitive will also be given so you can recognize the word, whatever case it's in. The first- and second-declension adjectives will have those endings; the third-declension endings are for ....

But hey! Forget all that. You'll recognize the endings in due time.

No-Brainer Adjectives

Romans created some adjectives from nouns by adding the suffix *osus,* meaning "full of." It doesn't take an Einstein to figure out *verbosus* means "full of words."

Nominative (Masculine Singular)	Genitive	Meaning	Derivative
absurdus	absurdi	absurd	absurd
Africanus	Africani	African	African
alienus	alieni	foreign	alien
Brittanicus	Brittanici	British	British
communis	communis	common	common
fungosus	fungosi	spongy	fungous
furiosus	furiosi	furious	furious
gloriosus	gloriosi	glorious	glorious
Graecus	Graeci	Greek	Greek
herbosus	herbosi	grassy	herbaceous
industriosus	industriosi	industrious	industrious
infirmus	infirmi	weak	infirm
immortalis	immortalis	immortal	immortal
medius	medius	middle of	median
mutilus	mutili	broken	mutilate
nervosus	nervosi	nervous	nervous
nobilis	nobilis	noble	noble
otiosus	otiosi	at leisure	otiose
Romanus	Romani	Roman	Roman
singulus	singuli	one at a time	single
triumphalis	triumphalis	triumphant	triumphal
verbosus	verbosi	wordy	verbosity

Note that the adjectives describing a country often end in *anus* or *icus*. And if you are *otiose,* you are on vacation or just a bum.

Harder-to-Remember Adjectives

Note that in the following list, some adjectives end in *er,* like some second-declension nouns (such as *puer, ager, vir*). Like their noun counterparts, you need to know the genitive to find the base.

Nominative (Masculine Singular)	Genitive	Meaning	Derivative
amplus	ampli	full, large, wide	ample
asper	asperi	bitter, sharp	asperity
ceterus	ceteri	the rest	et cetera
dexter	dextri	right	dexterity
durus	duri	harsh	endurable
latus	lati	wide	latitude
liber	liberi	free	liberty
nasutus	nasuti	long-nosed	nasute
notus	noti	known	notable
omnis	omnis	all	omniscient
pensilis	pensilis	hanging	pensile
praeacutus	praeacuti	very sharp	acute
propinquus	propinqui	neighboring	propinquity
reliquus	reliqui	remaining	relic
similis	similis	similar	similar
sinister	sinistri	left	sinister
suavis	suavis	polite, polished	suave
sumptuarius	sumptuarii	excessive spending	sumptuary

Pensile is used to describe something that hangs, like a bird's nest, not what happened to Great Uncle Obadiah when convicted of murder.

The Romans had *sumptuary* laws, which regulated the amount of money one could spend on a banquet. The American sumptuary law is called credit card limit.

Remember poor *nasicorn* Uncle Edwin? He's also *nasute.*

Irregular Adjectives

The following adjectives will be found in forms different from the regular adjectives. These are often irregular in English as well, such as *good, better, best* and *much, more, most.* As indicated, there are a group of adjectives whose forms resemble more the pronoun *hic, haec, hoc* (for more details, see Chapter 8, "Taking the Place of Nouns—Pronouns").

Nominative (Masculine Singular)	Genitive	Meaning	Derivative
bonus	boni	good	bonus
magnus	magni	large	magnify
multus	multi	much, many	multiply
inferus	inferi	below	inferior
superus	superi	above	superior
exterus	exteri	the last	extreme
alter	alterius	the other	alter ego
nullus	nullius	none	nullify
totus	totius	all, total	total
ullus	ullius	any	—

A *teetotum* is a small top, used in games of chance and inscribed with the letter T for *take all*—not to be confused with *teetotaler,* one who abstains completely from drink.

Practice Makes Perfect 1

Translate the following expressions into English:

1. Nobilis femina   _____
2. Triumphalis cena   _____
3. In media cauda   _____
4. Infirmum aedificium   _____
5. Populus Romanus   _____

Now translate the English into Latin:

1. The common land   _____
2. Sumptuary law   _____
3. The single cave man   _____
4. The lone oyster   _____
5. The irate elephant   _____

The Most Agreeable Words

The big grammatical rule is that adjectives must agree with the noun they modify in number, gender, and case. So if the noun is *puella* and the adjective *bonus,* the ending on *bonus* must be nominative, singular, and feminine: *bona.*

Easy, you would think. Just use the same letter. Unfortunately, there are five declensions of nouns and two declensions of adjectives, and here come all those endings that send students to loony town.

But hey! Forget all that. Just look at the front of the word and we'll let the hard-core grammarians worry about agreement. Of course, if you *are* a hard-core grammarian, just look at the forms in Appendix B, "Grammar Summary."

If you want to try to be agreeable, match the nouns in Column A with the adjectives in Column B.

Column A	Column B
senatoris	bonus
vasis	superius
coquus	suavem
prandium	Graecis
denti	nervosi
hospitam	longo
hippopotamus	absurdus

Tene Memoria

Remember that the *a* ending is a popular one with the Romans. It can be the nominative singular feminine, nominative plural neuter, or accusative plural neuter. Use the context of the sentence to help you decide.

The Goods on Adjectives as Nouns

The English language often uses adjectives as nouns: the goods, the evils, the blues. In Latin, also, adjectives can be used alone as nouns. Most frequently these noun/adjectives appear in the neuter nominative or accusative plural, ending in *a*. They should be translated "things"—*multa* ("many things"), *bona* ("good things"), *altera* ("the other things").

Adjective	Meaning	Derivative
alter	the other	alter
bona	goods	bonbon
cetera	other things	et cetera
dextra	the right hand	dexterity
maiores	ancestors	major

continues

continued

Adjective	Meaning	Derivative
multa	many things	multitude
nota	known facts	notable
nullum	nothing	nullification, null and void
omnes	all, everybody	omnipotent, omniscient
sinistra	the left hand	sinister

If you are *ambidextrous,* you have in effect two right hands—*ambi*. It also means you are unusually skillful in two areas, as T.S. Eliot was in both prose and poetry. Of course, ambidextrous can have a more sinister meaning of being a double dealer, a shyster. On top of that, you might be *sinistral,* a rather sinister-sounding synonym for *left-handed.*

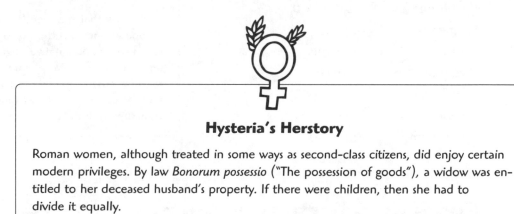

Hysteria's Herstory

Roman women, although treated in some ways as second-class citizens, did enjoy certain modern privileges. By law *Bonorum possessio* ("The possession of goods"), a widow was entitled to her deceased husband's property. If there were children, then she had to divide it equally.

Good, Gooder, Goodest—Degrees of Comparison

Not only do adjectives describe the noun they modify, they can also make comparisons. If your father is wise, your mother may be wiser, and, of course, you are the wisest of all. These suffixes—*er* and *est*—come from the Latin comparative and superlative forms, as we see in *longus, longior, longissimus*. These forms are also seen in music when you want to be the loudest—*fortissime*.

Perhaps you are *omnilegent*. You might know someone who reads even more than you, but it is awkward to say *omnilegenter*. So another form of the comparative is *more omnilegent* and the superlative, *most omnilegent*. In Latin we use *magis* and *maxime*, as in *magis intelligens* ("more intelligent") and *maxime intelligens* ("most intelligent").

Here are some examples of the degrees of an adjective:

Positive	Comparative	Superlative
praeacutus	praeacutior	praeacutissimus
suavis	suavior	suavissimus
nobilis	nobilior	nobilissimus

A very frequent form is the neuter, comparative form. This is translated as "more," just like the regular comparatives. It just lacks that telltale *ior*.

When you compare something with something else, you can use *quam* followed by the nominative. The ablative case is also used (for more details, see Chapter 9, "Where? When? How Many?"). For example …

> The pig is happier than the man.

Translates as …

> Porcus est laetior quam vir.

Comparative Neuter	Meaning	Derivative
asperius	more bitter	asperity
gloriosius	more glorious	glorious
iucundius	more pleasing	jocund
latius	more wide	lateral
suavius	more charming	suave

If you are the life of the party (the one with the lampshade on your head), you can be *jocund, jocose,* or filled with *jocundity*. At any rate, you will probably be making jokes.

On the other hand, if you are trying to impress your boss, remove the lampshade, take out your cell phone, and try to be *suave*.

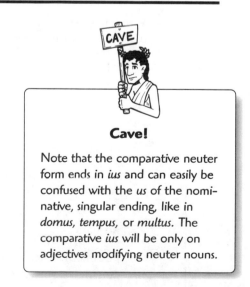

Cave!

Note that the comparative neuter form ends in *ius* and can easily be confused with the *us* of the nominative, singular ending, like in *domus, tempus,* or *multus*. The comparative *ius* will be only on adjectives modifying neuter nouns.

Practice Makes Perfect 2

Translate the following into English:

1. Nobilior _____
2. Longior _____
3. Iratissimus _____
4. Infirmissimus _____
5. Communior _____

Now change the English into Latin:

1. The right hand _____
2. More pleasing than (quam) salt _____
3. Larger than life (quam vita) _____

Now try matching the terms in Column A with those in Column B. Use your common sense and have the adjective agree in number, gender, and case.

Column A	Column B
1. Poplites	a. Medias
2. Dei	b. Publicis
3. Cibum	c. Praeacutum
4. Res	d. Alterius
5. Aedificiis	e. Nullum
6. Cornu	f. Immortales
7. Corporis	g. Mutili

More practice: From the pool of words at the end of the list, choose the adjective that agrees in number, gender, case, and common sense:

1. Opus _____
2. Lex _____
3. Homo _____
4. Arbores _____
5. Balineas _____
6. Cura _____
7. Apes _____
8. Graecia _____
9. Romani _____

publicum, populi, vetusta, tota, singuli, alienus, propinquas, magna, pensiles

I Object! The Accusative Case

The accusative case sounds very negative. *"J'accuse!"* exclaims Emile Zola, implying guilt. It is speculated that this case is so named because the attention is focused on the object you accuse. So the accusative case is used as the direct object of a verb as well as the object of a preposition.

The singular endings usually end with an *m*, the plural with an *s*. You find similar endings in *him*, the objective form of *he*, and *us*, the objective form of *we*. So, is it that easy? Let's try.

| | Accusative | | |
Nominative	Singular	Plural	Meaning
vita	vitam	vitas	life
dextra	dextram	dextras	right hand
cibus	cibum	cibos	food
lex	legem	leges	law
actus	actum	actus	act
res	rem	res	thing

What could be easier? Of course, it's highly unlikely you will need the form for plural of "right hand" unless you are talking about the traditional wedding ceremony in which the bride and groom are asked to join their right hands (*dextras iungere*).

The problem is with the neuter nouns. Look at these examples:

| | Accusative | | |
Nominative	Singular	Plural	Meaning
aurum	aurum	aura	gold
mare	mare	maria	sea
otium	otium	otia	leisure
tempus	tempus	tempora	time
vasum	vasum	vasa	vase

There is a pattern here. The nominative and accusative of neuter nouns are always the same. The plural neuter forms always end in *a*.

The accusative case endings are used on the direct object of verbs. The direct object is that which receives the action of the verb. If you are looking at something, that something will be in the accusative case. If you send something, bite something, peel something, wash something, run over something, paint something, or twist something, all the somethings must be in the accusative case.

Practice Makes Perfect 3

Try translating these phrases. The first one is done for you. Remember, in Latin word order does not indicate direct objects, as in English.

1. Capio vexillum.   <u>I capture the flag.</u>
2. Apprehendo anserem.   _____
3. Elephantum capio.   _____
4. Arbores subruo.   _____
5. Coquus cenam coquit.   _____
6. Labor tempus consumit.   _____
7. Caesarem peto.   _____

Time to translate into Latin:

1. I season the oyster.   _____
2. He decorates the eel.   _____
3. We leave behind the gladiators!   _____

Did You Know?

The word *miniature* comes from the Latin adjective *miniatus*, meaning "painted with red." In medieval times, a miniature was an illuminated manuscript where, ironically, the first letter was enlarged and elaborately decorated. The painter was called a *miniator* because he used a red paint from cinnabar, or *minium*. The color is also described as vermilion, which comes from the French *vermeil*, which comes from the Latin *vermis* ("worm").

How's That? Questions

Since the Romans did not use a lot of punctuation marks, a question was indicated at the beginning of the sentence by ...

➤ Using an interrogative word such as *quis* ("who"), *quid* ("what"), *ubi* ("where"), *quando* ("when"), *cur* ("why"), *quo modo* ("how"), *quantum* ("how much"), *quot* ("how many"), or *qualis* ("what kind of").

➤ Adding *ne* to the first word to show that a question was coming; for example, *Esne dictator?* ("Are you a dictator?") *Ambulatne in horto?* ("Is she walking in the garden?")

➤ Beginning the sentence with either *num* or *nonne. Num* would indicate a sentence was coming that needed a "no" answer, and *nonne* would indicate a sentence that needed a "yes" answer. These are fine distinctions not ever found on inscriptions, legal terms, or medical terminology. In fact, you rarely see these words except in conversation, and let's face it, how many dialogues do you expect to have in Latin riding on the elevator to work?

RETINEO

Grammar Guru

In English, the direct object almost always comes after the verb—*People eat potatoes. Potatoes* is the direct object. If the sentence was *Potatoes eat people,* then *people* would be the direct object and running for their lives from the GIANT KILLER POTATOES!!!

Practice Makes Perfect 4

Look back at the previous "Practice Makes Perfect" and turn the sentences into questions. Then translate them into English.

The Least You Need to Know

➤ Adjectives make our writing more defined and interesting.

➤ Adjectives agree with the noun they modify in number, gender, and case.

➤ Sometimes adjectives are nouns.

➤ Adjectives have degrees of comparison.

➤ The direct object is in the accusative case, which usually ends in *m* or *s*.

➤ Neuter nominative and accusative forms are always the same. The neuter plural nominative and accusative ending is *a*.

➤ Don't ask questions in Latin. It will only get you in trouble. Just use the universal shrug.

Chapter 8

Taking the Place of Nouns— Pronouns

If there were no pronouns, Shakespeare would have written:

> "Friends, Romans, countrymen, lend Mark Antony the ears of the friends, Romans, and countrymen;
>
> Mark Antony comes to bury Caesar, not to praise Caesar."

Pronouns are linguistic shortcuts, allowing us to use nice, short replacements for long, cumbersome names. English speakers automatically change cases—*I* see *him; he* sees *me; we* see *them*. So doing the same in Latin will be easy.

Words You Should Know Yourself

Personal pronouns are small and short, and just as in English, they will come in various cases:

Latin Pronoun	Case	Person	Number	English
ego	nominative	first	singular	I
me	accusative	first	singular	me
nos	nominative	first	plural	we
nos	accusative	first	plural	us
tu	nominative	second	singular	you
te	accusative	second	singular	you
vos	nominative	second	plural	you
vos	accusative	second	plural	you

The *ego*, made famous by Freud, is the "I" or "self" of any person. We all know that it can be very huge or fragile.

First- and Second-Person Pronouns and Adjectives

The personal pronouns in the first and second persons are very similar to the English: *ego* ("I"), *me* ("me"), *tu* ("you"). The plural varies a little, but can be remembered by *nos* meaning "us" and *vos* meaning "you guys." Here are some examples:

Ego te amo.	I love you.
Tu me amas.	You love me.
Nos familia laeta sumus.	We are a happy family.

Cave!

Remember that these are adjectives and therefore will have endings that agree with the noun they modify. So you will see *tuum, nostro, vestris,* but they still translate as "your," "our," and "your."

The personal pronoun is often omitted, as in this example: *Te amo* ("I love you"). When the personal pronoun is used, it shows emphasis: *Ego te amo* translates as "*I* love you" as opposed to your worst enemy, who does not.

Latin shows personal possession in the first and second person by using the possessive adjectives. Remember, they have to agree with the noun they modify and, therefore, will have varied endings.

Adjective	Base	Meaning
meus	me	my, mine
tuus	tu	your (singular)
vester	vestr	your (plural)
noster	nostr	our

Noster can be seen in the French *nôtre,* where the circumflex over the *o* denotes the missing *s*. Likewise, *votre* comes from the Latin *vester*.

The Lord's Prayer is often referred to as the Pater Noster, the first two words.

Practice Makes Perfect 1

Translate the following phrases into English:

1. Noster pater   _____
2. Tua soro   _____
3. Ego sum dictator   _____
4. Nos populus   _____
5. Vestra epistula   _____
6. Meus frater   _____
7. Te amo   _____
8. Mc appellate Ishmael   _____
9. Noli me vocare, ego te vocabo   _____
10. Ego mater sum   _____

This, That, and Whatever— Third-Person Pronouns and Demonstratives

Now for the third-person pronoun—*he, she, it, they, her, his, its, their, him,* and *them*. As you can see from the English, this is a bit more complicated, mainly because the pronouns designate gender and case. The English cases are …

➤ Subjective (for the subject): *he, she, it, they.*

➤ Possessive (to show ownership): *his, her, its,* and *their.*

➤ Objective (for the object of a verb or preposition): *him, her, them.*

Latin uses the demonstrative pronouns (*this, that, these, those*) as the third-person pronouns. Literally, Romans were saying *this man, this woman, this thing* or *that man, that woman, that thing* instead of *he, she, it.* A further distinction designates whether the third person is near the speaker, away from the speaker, or just anywhere. So we have *hic, haec,* and *hoc* to designate a person near, *ille, illa,* and *illud* for someone farther away.

But hey! Forget all that! Just remember that a very short word beginning with *h* will have something to do with this person, him or her or them. Another short word beginning with *ill* will also have something to do with that person, and a really short word beginning with *e* or *i* will designate all of the above. Don't be put off by all the forms, which are included here for reference.

Case	Singular	Plural
Nominative	hic, haec, hoc	hi, hae, haec
Genitive	huius, huius, huius	horum, harum, horum
Accusative	hunc, hanc, hoc	hos, has, haec
Nominative	ille, illa, illud	illi, illae, illa
Genitive	illius, illius, illius	illorum, illarum, illorum
Accusative	illum, illam, illud	illos, illas, illa
Nominative	is, ea, id	ei, eae, ea
Genitive	eius, eius, eius	eorum, earum, eorum
Accusative	eum, eam, id	eos, eas, ea

Just as adjectives can become nouns—*bona* ("good things")—so these pronouns can be translated as nouns—*ea* ("these things"), *illa* ("those things"), *haec* ("these things"). Don't confuse *haec* (nominative, singular, feminine) with *haec* (nominative and accusative, plural, neuter). We've faced this problem before with *puella* ("girl") and *tempora* ("times").

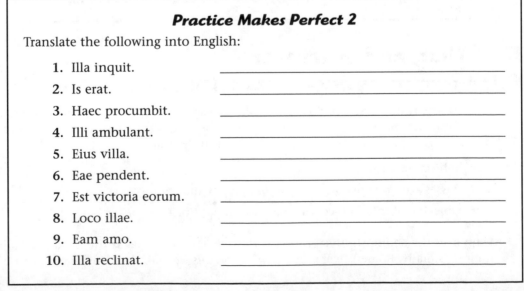

Practice Makes Perfect 2

Translate the following into English:

1. Illa inquit. _____

2. Is erat. _____

3. Haec procumbit. _____

4. Illi ambulant. _____

5. Eius villa. _____

6. Eae pendent. _____

7. Est victoria eorum. _____

8. Loco illae. _____

9. Eam amo. _____

10. Illa reclinat. _____

There is a related adjective—*idem, eadem, idem* ("the same"). All you need to remember is that the suffix *dem* translates as "the same." All the forms are very similar to the demonstrative pronoun *is, ea, id*.

All followers of Freud will recognize the *id*, the part of the psyche that is the source of unconscious and instinctive impulses.

An expression which is simply fun to say is *huc illuc*. This phrase—which can sound like a hiccough—can describe a tennis match, the promises of a politician, or a lawyer's arguments. *Huc illuc* means "this way and that."

Demonstrative pronouns can also be used as adjectives. These are recognized because there will be two words, and the adjective almost always comes first.

Tene Memoria

Remember that the genitive of *he* or *she* will be translated *his* or *hers*. So *eius, huius,* and *illius* will be translated *his*. Of course, you have noticed that *his* looks a lot like *eius*.

Adjective	Noun	Translation
hunc	librum	this book
hic	homo	this man
illae	arbores	those trees
eodem	modo	the same way
has	urinatores	these divers
ea	villa	this/that house

Did You Know?

Gaius Julius Caesar was killed on the *Ides* of March, not in the Senate House in the Roman Forum, but in Pompey's Portico where the senate was meeting. On that day Caesar was scheduled to be awarded a *diadem* and the title of King. Patriotic citizens had plotted to assassinate Caesar, and when he arrived at the building, the 62 conspirators swarmed around him. Tullius Cimber pretended to give him a petition. When Caesar brushed him aside, Cimber grabbed his cloak, the sign for the other conspirators to unsheath their weapons. Servilius Casca struck the first blow and others followed. Caesar soon gave up the fight and, wrapping his cloak around him, sank to the ground, muttering, "Et tu, Brute," speaking to his friend and using the nominative case of the personal pronoun. He fell at the foot of the statue of Pompey, a man he had defeated four years earlier.

Reflecting: Reflexive Pronouns

The English reflexive pronoun is *myself, yourself, himself, herself, ourselves, yourselves,* and *themselves*. It is used when the direct object refers to the subject of the sentence. In Latin, the personal pronoun accusative case is used for the first and second persons— *me, te, nos, vos.* But, as usual, the third person has to be different. The reflexive pronoun *se* or *sese* is used for both the singular and plural and, therefore, is surprisingly easy!

Subject	Verb	Pronoun	Translation
Ego	specto	me	I see myself.
Tu	audis	te	You hear yourself.
Nos	ornamus	nos	We decorate ourselves.
Vos	obruitis	vos	You bury yourselves.
Pueri	recipiunt	se	The boys retreat.
Illi	appellant	se	They call themselves.
Frater	pugnat	se	The brother fights himself.
Ostrea	applicat	se	The oyster attaches herself.

Tene Memoria

The reflexive adjective, *suus,* meaning "his/her/their own," will agree with the noun it modifies, *not* the person it is representing. So *suos agros* could be "his fields," if the subject was singular—*Curat suos agros* ("He watches over his fields").

The reflexive adjective, *suus* (base *su*) is similarly used for all parties of the third person. It will be translated "his own," "her own," or "their own," depending on the subject of the sentence.

The reflexive pronoun is not used for the subject. If you want to say *I myself,* then use the intensive pronoun, *ipse.* This is also sometimes translated as *very,* as in *the very idea!* This word can also be used as an adjective or a pronoun, as in this example:

Ipsa ad villam venit.

She herself comes to the house.

Don't confuse the intensive with the reflexive:

Se vidit in speculo.

She saw herself in the mirror.

Here are the singular and plural forms of *ipse:*

Singular		
ipse	ipsa	ipsum
ipsius	ipsius	ipsius
ipsi	ipsi	ipsi
ipsum	ipsam	ipsum
ipso	ipsa	ipso

Plural		
ipsi	ipsae	ipsa
ipsorum	ipsarum	ipsorum
ipsis	ipsis	ipsis
ipsos	ipsas	ipsa
ipsis	ipsis	ipsis

There is one more demonstrative adjective, *iste,* which has similar forms and is translated "that ---- of yours," often used in a derogative way, like *that mother-in-law of yours!*

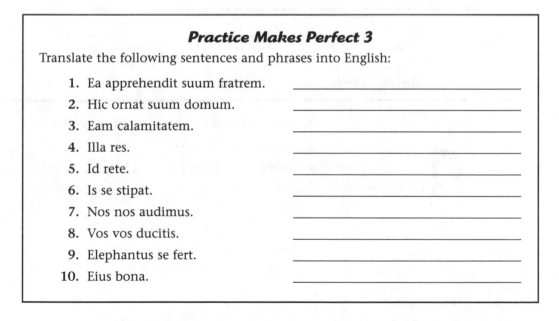

Practice Makes Perfect 3

Translate the following sentences and phrases into English:

1. Ea apprehendit suum fratrem. _____
2. Hic ornat suum domum. _____
3. Eam calamitatem. _____
4. Illa res. _____
5. Id rete. _____
6. Is se stipat. _____
7. Nos nos audimus. _____
8. Vos vos ducitis. _____
9. Elephantus se fert. _____
10. Eius bona. _____

There are many indefinite pronouns in Latin translating as *some, any, any at all, any one you please, some, someone, some few, a certain one, whoever, I don't know who.* These are discussed in Chapter 14, "Closing In on Clauses," together with relative pronouns, because these, for the most part, have forms similar to the relative pronoun.

Hysteria's Herstory

Fulvia, the Roman wife of Antony before he became besotted with Cleopatra, was famous for her boldness and verve. When Cicero was beheaded by Antony's soldiers in 43 B.C.E., his head and hands were brought to the Roman Forum where they were on display for all to see. Fulvia made a public spectacle of herself and subsequently a place in history by taking a large hair pin from her hair and vehemently piercing the inanimate and now powerless tongue of Cicero. Ouch!

You Can Go Now!

The verb *eo, ire,* is as short and irregular as its English counterpart. Here is the complete present tense:

Present Tense			
eo	I go	imus	we go
is	you go	itis	you go
it	he/she, it/goes	eunt	they go

Cave!

Do not confuse the third person pronoun *is, ea, id* with the irregular verb *ire* ("to go"). *Is* can also mean "you go," so try to use your common sense and the context of the sentence.

This little verb is often combined with prefixes:

exeo	I go out
redeo	I return
ineo	I go in
abeo	I go away
adeo	I go toward
obeo	I go to meet, I run over
praetereo	I go over or beyond

A preterite tense is one wholly in the past. This word is used in many Romance languages to describe a past tense. *Preterition,* also from *praetereo,* is the Calvinistic doctrine that having elected to eternal life certain chosen ones, God passed over the rest, leaving them to eternal death. Bummer.

You will notice that the second-person singular ending is *s* and the plural, *tis*. You can now use these endings on all the verbs you have learned.

Practice Makes Perfect 4

Try translating these:

1. Doletis _____
2. Consistis _____
3. Audis _____
4. Deletis _____
5. Adicis _____
6. Exit _____
7. Redeunt _____
8. Praeteris _____
9. Init _____
10. It is _____

The Least You Need to Know

➤ Personal pronouns are small and powerful and you know some already, like *ego* and *me*.

➤ The third-person pronouns come in many shapes and forms but look a lot like the English "his," "it," "him," and ... "hiccoughs."

➤ The reflexive pronoun is the beginning two letters in *self*, which is how it is translated.

Chapter 9

Where? When? How Many?

Imagine trying to determine your place and time without compass or digital watch. Imagine adding and subtracting Roman numerals with a few beads and wire. Fortunately, the Latin language makes up for some of those deficiencies by having many adverbs to describe when, where, and how, as well as a specific case for location. Specific time, unfortunately, never quite caught on.

Adverbs

Adverbs are used to modify verbs, adjectives, and other adverbs. Many adverbs in English end in *ly*, such as *largely, insipidly,* or *indisputably*. Other adverbs are simple words, often short, like *not, very,* or *easily*. In Latin, many adverbs are also short words that do not have other forms. Some are really easy to remember.

Easy Adverbs

The following adverbs should be easy to remember by their familiar derivatives. And the good news is that adverbs have only one form.

Adverb	Meaning	Derivative
foras	out	forum, door
non	not	nonexistent
primum	for the first time	prime time
privatim	privately	private

Primogeniture is "being the first born," formerly a good thing for the inheritance, nowadays not so good for breaking ground for younger siblings.

When and Where Adverbs

Adverbs are often used to add a little information to a sentence. They can tell us the when, where, and how of the word or phrase they modify. The following adverbs are a little harder to remember.

Adverb	Meaning
hic	here
hodie	today
interea	meanwhile
mane	in the morning
numquam	never
umquam	ever
nunc	now
olim	once upon a time
semper	always
tum	then
unde	from when, whence

Apart from the popular *Semper Fidelis* of the Marine Corps, we see *semper* in *sempervirent,* an "evergreen," which we hope will stay *sempervirent* for a *sempiternity*.

Tell-Me-How Adverbs

Finally, we have a few adverbs that will tell you how, in what way, or to what degree.

Adverb	Meaning
adeo	to such a degree
etiam	even, also

Adverb	Meaning
ita	in such a way
item	at the same time, likewise
paulo	a little
quot	how many
tot	so many
vero	truly

Try to be *veracious* and truthful, and not *voracious* or, heaven forbid, *bodacious*. *Ver* ("true") can be confused with *vert* ("turn"), *ver* ("spring"), or *verb* ("word").

Adverbs from Adjectives

The other method of forming adverbs is fairly consistent and logical, unlike the previous list. To form an adverb from an adjective, much like we do in English (with words such as *pretty, prettily; handsome, handsomely*), you change the ending of the *us* adjective to *e*, and the ending of an *is* adjective to *iter*. This doesn't always work, just as it does not in English, but it's a start.

Grammar Guru

Quot and *tot* can be used correlatively and translated "as many ---- as."

Adjective	Meaning	Adverb	Meaning
calidus	warm	calide	warmly
communis	common	communiter	commonly
durus	harsh	dure	harshly
fortis	brave	fortiter	bravely
humilis	humble	humiliter	humbly
infirmus	weak	infirme	weakly
iniquus	unfair	inique	unfairly
iratus	angry	irate	angrily
laetus	happy	laete	happily
miser	unhappy	misere	unhappily
similis	similar	similiter	similarly
triumphalis	triumphant	triumphaliter	triumphantly

Practice Makes Perfect 1

Match the face with the adverb:

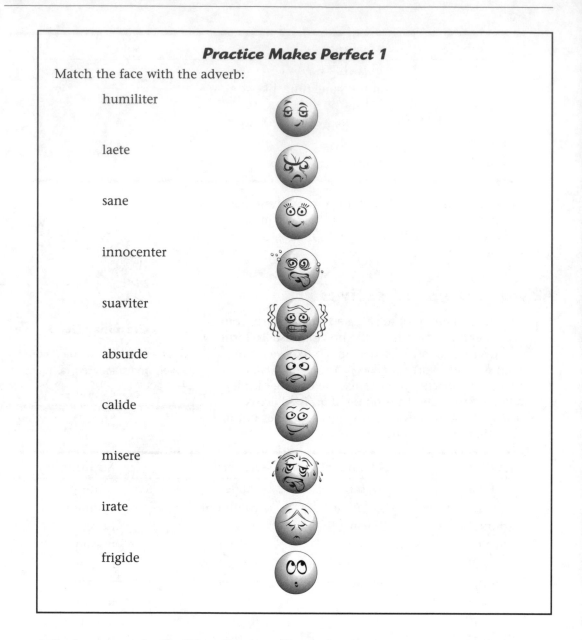

humiliter

laete

sane

innocenter

suaviter

absurde

calide

misere

irate

frigide

A final note on adverbs: Like adjectives, adverbs have a comparative and superlative degree. You can say *angrily, more angrily,* and *most angrily.* This is done by adding *ius* for the comparative and *issime* for the superlative. As with adjectives, the object of comparison can be in the ablative. The word *quam* is also used.

For example …

>He writes more clearly than I.

Translates as …

>Scribit clarius quam ego.

Or …

>Scribit clarius me.

Cave!

Watch out! The word with the *ius* ending can be a neuter adjective or a comparative adverb.

Ten Little Carthaginians—Numbers

Roman numerals are used in the modern world to designate a classic: Super Bowl XXIII is somehow a better thing, an event of stature, thanks to the addition of X's and I's. *Rocky II* is a movie to be seen because it is Roman numeralled, not because it's a weak remake of the first *Rocky*.

The Romans used numerals for the same reason we use them, to count. But their method of counting, using an abacus, is light-years away from our methods today. The mind truly boggles at the difference: A Roman had to carefully put beads into the tens, hundreds, and thousands columns, while I, at the click of a mouse, can count every word, every character, every space, and every line in this book instantly.

Did You Know?

The shape of Roman numerals originated with the finger movements of early merchants and traders—one finger, two fingers, three fingers, four fingers, and then the V, shaped by the thumb and fingers. Crossed hands made a 10, and the world became a better place.

Numbers are always tackled toward the end of the first-year Latin textbook because they have several forms that are like irregular adjectives. Luckily, endings and the correct form are not top priority, so we can enjoy this easy list of Latin words:

Number	Translation	Derivative
unus	one	unify
duo	two	duplex
tres	three	triplets
quattuor	four	quarter
quinque	five	quintuplets
sex	six	sextet
septem	seven	September
octo	eight	October
novem	nine	November
decem	ten	December
centum	one hundred	century
mille	one thousand	millennium

It's interesting to see the similarities in other languages:

Spanish	French	Italian	German
uno	une	uno	eins
dos	deux	due	zwei
tres	trois	tre	drei
cuatro	quatre	quattro	vier
cinco	cinq	cinque	fünf
seis	six	sei	sechs
siete	sept	sette	sieben
ocho	huit	otto	acht
nueve	neuf	nove	neun
diez	dix	dice	zehn

A.U.C., B.C., A.D., and B.C.E.—the Roman Calendar

What year is it really? We passed through the millennium without any ruckus because everyone has a different idea of what the date really is! The Romans counted the years from the founding of Rome (*ab urbe condita*), 753 B.C. in our reckoning. So their date for the assassination of Caesar was A.U.C. 710. When the calendar was established for Christianity, the Latin *Anno Domini* was used and nowadays some smart aleck has added another choice—Before the Common Era (B.C.E.).

Just in case you want to convert our modern years to the Roman way of thinking or vice versa, here are the formulae:

➤ If the A.U.C. date is 753 or less, subtract it from 754 for a B.C. date.

➤ If the A.U.C. date is 754 or more, subtract 753 from it for an A.D. date.

➤ If the year is B.C., subtract it from 754.

➤ If the year is A.D., add it to 753.

RETINEO

Grammar Guru

Mille (1,000) is an indeclinable adjective. *Milia* (thousands of any number) is a noun and takes the partitive genitive. So you have to say 2,000 soldiers, *duo milia militum,* but 1,000 soldiers, *mille milites.*

The Romans had a calendar that would give you a headache. Every day was reckoned from three fixed dates—the *Kalends,* the *Nones,* and the *Ides.* Unfortunately, the Nones was sometimes on the 5th and sometimes on the 7th, while the Ides was sometimes on the 13th, and other times on the 15th. Romans had to count backward from the Kalends to find out the days after the Ides and it really wasn't worth all that trouble. Furthermore, they reckoned the hours of the day by the hours after sunrise, so 3 o'clock in the winter was at a different time than 3 o'clock in the summer; it's no wonder Europeans to this day are late to everything.

They had several versions of the calendar from early times, all beginning the year in March. Julius Caesar made several revisions. Following the Egyptian method, he used a 365-day year, adopted a leap year in February and began his new year on the Kalends, or first day, of January, 45 B.C. He changed the month of Quinctilius, previously the fifth month, to July and later the sixth month was named by Augustus for himself. This explains why September, although derived from *septem,* is actually the ninth month in the year.

Here is a brief look at the Roman year:

➤ *Ianuarius* was named for Janus, the two-faced god of doorways and beginnings. The Romans didn't have wild New Year's Eve parties, but they did exchange gifts.

➤ *Februarius* was sacred to Mars and Juno. This month was devoted to life and death, fertility, and the fruits of the earth. The festival Lupercalia occurred in February, when young men sacrificed a goat, cut strips of goat skin, and ran through the street of Rome naked. Crowds of mostly women followed, for they believed that being touched by the Lupercali enhanced fertility.

➤ *Martius,* the month of Mars, was originally the first month and celebrated spring. Mars, god of war, also protected agriculture and business. The Salii, male dancers, leaped about often during the year in honor of Mars. These men, of noble birth, wore embroidered tunics with bronze belts and swords, breastplates, purple cloaks, and conical hats. A spear or stick in one hand and a shield in the other, they would leap and dance to the tune of a flute and sing a song in archaic Latin. This, of course, is reminiscent of Mardi Gras, which also has a lot of leaping and singing and occurs about this time.

➤ *Aprilis,* according to Ovid, got its name either from the Greek Aphrodite, since the month is devoted to Venus, or from *apertus,* "open," because in April everything in nature opens up. In any case, the Romans celebrated April Fools' Day and spent the day doing things backward, wearing women's clothes, and generally behaving like complete idiots.

➤ *Maius,* named for Maia, the wife of Mars, was a month of purification and festivals in honor of the dead. The Lemuria was a nine-day feast for the souls of the dead, called *lemures.* The lemur monkey with the big, ghostlike eyes is the singular of this word.

➤ *Junius* was sacred to Juno, goddess of marriage. Take heed! The first half was a period of religious purification and, therefore, not a time for weddings.

➤ *Julius,* originally Quinctilius, the fifth month, contained the Neptunalia, a holiday for Neptune. During the Neptunalia, all the city dwellers went out to fields and forests, built little huts from grass and leaves, and picnicked and camped out overnight.

➤ *Augustus* was named by Caesar Augustus himself. On August 24, 79 A.D., at 1 P.M., Mt. Vesuvius erupted during the festival of Vulcan, god of earthquakes, lightning, and volcanoes!

➤ *September* was the birth month of Augustus, who was deified on the 17th of this month in 14 A.D.

➤ *October* was the month in which the ancient battle between the Romans and the Albans was remembered. Three Horatii brothers fought three Curiatii brothers. Obviously, the Romans won.

➤ *November* began with a celebration of the foreign goddess Isis but from then on was dullsville.

Hysteria's Herstory

Although the victory of the Horatii was acclaimed throughout Rome, the real victim was the sister of the winning Horatius. She had been secretly engaged to the enemy, Curiatus, and when she learned they had all been killed, her lover included, she cried loudly and, one can imagine, passionately. Horatius, the victor, lost his patience, grabbed his sword, and killed his sister for being disloyal to Rome and such a whiner. The people forgave him and never punished him.

➤ *December* culminated with the festival of Saturn, the Titan who was supplanted by Jupiter and who fled to Italy to reign for many years. His rule was called the Golden Age as it was time of peace, happiness, and prosperity for all. The Saturnalia—a week-long time of feasting, gift-giving, and decorating of the home— was the precursor of Christmas. Look what the Romans started.

At Carthage—the Locative Case

Romans used special endings to show "at" someplace. *Romae* means "at Rome," *Carthagini* means "at Carthage." For nouns of the first and second declension, the locative is like the genitive; for third declension, like the ablative, or sometimes dative; and for plural words and names of cities, small islands, and towns ....

But hey! Forget all that! Just remember that sometimes, by changing a word ending, you can say *at Rome, at Carthage, at Brundisium.*

The Last of the Cases

You've noticed by now that the endings on nouns give you a clue as to how the word can be translated and how it is used in the sentence. The nominative case shows that the word is the subject. The genitive case shows possession and is translated *of* or *'s.* The accusative case is the direct object or the object of certain prepositions. The locative case shows location. Have courage! Only two more to go.

The Dative Case

The dative case is used for the indirect object and sometimes for possession. The indirect object usually occurs with verbs of giving, showing, or telling. For example:

> I give the book to him.

> I give him the book.

translates as ...

> Do librum ei.

The book is the direct object; it is what I gave. *Him* is the indirect object; it is to whom I gave the book.

The dative of possession is seen most often in the expression *Mihi nomen est Marcus* ("My name is Marcus," or literally, "The name Marcus is for me"). Here are the various singular and plural dative endings for all five declensions:

First Declension Singular/Plural		Second Declension Singular/Plural		Third Declension Singular/Plural		Fourth Declension Singular/Plural		Fifth Declension Singular/Plural	
ae	is	o	is	i	ibus	ui	ibus	ei	ebus

The Ablative Case

Notice that the ablative endings in the singular are simply one vowel. In the plural they are identical to the dative in all declensions. The ablative is the last case and is a kind of catchall. You can do just about anything in the ablative case. Here's a list of the various singular and plural ablative endings:

First Declension Singular/Plural		Second Declension Singular/Plural		Third Declension Singular/Plural		Fourth Declension Singular/Plural		Fifth Declension Singular/Plural	
a	*is*	*o*	*is*	*e*	*ibus*	*u*	*ibus*	*e*	*ebus*

The ablative case is used in the following ways:

➤ **Means or instrument.** To show with what instrument, tool, object, or thing something is done. For example …

> I cut the ham with a knife.

Translates as …

> Caedo pernam bipenni.

➤ **Agent.** The person by whom something is done, especially with passive verbs, is indicated by the preposition *a* or *ab* and the ablative. For example …

> The ham is cut by the cook.

Translates as …

> Perna a coquo caeditur.

➤ **Time.** To show when something is done. For example …

> I cut the ham at the second hour.

Translates as …

> Caedo pernam secunda hora.

➤ **With prepositions.** Many prepositions are followed by the noun in the ablative case, especially prepositions denoting place or from. For example …

> in the water

Translates as …

> in aqua

➤ **Manner.** To show how something is done. For example …

> I cut the ham with a great noise.

Translates as …

> Caedo pernam magno clamore.

➤ **Degree of difference.** To show the comparative degree with adjectives and adverbs. For example …

> The pig is fatter than a horse.

Translates as …

> Porcus pinguior equo est.

The personal pronouns also have dative and ablative endings:

Dative	*mihi*	*nobis*	*tibi*	*vobis*	*ei, eis*	*huic his*
Ablative	*me*	*nobis*	*te*	*vobis*	*eo, ea, eis*	*hoc hac his*

For example …

> I am longer than him.

Translates as …

> Sum longior eo.

And …

> These girls are wiser than those boys.

Translates as …

> Hae puellae illis sapientiores sunt.

Tene Memoria

Remember that adverbs end in *e*, *iter*, *ius*, or *issime*.

Practice Makes Perfect 2

Translate the following phrases and sentences:

1. Today, not in the morning _____
2. Never at the second hour _____
3. Angrily _____
4. Once upon a time _____

Now translate the Latin into English:

1. Duo et duo faciunt quattuor _____
2. Nunc aut numquam _____
3. Tum et nunc _____
4. Vero primum _____
5. Item, sum certus _____
6. Semper fidelis _____

> **The Least You Need to Know**
>
> ➤ Adverbs do not have a lot of confusing endings.
>
> ➤ Adverbs answer the questions of where, when, and how.
>
> ➤ We are indebted to the Romans for the word *calendar,* the names for months of July and August, and that crazy leap year.
>
> ➤ When in Rome, use the locative case.
>
> ➤ The dative case is used for the indirect object, and the ablative case is used for everything else.

Chapter 10

Expanding the Time Frame—Past and Future Tenses

It's time to look at verbs in their entirety. Dictionaries, vocabularies, and textbooks will give four parts to every verb—unless the verb is missing a part or two, in which case it is called defective. This doesn't mean there is anything wrong with the verb. It just isn't all there, like your second cousin Ollie.

The Principal Parts of Verbs

There are six tenses in Latin: present, imperfect, future, present perfect, past perfect, and future perfect, and they all come in both active and passive voices. The four principal parts give all the bases for the tenses, so you really need to know what principal parts are and how to use them:

➤ **First principal part.** *Amo* ("I love"), first person singular, present tense. Every verb will be listed under this form in a dictionary or vocabulary list.

➤ **Second principal part.** *Amare* ("to love"), the present active infinitive. By dropping the *re* ending, you've got the indication of the conjugation and the present stem, the basis for the present, imperfect, and future tenses, both active and passive.

➤ **Third principal part.** *Amavi* ("I have loved"), the first person singular, present perfect active tense; by dropping the *i*, the perfect stem is created, which is the basis for all the perfect active tense forms.

➤ **Fourth principal part.** *Amatus* ("having been loved"), the perfect passive participle and the basis for all the perfect passive tense forms.

Verbs with Easy Third Principal Parts

When the third principal part is the same as the first, it really is not a good thing, for how can you tell *ascendimus* ("we climb") from *ascendimus* ("we have climbed")? Answer: You can't, and you'll just have to deal with it.

Except for a few changes in the fourth principal part, the following verbs are easily recognized in all tenses:

First	Second	Third	Fourth	Meaning	Derivative
ascendo	ascendere	ascendi	ascensus	climb	ascend
invado	invadere	invadi	invasus	invade	invasion
moveo	movere	movi	motus	move	motion
prandeo	prandere	prandi	pransus	eat	prandial
respondeo	respondere	respondi	responsus	answer	response
venio	venire	veni	ventus	come	venture
video	videre	vidi	visus	see	vision

Many English derivatives come from the fourth principal part: *motion, vision, response, convention.*

What Latin words are the basis for *application? appellation? concoction? diffuse? ornate? petition? relate?* See Chapter 5, "Let's Have Some Action!" for answers.

Did You Know?

Those spectacular ruins of aqueducts are found as far from Rome as France, Spain, Turkey, and northern Africa. The covered channels for water were built on high arches, not to carry the water to the hills of Rome, but to slow down the flow of water which could burst the weak lead pipes of the city system. Today's engineers marvel at the skill of the aqueduct builders, who maintained a slope of 10 feet per 3,200 feet of rock cut or arch borne channel. Furthermore, of the 270 miles of aqueduct in Rome, 230 miles are underground.

Verbs with Slightly Changed Third Principal Parts

These verbs often follow a pattern within the conjugation. The first-conjugation verbs fairly regularly end in *are, avi,* and *atus.* Second-conjugation verbs (remember the ones whose first form ends in *eo?*) often have a third principal part ending in *ui.* Third-conjugation perfect stems often end in *s* or *x.* Fourth-conjugation verbs often end in *ire, ivi* or *ii, itus.*

First	Second	Third	Fourth	Meaning	Derivative
amo	amare	amavi	amatus	love	amative
dico	dicere	dixi	dictus	speak	diction
dissimulo	dissimulare	dissimulavi	dissimulatus	pretend	dissimulate
habeo	habere	habui	habitus	have	habit
habito	habitare	habitavi	habitatus	live	inhabit
includo	includere	inclusi	inclusus	include	include
invito	invitare	invitavi	invitatus	invite	invite
laboro	laborare	laboravi	laboratus	work	labor
mitto	mittere	misi	missus	send	mission
moneo	monere	monui	monitus	warn	admonition
peto	petere	petivi	petitus	beg, ask	petition
porto	portare	portavi	portatus	carry	portfolio
quaero	quaerere	quaesivi	quaesitus	ask	inquire
praetereo	praeterire	praeterivi	praeteritus	pass	preterite over
volo	velle	volui	—	want	volition

Your *portfolio*—the one with your artwork, not the one at your broker's—is used to carry around your work. A *portmanteau* is your traveling bag, and *porter beer* is what your porter, the man who carries your stuff, drinks when off duty. Porter beer is made from a weak stout rich in sugar with 4 percent alcohol. He might as well drink it on duty.

Verbs with Principal Parts You Really Need to Know

The following verbs are frequently used and have third and fourth principal parts that you might not recognize as remotely belonging to the first principal part. Most people will not find the word in the dictionary because it is listed under the first principal part. My advice is to always look around the dictionary page at the complete entries. Sometimes you will find the mystery word listed as a third or fourth principal part.

Cave!

Praetereo looks like a second conjugation verb ending in *eo,* but looks are misleading as the verb is a compound of *praeter* and *eo,* which is a fourth-conjugation verb.

First	Second	Third	Fourth	Meaning	Derivative
ago	agere	egi	actus	do, drive, live	agent
capio	capere	cepi	captus	capture	capture
do	dare	dedi	datus	give	data
facio	facere	feci	factus	do, make	fact
fero	ferre	tuli	latus	carry	elate
iacio	iacere	ieci	iactus	throw	reject
possum	posse	potui	—	be able	potent
sto	stare	steti	status	stand	status
sum	esse	fui	futurus	be	future
volo	velle	volui	—	want	volunteer

So many English words come from the fourth principal part: *status, data, future, fact, act. Jactation* is the tossing to and fro, jerking and twisting of the body or its parts. Something like dancing?

It's an Imperfect World

The imperfect tense is so named because it denotes action that is not finished, not perfected. It is translated "was/were ----ing," "kept ----ing," or "used to ----."

The imperfect is formed in Latin by adding *bas, bas, bat, bamus, batis,* or *bant* to the present stem. Here is the imperfect tense of the verb *sto, stare* ("to stand"):

stabam	I was standing
stabas	you were standing
stabat	he was standing
stabamus	we were standing
stabatis	you were standing
stabant	they were standing

The imperfect is the same for all conjugations and is easy to recognize.

The imperfect tense of the verb *esse* ("to be") is as follows:

eram	I was
eras	you were
erat	he was
eramus	we were
eratis	you were
erant	they were

As you can see, this is also regular and will be used as a helping verb in the past perfect tenses, active and passive.

Translate the following verb forms into English:

1. Faciebamus   _____

2. Ferebant   _____

3. Eramus   _____

4. Dabat   _____

5. Agebatis   _____

6. Poterat   _____

7. Iaciebam   _____

8. Capiebas   _____

What's in Your Future?

The future tense tells what will be. In the first and second conjugations, look for *bo, bi,* or *bu* added to the present stem. Here is the future tense of the verb *amare* ("to love"):

amabo	I will love
amabis	you will love
amabit	he will love
amabimus	we will love
amabitis	you will love
amabunt	they will love

Unfortunately, the third and fourth conjugations couldn't follow that simple rule. Instead, they have *a* in the first person and *e* in all the rest. Now if you say that a few times, stressing the *a* first and then *e,* you'll have a little thing going that you can sing in the shower or hum in the subway.

Here is the future tense of *mittere* ("to send"):

mittam	I will send
mittes	you will send
mittet	he will send
mittemus	we will send
mittetis	you will send
mittent	they will send

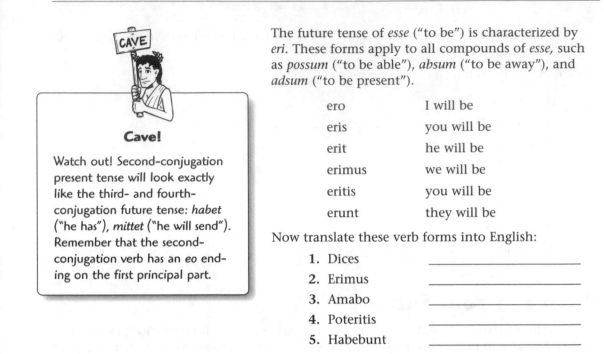

Cave!

Watch out! Second-conjugation present tense will look exactly like the third- and fourth-conjugation future tense: *habet* ("he has"), *mittet* ("he will send"). Remember that the second-conjugation verb has an *eo* ending on the first principal part.

The future tense of *esse* ("to be") is characterized by *eri*. These forms apply to all compounds of *esse,* such as *possum* ("to be able"), *absum* ("to be away"), and *adsum* ("to be present").

ero	I will be
eris	you will be
erit	he will be
erimus	we will be
eritis	you will be
erunt	they will be

Now translate these verb forms into English:

1. Dices   _____
2. Erimus   _____
3. Amabo   _____
4. Poteritis   _____
5. Habebunt   _____

The Perfect Tenses, Active and Passive

The perfect tenses in English use the verb *has/have* as a helping verb. The present tense of *have* is used for the present perfect (he *has* gone), the past tense of *have* for the past perfect (he *had* gone), and the future tense of *have* for the future perfect (he *will have* gone). All common sense and logical.

In Latin, the verb ending changes to indicate the tense. But all the perfect active tenses use the third principal part and all the perfect passives use the fourth principal part.

So let's put together the present perfect active (a.k.a. perfect active tense) of the verb *videre* ("to see"). Note the slightly different endings for the second person:

vidi	I have seen, saw, did see
vidisti	you have seen, saw, did see
vidit	he has seen, saw, did see
vidimus	we have seen, saw, did see
vidistis	you have seen, saw, did see
viderunt	they have seen, saw, did see

You can see immediately that the *t, mus, tis,* and *nt* endings are still there to remind you of *he, we,* and *they.* The *i, isti, istis,* and *evunt* endings and the third principal part will be the only indications that this is a perfect, and, therefore, a past, tense.

The past and future perfect tenses are not used as frequently as the present perfect, and they are easy to spot. They use a helping verb, the imperfect of *esse* and the future of *esse*, but it is added to the perfect stem like an ending.

Here is the past perfect active (a.k.a. pluperfect tense) of the same verb:

videram	I had seen
videras	you had seen
viderat	he had seen
videramus	we had seen
videratis	you had seen
viderant	they had seen

Tene Memoria

Just remember: third principal part, past tense. Third principal part with *era*, "had ----ed."

And here is the future perfect active tense:

videro	I will have seen
videris	you will have seen
viderit	he will have seen
viderimus	we will have seen
videritis	you will have seen
viderint	they will have seen

The perfect passive tenses really are logical and easy to remember. They use the fourth principal part, the perfect passive participle, and the verb *to be* as a helping verb; although, since this is Latin, the helping verb is out of order. It follows the participle as opposed to English, where the helping verb comes first.

Here is the present perfect passive tense of *videre:*

visus/a/um sum	I have been seen
visus/a/um es	you have been seen
visus/a/um est	he has been seen
visi/ae/a sumus	we have been seen
visi/ae/a estis	you have been seen
visi/ae/a sunt	they have been seen

The participle ending will change so as to agree with the subject. So if the subject is feminine, for example, the verb would be *visa sum* and if plural, *visae sunt.* If the subject is neuter, then *visum est* or *visa sunt.*

Here is the past perfect passive tense:

visus/a/um eram	I had been seen
visus/a/um eras	you had been seen
visus/a/um erat	he had been seen
visi/ae/a eramus	we had been seen
visi/ae/a eratis	you had been seen
visi/ae/a erant	they had been seen

The future perfect passive, should you ever use it, follows the same pattern:

visus/a/um ero	I will have been seen
visus/a/um eris	you will have been seen
visus/a/um erit	he will have been seen
visi/ae/a erimus	we will have been seen
visi/ae/a eritis	you will have been seen
visi/ae/a erunt	they will have been seen

But hey! Forget all that! Just watch for those third principal parts that will transport you to the past. Remember that *i* actually means "I," and you will have—or have had or had had—the perfect tense!

One last note: There is a perfect active infinitive that is easy to identify—*isse* on the perfect stem translates "to have ----ed." Of course, if the infinitive has a personal ending, which will immediately strike you as strange, then it's that subjunctive again; just translate it as a past tense.

The perfect passive infinitive will use the fourth principal part and the infinitive form of "to be," *esse*. For example …

amatus esse

Translates as …

to have been loved

Now translate the following:

1. Quaesivi   _____
2. Deportavit   _____
3. Noluit   _____
4. Antecesserat   _____
5. Commoverat   _____

6. Fuit _____

7. Fecerunt _____

8. Habuit _____

9. Incidissem _____

10. Potui _____

The Imperative—a Commanding Lead

While the Romans often used the subjunctive for a gentle command in the third person—*Fiat lux!* ("Let there be light!")—or an encouragement in the first person plural—*Eamus!* ("Let's go!")—they used the imperative form to give commands. And because commands are usually urgent, they made up a short imperative form, the present stem for the singular, and added *te* for the plural. So if your slaves were wasting time around the water cooler, you could yell, *Laborate!* Or if your mother-in-law was not moving fast enough, you could give her a little shove and say, *Festina!*

Negative command took a little more time. *Noli* (singular) and *nolite* (plural) plus the infinitive will get people to stop doing something—*Noli circumstare!* ("Stop standing around!"); *Nolite cantare!* ("Stop singing!"). Now try yelling these commands:

1. Prandite! _____

2. Move! _____

3. Noli movere! _____

4. Ite! _____

5. Porta! _____

6. Dicite! _____

RETINEO

Grammar Guru

The perfect passive participle, like all participles, can be used as a noun or adjective. Sometimes it is translated in a clause: *visus* is "which has been seen" or "the seen" (thing, person). But you are always correct to translate the fourth principal part as "having been ----ed."

Hysteria's Herstory

The Empress Poppaea, wife of Nero, will be remembered for her permanent wave. She sat for two weeks with her hair bound in curlers and packed in clay and mud. When the mud dried and was cracked off, her head was rippling like the sea. Nero was so entranced he had his hair waved likewise, setting off a trend. Of course, a bust of Poppaea survives to this day, making her hairdo really permanent.

Practice Makes Perfect

Identify the person, number, tense, and voice and then translate the verb; the first one is done for you. (If this is too onerous, just translate.)

1. Fuimus   <u>First person, plural, present perfect active; "We have been"</u>
2. Misit   _____
3. Veni   _____
4. Veniebant   _____
5. Potueram   _____
6. Amavit   _____
7. Factum est   _____
8. Data erant   _____
9. Steti   _____
10. Ceperint   _____
11. Respondit   _____
12. Prandimus   _____
13. Petitus erat   _____
14. Praeterivi   _____
15. Lati sunt   _____
16. Iecerunt   _____
17. Voluit   _____
18. Tuleram   _____
19. Invitavero   _____
20. Visum est   _____

Spot the seven! In the following sentences, find the seven verbs in the perfect tenses, then translate them into English:

1. Consulem vidi.   _____
2. Viros invitavero.   _____
3. Ipsa sum hospita.   _____
4. Multa praeterivi.   _____
5. Homo canem deportavit.   _____
6. Fungos et helvellas condiunt.   _____
7. Quaesivi diligenter.   _____
8. Femina fabulam narravit.   _____
9. Nuclei margaritae sunt.   _____
10. Unum cornu exstetit.   _____

Study Tips

The way to learn a language is to use it. Review the list at the beginning of this chapter. Cover the English and try to repeat the meaning. Or have a friend give the Latin or English and you give the translation.

When you have identified words you cannot remember, write them on cards or paper. Put the list over the kitchen sink, over your desk at the office, or in the bathroom. Read and repeat. Read and repeat.

Some people remember words better if associated with pictures. Organize a picture party, have everyone bring old magazines and find pictures that illustrate those words you can't remember. Cut out the picture, paste onto construction paper and write the Latin word prominently on the back of the picture. Keep these picture vocabulary cards near you.

Try to use the Latin derivatives as often as you can. When you read, note the words and expressions that are Latin or derived from Latin. Keep an eye out for articles about the Roman Empire or about Latin in education.

And above all, read Chapter 11, "Locutiones—Phrases." We are finally going to read phrases, clauses, and entire sentences in Latin.

The Least You Need to Know

➤ The third principal part is very important.

➤ The imperfect is translated as "was/were ----ing."

➤ The future tense has *a* in the first person and *e* in all the rest.

➤ Perfect tenses are past history.

➤ Commands are short.

Part 3

Expressing Yourself in Latin

Phrases, although incomplete grammatically, are often used for whole thoughts—like, whatever! Although hindered by a lack of verb, some phrases can still pack a punch—under 21?—or keep you going—nice work!—or make you very happy—no school!

Then there are those parts of speech that express a complete thought. A sentence is the coming together of all the parts of speech, a joining of those words, clauses, and phrases in order to make a statement about life, about nothing, about anything. The good news is that every sentence has a subject and predicate, so there is something going on in a logical and complete way. The bad news is that sentences can be complicated.

This part tells you everything you need to know about Latin phrases, clauses, and sentences.

Locutiones—
Phrases

Here are some definitions for the hard-core grammarian: A phrase is a group of words that does not have a subject and verb. A clause, on the other hand, has a subject and verb, although it may not always be a complete sentence. A prepositional phrase is a group of words that begins with a preposition, a word that shows a relationship of a noun or pronoun to some other word in the sentence.

But hey! Forget all that! A prepositional phrase begins with a little word, a preposition, and is followed by other words.

There used to be a grammatical rule: Don't end a sentence with a preposition. That's because a preposition is wedded to its object, the word that follows it. So you're not supposed to say, "Which car is the president in?" Instead, you should say "In which car is the president?" As far as English goes this rule probably went out with the undershirt; in Latin, however, you can count on the preposition and its object being very close together.

Words Without Which You Cannot Do

Some prepositions denote *coming toward*, or if you are not looking, *running into*. These generally are followed by the accusative case. *Ad murum* means "toward the wall" and *in murum* translates as "into the wall."

Other prepositions describe a *going away from*—*a muro* ("away from the wall"), *de muro* ("down from the wall"), and in case you are a mole or termite, *e muro* ("out of the wall"). These generally take the ablative case. The following table lists many common prepositions:

Preposition	Case	Meaning	Derivative
a/ab	ablative	away from	abience
ad	accusative	to, toward	adience
ante	accusative	before	anteroom
contra	accusative	against	contradict
cum	ablative	with	compress
de	ablative	down from	deride
e/ex	ablative	out of	extract
in	abl./acc.	in, on, into	insider
per	accusative	through	perfume
post	accusative	behind, after	postlude
praeter	accusative	past, beyond	preterite
pro	ablative	before, for	prosecute
prope	accusative	near	propinquity
propter	accusative	on account of	—
sine	ablative	without	sinecure
sub	abl./acc.	to the foot of, under	suburb
supra/super	accusative	over, above	superego
trans	accusative	across	transatlantic

Remember the *ego* and the *id*? The *superego* is the third part of Freud's psyche, which is partly unconscious and develops from the ego. It is *above the ego* partly to protect it from those nasty id impulses.

While we're psychoanalyzing, *abience* is that avoidance behavior we're all so fond of, while *adience* is the tendency to approach willingly a stimulus or situation. To avoid writing, I engage in abient behavior: walking the dog, cleaning the floor, ironing T-shirts, or reading junk mail.

A *sinecure* is a job without work, if such a thing is possible.

The following table list some common nouns and adjectives you will need. Notice that *agricola* is masculine, even though it belongs to the first declension.

Noun	Genitive	Gender	Meaning	Derivative
agricola	agricolae	m.	farmer	agriculture
alces	alcis	m./f.	elk	elk
articulus	articuli	m.	joint	articulate
auxilium	auxili	n.	aid	auxiliary
equus	equi	m.	horse	equine
iter	itineris	n.	journey, way	itinerary
magister	magistri	m.	teacher	magistrate
regina	reginae	f.	queen	regal
rex	regis	m.	king	regal
sacerdos	sacerdotis	m.	priest	sacerdotal
taberna	tabernae	f.	shop, bar	tavern
ursus/a	ursi/ursae	f.	bear	ursine
parvus/a/um	parvi/parvae/i	m./f./n.	small	parvitude
malus/a/um	mali/malae/i	m./f./n.	bad	malediction

To *articulate* is to unite with joints and to be *articulate* is to be able to join your syllables, words, and phrases into meaningful sentences.

A *malediction* is the opposite of a *benediction* and is something to avoid.

Parvitude is the state of being little. My troubles, for example, can differ in multitude and parvitude.

Here are more verbs without which you cannot read Latin:

Verb and Principal Parts	Meaning	Derivative
animadverto, ere, verti, sus	notice	animadversion
cedo, ere, cessi, cessus	move, yield	secede
decido, ere, cidi	fall down	decide
deporto, are, avi, atus	deport	deport
desilio, ire, ilui, sulturus	jump down	salient
intellego, ere, exi, ectus	know	intelligent
narro, are, avi, atus	tell	narrate
opprimo, ere, pressi, pressus	oppress	oppress

continues

continued

Verb and Principal Parts	Meaning	Derivative
pono, ere, posui, positus	put, place	deposit
reicio, ere, eci, ectus	reject	reject
remaneo, ere, mansi, mansus	remain	remain
salio, ire, salii/salui, salitus	jump	salient
sedo, are, avi, atus	sedate, sooth	sedate
statuo, ere, ui, tutus	decide	statute

Salient means "prominent," "conspicuous," "jumping," or "leaping." So if your salient talent is jumping and leaping, you could be famous for your salient salience.

In the Blink of an Eye—Coming or Going?

Two prepositions have different forms depending on whether the next word begins with a vowel or consonant, similar to the English *a* or *an* (for example, *a muro, ab arbore, e muro, ex arbore*).

Both *de* and *ex* are used with *numero* to mean "from the number of." *De* can also mean "about, concerning." For example, *aliqui ex numero militum relinquebantur* (some from the number of soldiers were left behind), or *tres de pueris clamabant* (three of the boys shouted).

Ad followed by a participle can be translated "for the purpose of"—*Ad cavendum praesidium ponitur* ("The guard is posted for the purpose of looking out").

A or *ab*, when used with a person, can mean "by"—*Ab puero canis amatur* ("The dog is loved by the boy").

Cum is usually combined with the reflexive and personal pronouns—*mecum* ("with me"), *secum* ("with himself"), *tecum* ("with you").

Tene Memoria

Remember that verbs whose first principal part ends in *eo* are in the second conjugation.

Finally, don't worry about getting the case correct. The object always follows the preposition closely, and what do you care what case it's in? The only word you might want to remember is *in,* and you should be able to tell by the context of the sentence whether the elephant is *in* the wall, or *running into* the wall.

Let's try translating the following prepositional phrases:

1. Ad villam   _____

2. A sorore   _____

3. E numero concharum

4. Post cenam _____

5. Ab sacerdote _____

6. Contra violentiam _____

7. Ad spectandum _____

8. Ad me _____

9. Vobiscum _____

10. E vita _____

Did You Know?

The Romans enjoyed theatrical performances of all kinds. The first plays were performed sporadically by Etruscan actors, who were imported to entertain the crowd at the chariot races in the Circus Maximus. They performed interpretive dance accompanied by the flute.

The Atellana, named for the town Atella in Campania, were plays similar to our Punch and Judy; these light-hearted farces featured stock characters like *pappus* (the old man easily fooled), *maccus* (the stupid one), and *bucco* (a fat-cheeked blockhead).

After the Atellan came the Mimes, which were considered lowbrow and tasteless and featured sex, violence, and nudity. Ironically, women were allowed to act in Mimes.

Prepositions as Prefixes—Preposterous!

The English language has thousands of words that begin with a Latin prefix, including *absent, adjunct, antedate, composite, excavate, invade,* and *submarine.* There are thousands of compound words in Latin as well. The compound words often change one letter or two, but generally they are easy to spot and translate. Here are a few formed from the prepositions we have learned already:

From *a/ab* ...

abstineo, ere, inui, tentus	abstain
appendo, ere, di, sus	pay out, weigh out
arripio, ere, ripi, raptus	snatch away

113

From *ad* ...

accedo, ere, cessi, cessus	move toward
accido, ere, cidi	happen, fall toward
accipio, ere, cepi, captus	accept
addo, ere, didi, additus	add
adduco, ere, dux, ductus	lead toward
admoneo, ere, ui, itus	warn

From *ante* ...

antecedo, ere, cessi, cessus	outdo, surpass
anteambulo, are, avi, atus	run before
antevenio, ire, veni, ventus	come before

From *co* (derived from *cum*, meaning "together, completely") ...

commoveo, ere, movi, motus	move thoroughly
comprehendo, ere, si, sus	unite, hold together, know
comporto, are, avi, atus	bring together
compello, ere, pulsi, pulsus	drive together

From *de* ...

decido, ere, cidi, cisus	cut down, fall down
decipio, ere, cepi, ceptus	take down
deduco, ere, duxi, ductus	lead down
deporto, are, avi, atus	carry away
desilio, ire, ui, itus	jump down

From *e/ex* ...

excipio, ere, cepi, ceptus	make exceptions
excogito, are, avi, atus	think out

From *in* ...

induco, ere, duxi, ductus	lead in
infundo, ere, fusi, fusus	pour on
inicio, ere, ieci, iectus	inject, throw on
insto, are, steti, status	stand on
invenio, ire, veni, ventus	come upon, find, invent

From *per* (meaning "thoroughly") ...

perficio, ere, feci, fectus	complete, finish
permisceo, ere, mixi, mictus	mix completely
pernocto, are, avi, atus	spend the night
permuto, are, avi, atus	change completely

From *praeter* ...

praetereo, ire, ii, itus	omit, go past

From *sub* ...

sublevo, are, avi, atus	get up, lift up
subruo, ere, rui, rutus	root out, uproot

Tene Memoria

Remember: *a, ab* means "by, from"; *ad* means "toward."

Can you guess the meaning of these compounds?

1. Exit _____
2. Init _____
3. Inambulo _____
4. Pervenit _____
5. Abduxit _____
6. Advenerunt _____
7. Deponit _____
8. Imposuit _____
9. Intramus _____
10. Transimus _____

Hysteria's Herstory

Pliny the Younger tells us about a remarkable woman, Ummidia Quadratilla, who lived to be almost 80. She owned a company of pantomime dancers and enjoyed their perform-ances more than the typical Roman noblewoman should. She brought her grandson up in her own home, supervising his education. Whenever she was about to either play checkers or watch the pantomimes, she sent him away to study. Way to go, Grandma!

Cave!

Watch out for the prefix *in*. The Greek prefix carries a negative meaning, as in *incomprehensible*, *intolerant*, and *indefensible*. The same warning for *ante*, not to be confused with the Greek *anti*, "against." So be *antiwar*, "against war," not *antebellum*, "before the war."

Cave!

Don't confuse *interjection* with *expletive*, an exclamation or oath that is frequently omitted. An expletive can also be that extra word in a sentence, like *there*, that really serves little purpose. Example: "There *is* a dog in the car."

Hey! Interjections!

The word *interjection* comes from *iacio*, "to throw," and *inter*, "between." When thrown in between a conversation, sentence, thought, or even total silence, an exclamation becomes a part of speech, the interjection, and is always followed by an exclamation point.

Like all human beings, the Romans had strong emotions, and we have evidence of what they said in times of surprise, anger, shock, or sadness. Letters about deaths or expressing indignation often used interjections. But our best and most valid sources are plays, particularly of Plautus, as he wrote about the daily life of the common people.

In *The Pot of Gold*, Eunonia says: *Heia! hoc face quod te iubet soror.* ("Come on now, do what your sister orders.")

And later, Megadora replies: *Neque edepol ego te derisum venio.* ("Good heavens! I didn't come here to make fun of you.")

Calling to someone, Megadora shouts: *Heus! Pythodicus!*

Here are some common interjections:

a, ah	alas! ah!
hem, ehem	oh! well! indeed! ha! so! (surprise)
hei, ei	hey! (alarm)
heia, eia	aha! (delight) come on! now, now! (playful remonstrance)
eheu	alas!
io	hurray! (joy) oh! (pain) ho there! (calling out)
ha, ha	ha ha! (laughter, hysterical laughter)
oh	oh! (surprise, joy, grief)
ohe	stop! enough!
oi	oh! oh, dear! (complaining, weeping)

At last, some one-word answers:

ita!	yes!
ita vero!	yes, indeed!
non!	no!
minime!	not at all!
certe!	definitely!

The Romans could and did swear, invoking the gods just as we do today. We, however, tend to curse the one God, while the Romans had a grand panoply of deities to call upon. Plautus has his characters frequently say *Pol! Edepol! Ecastor!* These rather mild imprecations call upon the minor god Pollux and his brother Castor. The *ede* is probably the preposition *e,* meaning "from," and a shortened form of *deus,* "god."

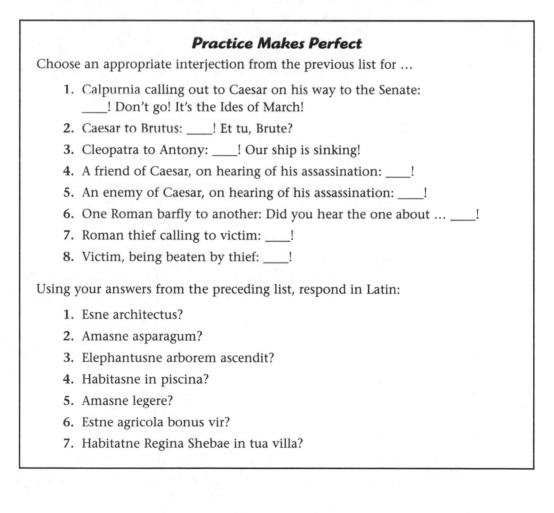

Practice Makes Perfect

Choose an appropriate interjection from the previous list for …

1. Calpurnia calling out to Caesar on his way to the Senate: ____! Don't go! It's the Ides of March!
2. Caesar to Brutus: ____! Et tu, Brute?
3. Cleopatra to Antony: ____! Our ship is sinking!
4. A friend of Caesar, on hearing of his assassination: ____!
5. An enemy of Caesar, on hearing of his assassination: ____!
6. One Roman barfly to another: Did you hear the one about … ____!
7. Roman thief calling to victim: ____!
8. Victim, being beaten by thief: ____!

Using your answers from the preceding list, respond in Latin:

1. Esne architectus?
2. Amasne asparagum?
3. Elephantusne arborem ascendit?
4. Habitasne in piscina?
5. Amasne legere?
6. Estne agricola bonus vir?
7. Habitatne Regina Shebae in tua villa?

The Least You Need to Know

➤ Prepositional phrases begin with a preposition and are short.

➤ Prepositions can be prefixes.

➤ Unlike injections, interjections can be fun.

➤ Now you can say *yes, no,* and *definitely* in Latin!

Chapter 12

Articuli—Clauses

In This Chapter

➤ Absolutely necessary words

➤ Time for temporal clauses

➤ The clause of much confusion: the ablative absolute

➤ Deponent verbs

A clause is a group of words that contains a subject and a verb. There are two basic kinds of clauses: independent and subordinate. The *independent clause* is like your oldest son and can stand alone. The *subordinate clause* is like your dog and depends on just about everybody to make his life meaningful.

A sentence is an independent clause. Two independent clauses can be joined to make one sentence. Another sentence can include both a subordinate and an independent clause.

But hey! Forget all that! I'll go into more detail on clauses in Part 4, "Reading Latin— Selections from Ancient Authors." Just try to learn the following words.

Absolutely Necessary Words

The following nouns and adjectives are from four different declensions. Remember that the fourth-declension nouns will have the genitive ending in *us*.

Nominative	Genitive	Gender	Meaning	Derivative
astrum	astri	n.	star	astrology
auris	auris	f.	ear	auricular
consuetudo	consuetudinis	f.	custom	consuetude
cornu	cornus	n.	horn	corniform
decretum	decreti	n.	decree	decree
hortus	horti	m.	garden	horticulture
lana	lanae	f.	wool	lanolin
liber	libri	m.	book	library
manus	manus	f.	hand, band	manuscript
mas	maris	m.	male	masculine
metus	metus	m.	fear	—
miles	militis	m.	soldier	military
plebs	plebis	f.	commoners	plebeian
puer	pueri	m.	boy	puerile
sapiens	sapientis		wise	sapient
stola	stolae	f.	dress	stole
urbs	urbis	f.	city	urban
via	viae	f.	road	viaduct
longus/a/um	longi/ae/a	m./f./n.	long	long
mortuus/a/um	mortui/ae/a	m./f./n.	dead	mortuary
novissimus/a/um	novissimi/ae/a	m./f./n.	latest	novice
transversus/a/um	transversi/ae/a	m./f./n.	lying across	transverse

Consuetude means "custom" or "use" and is a useful term for not tipping—*It's not my consuetude.* If your bicycle got run over by a truck and is now *corniform* ("in the shape of a horn"), that is probably not a good thing. A *cornada* is not a good thing, either; it's a wound inflicted by a bull in bullfighting.

Lanolin, used for ointments and cosmetics, is actually refined wool fat.

There are more useful verbs; remember that verbs with *eo* ending on first principal part are second conjugation:

First	Second	Third	Fourth	Meaning	Derivative
affero	afferre	attuli	allatus	carry to	afferent
alo	alere	alui	alitus	eat	aliment
canto	cantare	cantavi	cantatus	sing	cantabile
cedo	cedere	cessi	cessus	yield, go	process

First	Second	Third	Fourth	Meaning	Derivative
constituo	constituere	constitui	constitutus	decide	constitute
exanimo	exanimare	exanavi	exanatus	die	exanimate
gero	gerere	gessi	gestus	wear	gesticulant
lego	legere	legi	lectus	choose, read	lectern
placo	placare	placavi	placatus	please	placate
recipio	recipere	recepi	receptus	receive	receipt
rideo	ridere	risi	risus	laugh	risible
rodo	rodere	rodi	rosus	wear down	erode
scio	scire	scivi	scitus	know	science
specto	spectare	spectavi	spectatus	look at	spectator
spero	sperare	speravi	speratus	hope	aspiration
tardo	tardare	tardavi	tardatus	slow down	retard

An *afferent* nerve conveys the impulse toward the central nervous system.

If your spouse comes home and appears *exanimate,* he's probably had a very bad day.

Some people can't seem to talk without punctuating their thoughts with their fingers, waving their arms, and generally causing a lot of distraction with gestures. A nice way of describing this person is *gesticulant.*

And *risible* is a favorite on SAT tests. It means "laughable," so don't confuse it with *erasable.*

Time for Temporal and Causal Clauses

Temporal clauses are introduced by words denoting time: *ubi* ("when"), *antequam* ("before"), *postquam* ("after"), *quamquam* ("although"), *quod* ("because"), *simul* ("at the same time as").

The Clause of Much Confusion—Ablative Absolute

The word *absolute* comes from *ab* and *solvo,* the latter meaning "to loosen" or "let go." Caesar uses *absolvo* to describe the letting go of the ships from their moorings. In English, your church will *absolve* or *free* you from your sins (should you have any).

Tene Memoria

Remember that if there is no noun subject, the personal ending of the verb will be the subject: *o [es]* "I"; *s [es]* "you"; *t [es]* "he," *it [es]* "she"; *mus [es]* "we"; *tis [es]* "you"; and *nt [es]* "they."

Practice Makes Perfect 1

Translate the following into English; note that these are all sentence fragments:

1. Ubi astrum spectas _____
2. Antequam librum lego _____
3. Postquam miles trans viam ambulat _____
4. Simul cantant _____
5. Quamquam via longa est _____
6. Quod mortuus est _____
7. Quod stolam gerit _____
8. Ubi decretum ad consulem affertur _____
9. Ubi puer ridet _____
10. Quamquam consuetudo novissima magnopere aures movere est _____

In English grammar, an absolute is a phrase, usually a noun and a participle, that is not connected grammatically to the rest of the sentence. Absolutes are often used to add specifics to a generalization. For example: *Feet propped up on desk, light turned off, music turned on, George was ready for work.*

In Latin, the ablative absolute is a similar construction, but often translated as a clause. The ablative absolute consists usually of a noun and perfect passive participle, but sometimes present participle, sometimes two nouns, and always in the ablative case. It can express time, circumstance, cause, condition, concession, means, or manner.

But hey! Forget all that! Just remember that you can translate the ablative absolute with "after," "when," "since," "although," "because," "if," or "in the time of." Common sense is another key to translating the ablative absolute. Take a look at the following examples:

Inauribus gestis, omnes risimus.

> The earrings having been worn, we all laughed.

> Because the earrings were worn, we all laughed.

> When the earrings were worn, we all laughed.

Illis ursis captis, pueri laeti erant.

> Those bears having been seized, the boys were happy.

> Because those bears were seized, the boys were happy.

When those bears were seized, the boys were happy.

Although those bears were seized, the boys were happy.

Since those bears were seized, the boys were happy.

M. Antonio et Cicerone consulibus, Roma urbs magna erat.

In the consulship of Antonius and Cicero, Rome was a large city.

Rosa carne omni, margaritae ad imum cadunt.

All the meat having been worn away, the pearls fall to the bottom.

When all the meat has been worn away, the pearls fall to the bottom.

Because all the meat has been worn away, the pearls fall to the bottom.

All these translations, although different in meaning, are grammatically correct. Which one do you use? The one that fits best the context of the sentence or paragraph. Thus is the curse of Latin: two words, two hundred possible translations.

Novissimo totius agminis spectato, agricola viam transit.

The last of the whole line having been seen, the farmer crosses the road.

When the last of the line is seen, the farmer crosses the road.

Remember that the ablative absolute can be translated many different ways. But it will always be in the ablative (duh) and most often is separated from the sentence with commas.

Cave!

The ablative singular feminine often looks like the nominative singular feminine. Look to other words in the phrase for hints that it's an ablative.

Did You Know?

When Augustus was 76 years old, he wrote a treatise called *Res Gestae* in which he documented all the events and achievements of his life. He then had tablets inscribed and set them up in the provinces. This invaluable record, although just a little biased toward Augustus himself, has been praised as a major contribution to history. It is as famous for its omissions as its contents: Not one enemy of Augustus is named, nor is his wife of many years.

Practice Makes Perfect 2

Translate these sentences:

1. Cane alito, iter fecimus. _____
2. Agricola placata, equi ex urbe ducti sunt. _____
3. Toga induta, senator ex villa ambulavit. _____
4. Domino nato, in ecclesia cantamus. _____
5. Servata republica, Cicero laudatus est. _____
6. C. Mario et L. Valerio consulibus, Graecus non iucundus erat. _____
7. Convivium coepit, mensa allata. _____
8. His rebus dictis, Caesar rostrum relinquit. _____
9. Te duce, meum fratrem portabo. _____

Now try writing some Latin:

1. When the boy was seen, the father laughed. _____
2. The water having been received, Caesar slowed down. _____
3. When the food was eaten, the woman wore the dress. _____
4. The day having been decided, we watched the stars. _____
5. After the book was read, the mother-in-law was wise. _____

Or ... Deponent Verbs

It's time to review the passive forms of verbs. The passive voice is formed by adding special passive endings to the base. You learned about the endings for first person (*or*) and third person (*tur*) singular, and third person plural (*ntur*) in Chapter 5, "Let's Have Some Action!" Here is the complete passive conjugation:

Present Tense Ending	Imperfect Ending	Future Ending (First and Second/Third and Fourth)
or	bar	bor/ar
ris	baris	beris/eris
tur	batur	bitur/etur
mur	bamur	bimur/emur
mini	bamini	bimini/emini
ntur	bantur	buntur/entur

Examples: *amaris* ("you are loved"), *relinquemini* ("you will be left behind"), *laudamur* ("we are praised"), and *capientur* ("they will be seized").

Present Perfect	Past Perfect	Future Perfect
Fourth Principle Part Plus …	Fourth Principle Part Plus …	Fourth Principle Part Plus …
sum	eram	ero
es	eras	eris
est	erat	erit
sumus	eramus	erimus
estis	eratis	eritis
sunt	erant	erunt

Examples: *allata sunt* ("they have been carried away"), *ductus eram* ("I had been led"), *recepti erimus* ("we will have been received").

Deponent comes from the Latin *depono,* "to put aside," because these verbs have put aside all their active voice forms. Deponent verbs will have passive endings, but will be translated in the active voice. So *loquor* means "I speak," not "I am spoken," even though it has a passive ending.

Or … you can just remember that if the first principal part ends in *or,* it's deponent and always active, even though it has those passive endings. Here's a partial list of deponents. Notice that the infinitive is the present passive: The *e* of the present active infinitive changes to *i* except for the third conjugation, which has to do something different.

First Present Passive	Second Present Passive	Third Present Passive	Meaning	Derivative
creor	creari	creatus sum	create	create
loquor	loqui	locutus sum	speak	loquacious

continues

continued

First Present Passive	Second Present Passive	Third Present Passive	Meaning	Derivative
nascor	nasci	natus sum	be born	natal
palor	palari	palatus sum	wander	—
patior	pati	passus sum	suffer	patient
polliceor	polliceri	pollicitus sum	promise	pollicitation
proficiscor	proficisci	profectus sum	leave, go forward	proficient
sequor	sequi	secutus sum	follow	sequel

Pollicitation is a promise that is not accepted. If, for example, your neighbor dies and wills you her extremely scrawny and mean cat, and you reject the offer, that is a *pollicitation*. Not to be confused with *solicitation,* which has only one *l* but could also contain a promise.

Hysteria's Herstory

The Emperor Augustus was devoted to his wife, Livia Drusilla, and died in her arms on August 29, A.D. 14. When asked how she kept the love and affection of such an important and influential man, she replied, "My secret is simple: I have made it the work of my life to please him."

Practice Makes Perfect 3

Translate the following clauses:

1. Natus est. _____
2. Ego loquor. _____
3. Proficiscebantur. _____
4. Pati. _____
5. Palarisne? _____

Now change the following into Latin:

1. We create. _____
2. I am suffering. _____
3. They spoke. _____
4. Are you following? _____
5. I promise to do my best. _____

More Deponent Verbs

The Romans loved prefixes and sprinkled them liberally around their language. Three deponent verbs offer excellent examples of this make-another-word-with-a-prefix syndrome.

Prefix	Verb and Parts	Meaning	Derivative
	loquor, loqui, locutus	*to speak*	*locution*
ad	alloquor	speak to	allocution
com	colloquor	speak with	colloquy
ex	eloquor	speak out	eloquence
ob	obloquor	speak against	obloquy
pro	proloquor	speak out	prolocutor
trans	transloquor	recount from the beginning	—
	gradior, gredi, gressus	*to step, walk, go*	—
ad	aggredior	approach	aggressive
com	congredior	come together	congress
de	degredior	go down	degrade
di	digredior	go apart	digress
ex	egredior	go out	egress
in	ingredior	go in	ingredient
pro	progredior	go forward	progress
re	regredior	go back	regress
sub	suggredior	approach	subgrade
trans	transgredior	go across	transgress
	sequor, sequi, secutus	*to follow*	*sequence*
ad	assequor	go after	—
com	consequor	pursue	consequent

continues

continued

Prefix	Verb and Parts	Meaning	Derivative
ex	exsequor	follow out	executive
in	insequor	follow in	—
ob	obsequor	comply	obsequious
pro	prosequor	follow to	prosecute
re	resequor	reply	resequent
sub	subsequor	follow	subsequent

An *egress* is a synonym for "exit." The famous entrepreneur, P. T. Barnum, wanted to empty the circus tent to be ready for the next show. So he put a sign over the exit, *This Way to the Egress,* and everyone eagerly flocked out to see the exotic new animal—everyone except Latin students, of course.

An *obloquy* is "censure" or "blame." A *prolocutor* is a chairperson who might be giving an *allocution,* or an address.

Resequent is a geological term meaning a stream that flows down the dip of underlying formations in the same direction as the original stream.

The Least You Need to Know

➤ Temporal clauses indicate time and are fragments.

➤ Absolutes are separated from the sentence with commas.

➤ Deponent verbs are passive in form, active in meaning.

➤ If you want your deeds to be eternal, write them in stone.

Chapter 13

THE CLAUSE FAMILY

The Theory of Relative Clauses

In This Chapter

➤ Words that must be learned

➤ Recognizing your relatives

➤ Whoosier relative pronoun?

➤ Indefinites, intensives, interrogatives ... whatever

Your relatives are people you are pretty much stuck with. They are connected to you for birthday parties, family reunions, and obligatory correspondence like congratulations or condolences. Although you are closely related, your life would go on without them. So it is with relative clauses. The sentence will be complete without them, but the relative clause brings information and adds a little excitement to the sentence, just as Uncle Edwin does to Thanksgiving dinner.

Words That Must Be Learned

The following table contains a few new words you need to learn so you can read the relative clauses.

A *tenet* is a belief you hold dearly.

And let's hope that poor Uncle Edwin, who is nasicorn, hirsute, and nasute, is not also *cervicorn*, because then, to add to his troubles, he'd have antlers on his head.

Latin	Parts	Meaning	Derivative
apud	(preposition with acc.)	among, at the home of	—
bos	bovis, m./f.	cow	bovine
casus	casus, m.	chance	casual
celer	celeris	swift	celerity
cervus	cervi, m.	deer	cervicorn
fleo	flere, flevi, fletus	cry	flow
itaque	(conjunction)	and so	—
nam	(conjunction)	for	—
nomen	nominis, n.	name	nomenclature
scribo	ere, scripsi, scriptus	write	scripture
sella	sellae, f.	chair	—
teneo	ere, tenui, tentus	hold	tenet

Review time! Cover the column on the right and provide the correct translation. You've seen these words before.

Latin	Meaning
ago, agere, egi, actus	do, drive, live
balinea, ae, f.	bath
illa	she, that woman
ille	he, that man
inaures, ium, f. pl.	earrings
licuit	it was permitted
margarita, ae, f.	pearl
mensa, ae, f.	table, meal
murena, ae, f.	eel
natus, a, um	born, taken from
pensilis, e	hanging
terra, ae, f.	earth

Recognizing Your Relatives

You will remember that clauses are more complicated than phrases because they have a subject and a verb. An independent clause can stand alone, but a subordinate clause depends on the rest of the sentence for meaning.

There are several kinds of subordinate clauses, one of which is the relative clause.

Relative clauses are found within complete sentences. The relative pronoun will take the place of a noun, its antecedent, and act within its own clause.

But hey! Forget all that! Just remember:

➤ A relative clause begins with a relative pronoun: who, whose, whom, which, that.

➤ You can put mental (or real) parentheses around the relative clause and still have a meaningful sentence.

Tene Memoria

Remember, you can study words by sticking them on your fridge, TV, bathroom mirror, or the back of your cell phone.

And to get your exercise regimen started, pick out the relative clause from these four sentences:

1. I saw the boy who was eating peanuts.
2. The eel that was in the bathtub frightened the man.
3. My country, which I love, is America.
4. The car in which the President was riding turned the corner.

The other problem: You have to identify the antecedent. The antecedent (coming from the Latin *antecedo,* "go before") is the word directly before the pronoun. This is not difficult. In sentence 1, the antecedent is *boy;* in sentence 2, *eel.* The other antecedents are *country* and *car.*

In English, how do you know when to use *who, whom, whose, which,* or *that?* Some people don't know, or use the relative pronouns incorrectly. Here are some rules:

➤ **First rule.** Use *who, whom,* or *whose* for people, *which* or *that* for things.

➤ **Second rule.** *Who,* the nominative/subjective form, is used for the subject of the clause. *Whose,* the genitive/possessive form, is used to show possession. *Whom,* the accusative/objective form, is used as the object of the verb or object of a preposition.

➤ **Most important rule.** Decide the case by its use in its own clause.

For example:

The boy whose father is a teacher eats peanuts.

If you replace *whose* with its antecedent, the clause reads *The boy's father is a teacher.* Obviously, the *boy's* shows possession and, hence, is in the genitive form.

Another example:

> The girl whom I see is strong.

If you replace *whom* with its antecedent, the clause reads *I see the girl. Girl* is the direct object of the verb and, therefore, in the accusative/objective form.

This is the reason you say *to whom*. You need to use the objective form because the pronoun is the object of a preposition.

Practice Makes Perfect 1

Fill in the blanks with the correct relative pronoun:

1. The boat ___ is moored doesn't move.
2. The person of ___ you speak is Caesar.
3. I saw your mother ___ was walking down the street.
4. Your mother ___ I saw was walking down the street.
5. Dali, ___ paintings are very modern, had a prodigious mustache.
6. The cow ___ jumped over the moon was unusual.
7. It is I ___ you seek.
8. I am she of ___ you speak.
9. Give me the book ___ you are reading.

Whoosier Relative Pronoun?

In Latin, the relative clause is a little more complicated because of the cases. The relative pronoun must agree with its antecedent in number and gender, but, just as in English, it takes its case from its use in its own clause.

Here are the forms of the relative pronouns:

Case	Singular Masculine	Feminine	Neuter	Plural Masculine	Feminine	Neuter
Nominative	qui	quae	quod	qui	quae	quae
Genitive	cuius	cuius	cuius	quorum	quarum	quorum
Dative	cui	cui	cui	quibus	quibus	quibus
Accusative	quem	quam	quod	quos	quas	quae
Ablative	quo	qua	quo	quibus	quibus	quibus

Note the pattern in the relative pronoun forms: *ius* for genitive singular, like the demonstrative pronouns. The dative and ablative plurals are always the same. The ablative singulars end in single letters and the accusatives are reminiscent of the declensions.

Look at these examples:

Vidi Caesarem qui ab Gallia venit.

I saw Caesar who came from Gaul.

Vidi Caesarem cuius filia Julia appellata est.

I saw Caesar whose daughter was called Julia.

Vidi Caesarem cui honor datur.

I saw Caesar to whom honor is given.

Vidi Caesarem quem omnes laudant.

I saw Caesar whom all praise.

Vidi Caesarem ab quo laudor.

I saw Caesar by whom I am praised.

The relative pronoun will agree with its antecedent in number and case. Imagine that the pronoun is taking the antecedent's place; if the antecedent is a woman, then the pronoun should be a woman, and if the antecedent is two men, then the pronoun should be masculine plural. But because the pronoun is doing something in its clause, either being the subject or the direct object or object of a preposition, then its case is determined by its behavior in its own clause.

Fill in the blanks, using the words from the following pool of words:

Caesar cervus bos epistula vir femina

Grammar Guru

Remember: nominative case, subject; genitive case, possession; dative case, indirect object; accusative case, direct object; ablative case, everything else.

Several answers are correct, but common sense will probably exclude the cow from jumping or the letter being given food.

1. ____ qui salire amat.

   (Hint: The noun will be singular and masculine because *qui* is singular. How do you know? The verb has a singular ending.)

2. ____ quae domum remanet.

(Hint: The noun will be singular and feminine because *quae* is singular, feminine.)

3. ____ quam scripsi.

(Hint: *quam* is singular, feminine.)

4. ____ qui in piscina cecidit.

5. ____ cui cibum datum est.

6. ____ ab quo canes vocati sunt.

Practice Makes Perfect 2

Translate the following clauses; remember that they are subordinate clauses and, therefore, are not complete thoughts.

1. Versiculum in quo me admones   _____

2. Illam, cui Quintus mensam misit   _____

3. Ego qui ab ostreis abstinebam   _____

4. Nuclei qui margaritae sunt   _____

5. Is qui primus pensiles balineas invenit _____

6. Murenae (dative) quam ille amabat   _____

7. "Hecyram" quam mihi in silentio numquam agere licuit   _____

8. Membra inter quae manus, os, dentes sunt _____

9. Bos cuius unum cornu exsistit   _____

10. Sunt quae appellantur alces   _____

Did You Know?

Showers, or hanging baths, did not come in with modern plumbing. A fourth-century B.C.E. artwork depicts a bevy of women enjoying water piped into overhead devices and spraying out through showerheads shaped like boars and lions.

Indefinites, Intensives, Interrogatives ... Whatever

The following words follow the pattern set by the relative pronoun: genitive ending in *ius*, dative ending in *i*, accusatives following the first and second declensions, dative and ablative plurals with third-declension ending *ibus*.

Nominative (Masculine, Feminine, Neuter)	Meaning
aliquis, aliquis, aliquid	someone, anyone
ipse, ipsa, ipsum	-self (reflexive)
quidam, quaedam, quiddam	a certain
quis, quis, quid	who? what? (interrogative)
quinam, quinam, quidnam	who, pray? what?
quisque, quisque, quidque	each, every
quisquis, quisquis, quidquis	whoever
quisvis, quisvis, quidvis	whomever you want

It is lists like this that make you curse the Roman precision. They were maddeningly detailed, even about being indefinite!

You don't have to learn every form for every pronoun, since the endings are similar to the relative pronoun and often the prefix or suffix hints as to the meaning. For example:

1. *Aliquis* is made up of *alius* ("other") and *quis* ("who").

2. *Quinam* has the suffix *nam* ("for"), adding a little urgency to the question.

3. *Quisvis* has the suffix *vis* ("you want").

Tene Memoria

The suffix or prefix on these pronouns does not change. Look to the beginning or ending of these words for the case endings.

The forms of the interrogative pronoun are just a little different from the relative pronoun. Here's the singular:

Case	Masculine and Feminine	Neuter
Nominative	quis	quid
Genitive	cuius	cuius
Dative	cui	cui
Accusative	quem	quid
Ablative	quo	quo

The plural is exactly like the relative pronoun. The interrogative adjective—*what god, what road, what gift*—is declined completely like the relative pronoun *qui deus, quae via, quod donum.*

135

Practice Makes Perfect 3

Translate the following into English:

1. Quidam cervus nasum rubicundum habet. _____
2. Qui bos super lunam salit? _____
3. Invitate quemvis. _____
4. Caesar ipse in balneis erat. _____

Now swap the English for Latin:

1. Each slave washes his ears. _____
2. The chance of victory is great. _____

A couple more Latin phrases:

1. Alo aliquid. _____
2. Ede quidvis. _____

Hysteria's Herstory

During the siege of Saguntum by Hannibal, after all the food was gone, the people piled up a heap of all their treasures in the center of town. Then the men made a last ditch foray against the Carthaginians, who promptly slaughtered them all. Upon hearing of the disaster, the women set fire to the pile and cast themselves and their children on it to avoid capture and dishonor. This was not a good thing and began the Second Punic War.

The Least You Need to Know

➤ A relative clause begins with a relative pronoun.

➤ The relative pronouns begin with *qu* or *cu* just as the English relative pronouns begin with *wh*.

➤ There are many Latin words that have *quis* with a suffix or prefix.

➤ Whatever. Quicquid.

Chapter 14

Closing In
on Clauses

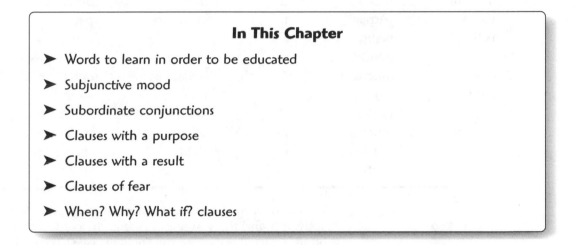

In This Chapter

➤ Words to learn in order to be educated

➤ Subjunctive mood

➤ Subordinate conjunctions

➤ Clauses with a purpose

➤ Clauses with a result

➤ Clauses of fear

➤ When? Why? What if? clauses

Let's face it. Some days you're in a good mood, others, not so hot. Verbs, too, have their moods. The imperative mood is bossy. The indicative mood is just your everyday normal state, while the subjunctive mood is wistful and dreamy. You've already learned the indicative and imperative. It's time for the subjunctive.

Words to Learn in Order to Be Educated

The following words have been separated into parts of speech. Some should be included in the idiotically easy category, like *fabula* ("story") or *figura* ("figure").

Nominative	Genitive	Gender	Meaning	Derivative
canis	canis	m./f.	dog	canine
cibum	cibi	n.	food	ciborium
civis	civis	m./f.	citizen	civil
exspectatio	exspectationis	f.	anticipation	expect
fabula	fabulae	f.	story	fabulous
figura	figurae	f.	shape	figure
frons	frontis	f.	forehead	front
ludus	ludi	m.	game, school	ludicrous
nihil	—	—	nothing	nil
os	oris	n.	mouth	oral
officium	offici	n.	duty	office
patria	patriae	f.	fatherland	patriotic
pellis	pellis	f.	skin, hide	pelt
pondus	ponderis	n.	weight	ponderous
quies	quietis	f.	quiet, rest	quiet
radix	radicis	f.	root	radical
ramus	rami	m.	branch	ramification
senatus	senatus	m.	senate	senate
species	speciei	f.	sight	species
venter	ventris	m.	stomach	ventral

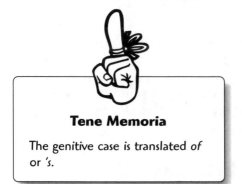

Tene Memoria

The genitive case is translated *of* or *'s*.

The *ciborium* is a permanent canopy over an altar. More aptly, it is also the vessel for holding the consecrated bread or sacred wafers for the Eucharist (see Chapter 22, "Late Latin and Church Latin").

You *ponder* while thinking weighty thoughts, and you will become *ponderous* if you eat doughnuts at the same time. Other *ramifications?* An enlarged *ventral* area.

To make sure it all sticks, translate the following genitives:

1. The anticipation of school _____

2. The hide of the deer _____

3. The food of the dog _____

4. The shape of the forehead _____

5. The quiet of leisure _____

6. The weight of duty _____
7. The sight of land _____
8. The root of the tree _____
9. The stomach of the oyster _____
10. The citizen's story _____

Did You Know?

Roman schools were called *ludi* or *scholae*. The *ludi* were basically elementary schools, where children would learn reading, writing, and arithmetic. They could go on to the *grammaticus*, who would teach them literature and languages—Latin and Greek. To finish the education, a young man might then study under a *rhetor*, to polish his writing skills, elocution, and philosophy.

There were *ludi* for special subjects like gladiatorial skills, music, fencing, cooking, military, and barbers.

Scholae, which in Greek means *leisure*, were schools where study was continued at a pace set by the student and focused on literary topics.

Adjective/Adverb	Genitive	Meaning	Derivative
alius	ali	other	alias
cotidie	—	daily	—
deinde	—	then, next	—
dulcis	dulcis	sweet	dulcimer
excelsus	excelsi	high, lofty	excel
fictilis	fictilis	clay, earthenware	fictile
imus	imi	deepest	—
iniquus	iniqui	unfair	iniquity
istuc	—	there, to that place	—

continues

continued

Adjective/Adverb	Genitive	Meaning	Derivative
item	—	at the same time, likewise, besides	—
lenis	lenis	gentle, kind	lenient
magis	magius	more	magnify
mirus	miri	wonderful	miracle
mitis	mitis	sweet, gentle	mitigate
mutuus	mutui	borrowed	mutual
praeceler	praeceleris	very swift	celerity
praecipuus	praecipui	special	—
sic	—	thus	—
sollertius	sollerti	skilled	—
subinde	—	immediately afterward	—
subito	—	suddenly	—
vetustus	vetusti	old	veteran

Several other words come from *dulcis; dulcet* is an adjective meaning "pleasant to listen to," *dulcify* means "to make more agreeable," and a *dulcinea* is a "sweetheart" or "girlfriend," named for Dulcinea, the ladylove of Don Quixote.

Principal Parts	Meaning	Derivative
committo, committere, commisi, commissus	begin	commit
conspicio, conspicere, conspexi, conspectus	catch sight of	conspicuous
curo, curare, curavi, curatus	care for	curative
includo, includere, includi, inclusus	include	include
libero, liberare, liberavi, liberatus	free	liberate
salveo, salvere, salve, salvus	be in good health	salve
sedeo, sedere, sedi, sessus	sit	session
terreo, terrere, terrui, territus	frighten	terror
trado, tradere, tradidi, traditus	hand over	trade
vereor, vereri, veritus sum	fear	—
vivo, vivere, vixi, victus	live	vivacity

Romans greeted each other with *Salve!* ("Be well!") Other derivatives are *salutation, salubrious,* and *salutary.*

Subjunctive Mood

So far all the verbs in the finite tenses (those with personal endings) have been in the indicative mood. The indicative mood indicates that something is happening—*it is, it was, it will be,* and *it has been.* No discussion.

The subjunctive is used to show that the action is not straightforward. The subjunctive mood shows action that might happen, would happen, should happen if all goes well, or just wishful thinking. The subjunctive mood, a whole new set of endings for verbs, is used frequently in subordinate clauses.

> **Cave!**
>
> Don't confuse *saltation* (jumping) with *salutation* (welcoming), although the two often happen simultaneously, especially with your dog.

Here's a list of what you need to form the subjunctive:

➤ **Present active.** Use *e* in the first conjugation, *a* in all the rest. For example, *portet* ("he might carry"), *mittat* ("he might send"), or *audiam* ("I may hear").

➤ **Present passive.** Add passive endings. For example, *portetur* ("he might be carried"), *mittatur* ("he might be sent"), or *audiar* ("he might be heard").

➤ **Imperfect active.** Use the present infinitive plus an ending. For example, *portaret* ("he was carrying") or *mitterem* ("I was sending").

➤ **Imperfect passive.** Add passive endings. For example, *portaretur* ("he was being carried").

➤ **Perfect active.** Add *eri* and endings to the perfect stem. This will look a lot like the future perfect. For example, *portaverim* ("I carried") or *dederint* ("they gave").

➤ **Perfect passive.** Use the fourth principal part plus the subjunctive of the verb *esse* ("to be"). For example, *portatus sim* ("I have been carried") or *portati sint* ("they have been carried").

➤ **Pluperfect active.** Use the perfect infinitive plus endings. For example, *portavissem* ("I had carried") or *monuisset* ("he had warned").

➤ **Pluperfect passive.** Use the fourth principal part plus the imperfect subjunctive of the verb *esse* ("to be"). For example, *portatus essem* ("I had been carried") or *moniti essemus* ("we had been warned").

> **Grammar Guru**
>
> The subjunctive is often translated exactly like the indicative. Other times it can be translated "may," "might," "in order to," or "should," depending on the construction. It is also used for first- and third-person commands: *Fiat lux!* "Let there be light!" *Eamus!* "Let's go!"

The subjunctive of *esse* is easily recognized:

Present		Imperfect	
sim	simus	essem	essemus
sis	sitis	esses	essetis
sit	sint	esset	essent

The following table presents the first and second conjugation. All the other conjugations form the subjunctive exactly like the second.

amo, amare, amavi, amatus ("to love")

Present

Active		Passive	
amem	amemus	amer	amemur
ames	ametis	ameris	amemini
amet	ament	ametur	amentur

Imperfect

Active		Passive	
amarem	amaremus	amarer	amaremur
amares	amaretis	amareris	amaremini
amaret	amarent	amaretur	amarentur

Perfect

Active		Passive	
amaverim	amaverimus	amatus sim	amati simus
amaveris	amaveritis	amatus sis	amati sitis
amaverit	amaverint	amatus sit	amati sint

Pluperfect

Active		Passive	
amavissem	amavissemus	amatus essem	amati essemus
amavisses	amavissetis	amatus esses	amati essetis
amavisset	amavissent	amatus esset	amati essent

moneo, monere, monui, monitus ("to warn")

Present

Active		Passive	
moneam	moneamus	monear	moneamur
moneas	moneatis	monearis	moneamini
moneat	moneant	moneatur	moneantur

All other tenses are formed exactly like the first conjugation.

Subordinate Conjunctions

Here is a list of conjunctions that will introduce a subordinate clause, usually in the subjunctive mood.

Conjunction	Meaning	Derivative
antequam	before	—
cum	when, since, although	—
donec	until	—
dum	while	—
ita	in such a way	—
quanto	how much	quantify
quo	where	—
si	if	—
sic	thus	—
tam	so	—
tantum	so great	tantamount
unde	whence	—
ut	in order that, that	—
veluti	just as	—

Hysteria's Herstory

Twenty-four letters from Cicero to his wife, Terentia, survive and reveal that as a dutiful Roman wife she kept a home for him until he became obsessed with the idea that she was stealing his money and divorced her in 46 B.C.E. He was probably turned off by her strong will and independence. Cicero had arranged two marriages for his daughter Tullia, but the third husband was chosen by Tullia and her mother while Cicero was away.

Unlike the hapless Cicero, whose head and pierced tongue ended up impaled on the Forum, Terentia was said to have lived to the ripe old age of 103.

Clauses with a Purpose

Purpose clauses begin with *in order that, with the purpose of,* or just plain *to.* For example:

> I went into the kitchen to see to dinner.
>
> I went into the kitchen in order to see to dinner.

In Latin, the verb in the purpose clause will be in the subjunctive. For example:

> In culinam ivi ut prandium viderem.

Sometimes the purpose clause begins with a relative pronoun, translated *who were to ....* For example:

> Servos in culinam misi qui prandium viderent.
>
> I sent the slaves into the kitchen who were to fix dinner.

Now it's your turn. Translate these sentences:

1. Multi alios laudant, ut ab illis laudentur.

   _____

2. Multi alios laudabant, ut ab illis laudarentur.

   _____

3. Servos in tabernam misit ut amicum occuparent.

   _____

The negative purpose clause is introduced by *ne*. For example:

> Epistulam mittit ne fleas.

> He sends a letter in order that you not cry.

Clauses with a Result

Subordinate clauses of result sometimes follow a word such as *in such a way, so that, so much, to the point that, so great*, and begin with *with the result that* or sometimes simply *that*. Result clauses are always in the subjunctive. For example:

> Pisces tantum condiunt ut nemo edere possit.

> They season the fish so much that no one is able to eat.

Now translate the following sentences:

1. Ita clamorem fecit ut exire necesse esset.

   _____

2. Amabat murenam adeo ut in piscina sederet.

   _____

The negative result clause uses *ut ... non*. For example:

> Tanta fabula fuit ut ego ei credere non possem.

> The story was of such a kind that I was not able to believe it.

Clauses of Fear

These aren't clauses to be afraid of. These are clauses that show fear and are always in the subjunctive. Even more perverse, they use *ut* for the negative and *ne* for the positive. For example:

> Vereor ut cibum habeam.

> I fear that I may not have food.

> Verebatur ne hostes urbem occuparent.

> He was afraid that the enemy would seize the city.

When? Why? What If? Clauses

Subordinate clauses that indicate time are usually in the indicative. For example:

> Haec feci, dum licuit.

> I did these things while it was permitted.

Ubi haec audivit, abiit.

When he heard these things, he went away.

Subordinate clauses that indicate cause are also in the indicative. For example:

Quod hoc emi, meum est.

Because I bought it, it is mine.

Clauses that indicate conditions are sometimes indicative, sometimes, subjunctive.

If it is an open condition, where there is no doubt as to its fulfillment or probability, the indicative is used. For example:

Si spirat, vivit.

If he is breathing, he is living.

If, on the other hand, there is some doubt as to the actuality, if it is contrary to fact, then the subjunctive is used. For example:

Si venisses, gavisus essem.

If you had come, I would have been glad.

Practice Makes Perfect

Choose a clause that would complete the sentence:

1. He was a general ...
2. We go shopping ...
3. The men took the rope ...
4. We have fun ...
5. I would cry ...

a. ... si meus canis aberat.
b. ... cum fabulam audimus.
c. ... ut cervum caperent.
d. ... quod praecipuus erat.
e. ... cum nihil facere sit.

Now translate the following sentences:

1. Cum Caesar haec audiret, se recipere milites iussit.

   _____

2. Quae cum ita sint, Romam ibo.

   _____

3. Haec feci, dum licuit.

   _____

4. Dum haec agebantur, servi discesserunt.

    _____

5. Mane domum donec redibo.

    _____

6. Si stat, vivit.

    _____

For all intents and purposes, differentiating between the indicative and the subjunctive is not necessary for your enjoyment of learning Latin. When you decide to write in Latin extensively, then you will need to know the finer distinctions. If you are simply translating, it usually works to just follow your common sense. However, you could remember that the subjunctive can be translated with such waffling words as *may, might, could, would,* or *were to.*

The Least You Need to Know

➤ Subjunctive forms are not like the indicative.

➤ If it's not real, it's subjunctive.

➤ Latin has too many little words.

➤ Clauses complete thoughts and complicate sentences.

Chapter 15

Simple and Not-So-Simple Sentences

Sentences can be as short as one word—*Go!*—or as long as William Faulkner's sentences that stretch from Mississippi to Tennessee. But every sentence has at least one subject and one predicate because that's what makes the complete thought.

Sentences work in different ways. Some declare their thought and are called *declarative* sentences. Others ask questions and are *interrogatives*. Still others give commands and are called *imperative* sentences. They often have the subject *you* understood (that is, not written), like the imperative sentence above: *Go!*

I Will Learn These Words

More verbs to learn and enjoy! Watch out for the fourth principal part that sometimes looks like an alien. There are deponent verbs as well. They end in *or* and have passive forms but active meanings.

Principal Parts	Meaning	Derivative
absum, abesse, afui, afuturus	be away	absent
ambulo, ambulare, ambulavi, atus	walk	ambulatory
credo, credere, credidi, creditus	believe	credible
exeo, exire, exii, exitus	go out	exit
gaudeo, gaudere, gavisus sum	rejoice	gaudy
incido, incidere, incidi, incissus	cut into	incisor
iubeo, iubere, iussi, iussus	order	jussive
lacrimo, lacrimare, avi, atus	cry	lachrymose
ludo, ludere, ludi, lusus	play	ludicrous
miror, mirari, miratus sum	wonder	iracle
soleo, solere, solui, solitus	be accustomed	—
taceo, tacere, tacui, tacitus	be quiet	taciturn
traho, trahere, traxi, tractus	draw, drag	traction
tutor, tutari, tutatus sum	watch over	tutor
valeo, valere, valui, valiturus	be well	value

If you are an *ambulatory* patient, you are walking around, unlike the British babies, who are pushed around in a *perambulator.*

Iussive comes from the Sanskrit *udyodhati,* which means "boils up, rages." I guess it's based on the idea that if you are boiling up and raging, someone will take what you say as an order.

Lachrymose means "teary," having those wet things coming from your *lacrimal* glands and causing much *lacrimation.*

Here are some nouns and adjectives you will need. Remember that every noun has a gender. Adjectives, on the other hand, have forms for all three genders. Numbers, like adverbs, blessedly have only one form.

Word and Base	Meaning	Derivative
ager, agri (m.)	field	agriculture
bellum, belli (n.)	war	bellicose
brevis, breve	short	brief
caput, capitis (n.)	head	capital
centum	one hundred	century
corpus, corporis (n.)	body	corporal
cubile, cubilis (n.)	bed	concubine
culpa, culpae (f.)	fault	culpable

150

Word and Base	Meaning	Derivative
deceptus, decepta, deceptum	deceived	deception
derectus, derecta, derectum	straight	direct
domus, domus (f.)	house	domestic
frigidus, frigida, frigidum	cold	frigid
hora, horae (f.)	hour	hour
iratus, irata, iratum	angry	irate
iucundus, iucunda, iucundum	happy	jocund
luna, lunae (f.)	moon	lunar
lupus, lupi (m.)	wolf	lupine
nemo, neminis (m./f.)	no one	—
nodus, nodi (m.)	knot, joint	node
nox, noctis (f.)	night	nocturnal
onus, oneris (n.)	burden	onerous
palla, pallae (f.)	dress	—
servus, servi (m.)	slave	servile

Corporal punishment relates to blows to the body, while *capital* punishment afflicts the head and is therefore more deadly.

Did You Know?

The ancient public baths were much like the health club or the YMCA of today. Men and women would retire to the baths for saunas, exercise, massages, and socializing. The largest baths in Rome were those of Caracalla, which are almost equal in size to the Colosseum. The baths of Caracalla were almost one mile in circumference and could accommodate 1,600 bathers. Romans were enthusiastic bathers. Unfortunately, they didn't use soap.

Adverb	Meaning
diu	for a long time
iam	now, already
igitur	therefore
mox	soon
quando	when
quoque	also
saepe	often
statim	immediately
ubi	where, when
utinam	would that!

Simple Sentences—I can learn Latin.

Simply put, every sentence has a subject and a verb. The subject is always in the nominative case.

Remember, nominative case endings are often one of the following: *a, ae, r, us, um, i, a, es*. Unfortunately, the maverick third declension (nominative singular) can end in any letter. In Latin, sometimes the subject is attached to the verb. The personal pronoun is indicated by the following endings: *i* ("I"), *s* or *tis* ("you"), *t* ("he," "she," "it"), *mus* ("we"), *tis* ("you" pl.), and *nt* or *erunt* ("they").

The passive personal endings are *or* ("I"), *eris* or *re* ("you"), *tur* ("he," "she," "it"), *mur* ("we"), *mini* ("you" pl.), and *ntur* ("they").

> Here's a translation tip: Look for a noun in the nominative case. If there is none, look for the verb, usually at the end of the sentence. Use the personal pronoun ending for your subject. Take, for example; *Viros invitabo.*

Since *viros* is not nominative, look at *invitabo* and begin the sentence "I will invite …."

Now it's your turn again. Translate these simple sentences:

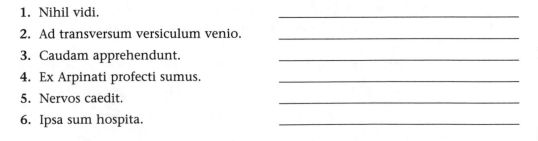

1. Nihil vidi.
2. Ad transversum versiculum venio.
3. Caudam apprehendunt.
4. Ex Arpinati profecti sumus.
5. Nervos caedit.
6. Ipsa sum hospita.

7. Cotidie patior. _____

8. Multa praetereo. _____

9. Ipsae concidunt. _____

10. Habent crura sine nodis. _____

11. Utinam mundum vincam! _____

Some sentences will have a subject and a direct object. The verbs in these sentences will have a transitive verb, a verb that *transits* or *goes across* to an object. Because of the lackadaisical attitude toward word order, the reader must distinguish the nominative from the accusative endings. For your review, here are the accusative endings: *am, as, um, os, a, em, es,* and *us.* For example:

Bellum agros delebat.

The obvious accusative is *agros. Bellum* could be in the accusative since it is a neuter noun. But there is no conjunction to show that something destroys fields and war, and, furthermore, that just doesn't make sense. It is more sensible to use *bellum* as the subject.

A further helpful hint is to check out the verb. It is singular, third person, agreeing very nicely with *war.*

Now it's your turn again. Translate the following sentences:

1. Lauti fungos, helvellas, herbasque condiunt.

   _____

2. Homo nobilis hoc simulacrum deportat.

   _____

3. Sergius Orata vivaria invenit.

   _____

4. Uxor inaures addidit.

   _____

5. Troglodytae arbores conscendunt.

   _____

6. Corpus humanum membra habet.

   _____

7. Plebs fabulam intellexit.

   _____

Finally, some sentences will not have a direct object because their verb is intransitive, *not going across* to an object. Often these verbs are followed by a predicate noun, a word that renames the subject and therefore is in the nominative case.

Typical intransitive verbs that take a predicate noun are *is, am, are, was, were, feel, be called,* and *seem.*

Other intransitive verbs are action words or states of being, like *run, jump, stand,* and *happen.* For example …

> Vir agricola esse videtur.

You can see that the two nouns are in the nominative. So it would be correct either to say …

> The man seems to be a farmer.

Or …

> The farmer seems to be a man.

Remember, your translations can be flexible! Try it:

1. Diligenter quaesivi. _____
2. Alii singuli sunt. _____
3. Silentium est. _____
4. Unum cornu exsistit. _____
5. Nuclei decidunt. _____
6. Equi non boves sunt. _____
7. Gaudeamus. _____
8. Frigida cubila sunt. _____
9. Tibi credo. _____
10. Omnes vobis credimus. _____

Interrogative Sentences: Can I learn Latin?

We form questions by using an interrogative word—*Why? How? When? Where?* We also ask questions by inverting the word order—*Can I learn Latin?* Sometimes we indicate written questions by using the question mark—*The movie is over?*

The Latin equivalent of the question mark is the enclitic *ne* added to the first word of the sentence. For example:

> Esne agricola?
>
> Are you a farmer?

Latin also has interrogative words that will begin the sentence. For example:

> Quo vadis?
>
> Where are you going?

Now translate these:

1. Invitabisne viros et clientes? _____
2. Ubi corpus pones? _____
3. Quot togas habes? _____
4. Tenebis memoria omnes leges? _____
5. Afuisti ab tua villa? _____
6. Estne domus procul? _____

Complex Sentences: Although I am a complete idiot, I can learn Latin.

A complex sentence is a simple sentence that contains a subordinate clause. There are four ways you can recognize a subordinate clause in Latin:

1. A relative pronoun begins the clause. The forms of the relative pronoun begin with *qu* or *cu*. The clause usually ends with its own verb. For example:

   > Video canem qui in via stat.

   The simple sentence is *Video canem,* "I see the dog." The subordinate clause, which you can lift out and still have a complete thought, is "which is standing in the road."

2. The result clause begins with *ut* or *ne,* fol-lowed by the subjunctive and is translated "for the purpose of" or "with the result that." For example:

   > Tantum cibum edit ut obesus fiat.

   Words like *tantum, ita, adeo,* and *tam* often signal a result clause.

3. A subordinate conjunction begins the clause. *When, since, although,* and *while* are fre-quently used. For example:

   > Dum dominus abest, servi ludent.

Cave!

There is nothing to prevent a writer from inserting clauses within clauses: *I see the dog that is standing in the road that runs from Boston to New York that is a large city.*

4. The clause contains the ablative absolute—two or three words, usually set off by commas, in the ablative case, without any recognizable connection to the sentence. For example:

> Viris captis, feminae clamabant.

Remember, the ablative absolute can be translated with a subordinate conjunction, even though there is none there in the Latin (for example, *Because the men were captured, the women were shouting*).

With any complex sentence, you can remove the clause and still have a complete thought.

Hysteria's Herstory

Upper-class Roman women used cosmetics extensively. They painted the underlid of the eye green, while the upperlid, eyelashes, and eyebrows were blackened. They painted their fingernails and toenails red and often used an orange-red dye to color the palms of their hands and the soles of their feet. White lead was used to beautify their faces but because women often became sick from lead poisoning, they substituted chalk.

Practice Makes Perfect

Your turn again. Translate the following sentences into English:

1. Venio ad transversum versiculum in quo me admones.

   _____

2. Dies fecit (made it happen) ut Quintus in Arcano maneret.

   _____

3. Illa inquit, "Ego ipsa sum hospita," quod antecesserat Statius ut prandium nobis videret.

   _____

4. Discubuimus omnes praeter illam, cui Quintus mensam misit.

   _____

5. Lauti volunt in honorem adducere terra nata quae lege excepta sunt.

   _____

6. Fungos, helvellas, herbas ita condiunt ut nihil possit esse suavius.

   _____

7. Ego, qui a ostreis et murenis abstinebam, a beta et malva deceptus sum. _____

8. Rosa carne omni, nuclei corporum, qui margaritae sunt, in ima decidunt.

   _____

9. Antonia murenae quam ille amabat, inaures addidit.

   _____

10. Crure tardato, alterius poplitis nervos caedit.

    _____

11. Hecyram ad vos refero, quam mihi in silentio numquam agere licuit.

    _____

12. Cum rumor de gladiatoribus venit, ego meum locum non potui tutari.

    _____

13. Corpus humanum multa membra habet inter quae manus, os, dentes, venter sunt.

    _____

14. Accidunt arbores tantum ut summa species earum stantium relinquatur. _____

15. Sum irata quod nunc non valeo.

    _____

16. Femina pallam quae longa est gerere solet.

    _____

17. Servus tunicam quae brevis est gerere solet.

    _____

The Least You Need to Know

➤ Simple sentences have a subject and verb.

➤ Complex sentences contain a subordinate clause.

➤ Questions are indicated by the suffix *ne* on the first word.

➤ Some of the sentences in this chapter were made up 2,000 years ago.

Chapter 16

Compound Sentences and Beyond

In This Chapter

➤ More words to learn and memorize

➤ Simple and complex compound sentences

➤ Compound–complex sentences

➤ Indirect statements, questions, and commands

Most first-time readers of Cicero's orations curse his use of clauses within clauses. His famous periodic sentences are also infamous for their length. Students struggling through Caesar's *Gallic Wars* will agree that all his sentences are too complex and wonder why he didn't have shorter thoughts.

A reader of original Latin has to get used to stopping at the conjunctions and breaking up some of those long sentences into more readable, understandable ideas.

So we end our formal grammar section with clausal constructions that you can make into sentences themselves.

More Words to Learn and Memorize

Many of these conjunctions you have seen before. Remember that coordinating conjunctions will join two independent clauses. Subordinating conjunctions will have one clause depending on the other to complete its meaning. The good news is that conjunctions have only one form.

Coordinating Conjunctions	Meaning	Subordinating Conjunctions	Meaning
at	but		
aut	either	antequam	before
aut … aut	either/or	cum	when, since, although
autem	moreover, nevertheless, on the other hand	donec	until
et	and	dum	while
et … et	both/and	ita	in such a way
etiam	also	si	if
que	and	sic	thus
sed	but	tam	so
sicut	just as	tantum	so great
		unde	whence
		ut	in order to, that
		veluti	just as

You have seen a few forms of two irregular verbs. Here is the complete conjugation of *volo, velle, volui* ("to be willing, wish"), and *nolo, nolle, nolui* ("to be unwilling").

Volo, Velle, Volui

Present			
volo	I wish	volumus	we wish
vis	you wish	vultis	you wish
vult	he wishes	volunt	they wish

Future			
volam	I will wish	volemus	we will wish
voles	you will wish	voletis	you will wish
volet	he will wish	volent	they will wish

All other forms of *volo* are regular.

Nolo, Nolle, Nolui

Present			
nolo	I do not want	nolumus	we do not want
non vis	you do not want	non vultis	you don't want
non vult	he doesn't want	nolunt	they don't want

Future			
nolam	I will not want	nolemus	we will not want
noles	you will not want	noletis	you will not want
nolet	he will not want	nolent	they will not want

All other forms are regular.

Remember that the imperative form of *nolo, noli* (singular), and *nolite* (plural) is used for the negative command. For example,

> Noli in via stare.

> Don't stand in the road.

> Nolite clamare.

> Don't shout (you all).

The other irregular verb is *fio, fieri, factus sum.*

This verb is actually the passive of *facio, facere* ("to do" or "to make"). As such it is translated as "to become, to be done, to be made."

Tene Memoria

Remember that an infinitive usually follows *volo*, as in *Volo legere* ("I wish to read").

Present			
fio	I become	fimus	we become
fis	you become	fitis	you become
fit	he becomes	fiunt	they become

The future tense of this verb is like a third conjugation, and all other tenses are regular.

Compound Sentences

Compound sentences have two or more simple sentences joined by a coordinating conjunction. In English we can use the semicolon, an idea not yet in vogue for the Roman scribes. For example:

Canem video et pullus trans viam it.

I see the dog and the chicken go across the road.

To foster your Latin skills, translate the following compound sentences culled from the original Latin selections in Chapters 18, "Selections from Vitruvius *et al.,*" and 19, "Look Ma! I'm Reading Latin!"

1. In nobile civitate Ephesi, Graeci habitaverunt et lex iniqua constituta esse dicitur.

   _____

2. Architectus publicum opus recipit et pretium dat.

   _____

3. Figura alcis similis capro est sed magnitudine paulo antecedit.

   _____

4. Ad arbores se applicant et ita quietem capiunt.

   _____

5. Aut arbores ab radicibus subruunt aut eas accidunt.

   _____

6. Infirmas arbores pondere affigunt atque ipsae concidunt.

   _____

7. Troglodytae Aethiopiae solo venatu se alunt et cotidie arbores ascendunt.

   _____

8. Pedes stipat in sinistro femine itaque poplitem dextra caedit.

   _____

9. Elephantus crure tardatur et breve tempore mortuus est.

   _____

10. Itaque id me commoverat sic illa aspere responderat.

    _____

Compound–Complex Sentences

Compound-complex sentences are those compound sentences that also include clauses. Latin writers were fond of putting clauses into clauses into clauses, *ad infinitum,* all of which were in the subjunctive. For example:

Canem video et pullum qui trans viam it etiam video.

I see the dog and I see the chicken which is crossing the road.

Your turn again. Translate the following gems:

1. Si non amplius quam quarta sumptui in opere consumitur, ad aestimationem eam addit neque ulla poena tenetur.

   _____

   _____

2. Neque quietis causa procumbunt neque, si quo afflictae casu conciderunt, erigere sese ac sublevare possunt (si quo = "if any").

   _____

   _____

Did You Know?

Julius Caesar was given the province of Gaul at the end of his consulship. Situated beyond the Alps and considered a pretty poor prize for a proconsul, Gaul nevertheless was for Julius Caesar's taking, and he advanced with his troops in 58 B.C.E. During his seven years there he acquired control over what is now France and Belgium and continuously sent back to the citizens of Rome his *Commentaries*—a running account of his victories and his description of the people.

Indirect Statements

An indirect statement comes after verbs of stating— *say, know, think, tell, believe,* and the like.

An indirect statement reports a direct statement in a subordinate clause introduced by *that*. For example:

> Direct statement: The chicken is old.
>
> Direct statement: He said, "The chicken is old."
>
> Indirect statement: He said that the chicken is old.

In English, we sometimes omit the introductory word *that:*

> He said the chicken was old.

RETINEO

Grammar Guru

The English subjunctive uses *were, be,* and *would* (among others) to show contrary-to-fact conditions and other nonrealistic states. For example, *If I were a complete idiot, would I be here today?*

163

In Latin there is no introductory word. Instead, we have the subject of the indirect statement in the accusative case, and the verb in the infinitive. For example:

> Dixit pullum vetustum esse.

> He said that the chicken was old.

You will notice that the present infinitive is used here, although it's translated as the past tense. The infinitive in an indirect statement shows a relationship between the main verb and the subordinate verb. The present infinitive shows that both actions are going on at the same time. For example:

> Dicit pullum vetustum esse.

> He says that the chicken is old.

> Dixit pullum vetustum esse.

> He said that the chicken was old.

The perfect infinitive is used to show time before that of the main verb.

> Dicit pullum vetustum fuisse.

> He says that the chicken was old.

> Dixit pullum vetustum fuisse.

> He said that the chicken had been old.

The future infinitive is used to show time after that of the main verb.

> Dicit pullum vetustum futurum esse.
> He says the chicken will be old.

> Dixit pullum vetustum futurum esse.

> He said that the chicken would be old.

Did You Know?

There existed in Rome a school for chicken breeders. The course lasted eight months and the tuition was 40 chickens, which were used as a basis of instruction for labs. Profits from the sale of eggs and occasionally of the chickens themselves provided for the faculty salaries and maintenance of the school.

Here are some indirect statements from ancient authors that you can practice translating:

Quintus mihi narravit illam secum dormire non voluisse. (Cicero)

Sapientissimum esse dicunt eum cui quod opus sit ipsi veniat. (Cicero)

Credula spes vitam fovet et futurum esse melius cras semper dicit. (Tibullus)

Nemo enim est tam senex qui annum vivere se posse putet. (Cicero)

Indirect Questions

Like the indirect statement, the indirect question comes after verbs of *saying, knowing, thinking,* or *asking* and takes the subjunctive. For example:

Quaesit qui ad cenam veniat.

He asks who is coming to dinner.

Some words that will introduce an indirect question are *qui* ("who"), *quid* ("what"), *quomodo* ("how"), *unde* ("wherefrom"), and *quantum* ("how much").

Here are some examples from Latin authors:

Ne mireris unde hoc accideret et quomodo commiserim. (Cicero)

Pollicetur dicere quantus sumptus futurus sit. (Vitruvius)

Nescire quid antequam natus sis acciderit, id est semper esse puerum. (Cicero)

Nunc scio quid sit amor. (Vergil)

Multi dubitabant quid optimum esset. (Cicero)

Indirect Commands

Although indirect commands can come in the guise of the accusative and an infinitive, they also come with *ut* or *ne* plus the subjunctive. The most common verbs implying an act of will or command are *mando* ("to command"), *rogo* ("to ask"), *peto* ("to ask"), *persuadeo* ("to persuade"), *moneo* ("to warn"), *hortor* ("to urge"), *video* ("to see to it"), and *permitto* ("to permit").

Here are some examples:

Caesar suos milites hortatus est ne timerent.

Puellas monuit ne hoc facerent.

Persuasit eis ut hoc facerent.

165

Practice Makes Perfect

Time to hand the pen to you again. Translate the following sentences:

1. Quintus in Arcano remansit et Aquinum ad me postridie mane venit mihique narravit nec secum illam dormire voluisse et, cum discessura esset,eam fuisse eius modi, qualem ego vidissem. (Hint: Translate in sections.)

   _____

   _____

   _____

2. Quintus in Arcano remansit.

   _____

3. Aquinum ad me postridie mane venit.

   _____

4. Mihi narravit nec secum illam dormire voluisse.

   _____

5. Cum discessura esset, eam fuisse eius modi qualem ego eam vidissem.

   _____

The famous first line, *Gaul is divided into three parts,* is part of a compound-complex sentence that can be divided into six parts:

1. Gallia est omnia divisa in partes tres.
2. Belgae unam partem incolunt.
3. Aquitani aliam partem incolunt.
4. Celtae tertiam partem incolunt.
5. Celtae ipsorum lingua Celtae appellantur.
6. Celtae nostra lingua Galli appellantur.

Try translating the original sentence:

> Gallia est omnis divisa in partes tres, quarum unam incolunt Belgae, aliam Aquitani, tertiam, qui ipsorum lingua Celtae, nostra Galli appellantur.

Hysteria's Herstory

When Pliny the Younger was 40, he married a young girl, Calpurnia. He was inordinately proud of this model wife who was sensible and thrifty and took an interest in literature, especially Pliny's writings. He boasts that when he gave public readings of his works, she would station herself behind a curtain and listen carefully to the praise heaped upon him. She even took his poetry, set it to music, and then serenaded her husband with his own poems. No wonder he thought she was terrific!

The Least You Need to Know

➤ In spite of all the grammatical terminology, thoughts can be broken down into bytes.

➤ Indirect statements take the subject in the accusative case, and the verb in the infinitive.

➤ Indirect questions and commands take the subjunctive.

➤ If the Romans wanted to string their thoughts into one unbroken, tediously long sentence, we are up to the challenge.

➤ We've come a long way from the ideal Roman wife, baby.

Part 4

Reading Latin—Selections from Ancient Authors

These selections are arranged in chronological order and represent various aspects of life: art, politics, sports, natural history, family life. The readings show that contractors underestimated their bids, wives were insulted by their husbands' behavior, some people had to watch what they ate, and there was more than one way to catch an elephant.

It's hard to imagine that some of these events happened 2,000 years ago and not yesterday.

Selections from Republican Rome

After the expulsion of the kings in 509 B.C. and the formation of the Republic, the inhabitants of Rome gradually expanded their power and influence, first throughout Italy and then gradually to the whole Mediterranean world. By 166 B.C., the time of Terence, many Romans had become well-educated citizens, knowing Greek as well as their own developing language, Latin.

The literature that remains from early Rome through the fall of the Republic is wonderfully varied. Letters, though often edited for publication, reveal personal life. The *Commentaries* from Caesar are the first historical record of Europe. Through his letters, orations, and essays, Cicero gives us a thorough picture of the contemporary mind. The plays of Terence give us a taste of the language and behavior of the people in the street.

Vita Terenti (The Life of Terence)

At the end of the second century B.C., Rome had expanded its power from Spain to Africa, from Asia Minor to Macedonia. Roman life was imitated in art and architecture, politics and government. Some Roman citizens became wealthy. They had slaves to do the housework and take care of business. Money was rolling in from the provinces. What was left to do? Luckily, some talented people could write plays, and the wealthy citizens were quick to sponsor such endeavors.

Publius Terentius Afer was born in Carthage in 185 B.C. and came to Rome as a slave of a senator who educated him and then gave him his freedom. Sponsored by Scipio Africanus Minor, Terence wrote many plays, adapted into the Latin language from Greek.

This selection is from the prologue, 21–36, to *Hecyra, The Mother-in-Law,* and shows how plays attracted all kinds of people in the streets. At this time there were no theaters, so plays were produced on hastily built stages that were often dismantled at the end of the day.

The speaker was also the producer.

With the help of the following notes, you should be able to read this adaptation from *Hecyra.* Remember to find the subject and verb; if it seems like Greek to you, find the translation in Appendix D, "Answer Keys."

Latin	Form	Meaning
refero	first person, singular, present	I bring back
eam	accusative, singular, feminine	it (referring to *Hecyra*)
erit	third person, singular, future	it will be
pugilum	genitive, plural	of the boxers
fecerunt	third person, plural, perfect	made it so
tutari	present infinitive	(deponent verb) to save

Hecyram ad vos refero, quam mihi in silentio numquam agere licuit. Ita eam oppressit calamitas.

Eam calamitatem vestra intellegentia sedabit, si erit adiutrix nostrae industriae. Cum primum eam agere coepi, pugilum gloria, funambuli exspectatio, comitum conventus, strepitus, clamor mulierum fecerunt ut ante tempus exirem foras.

Refero denuo. Primo actu placeo. Cum interea rumor venit de gladiatoribus, populus convolat,clamant, pugnant de loco; ego interea meum non potui tutari locum.

Nunc turba non est; otium et silentium est. Agendi tempus mihi est.

Caesar: More Than Just a Salad

Gaius Iulius Caesar, renowned for his military conquests, his mastery over a certain Egyptian queen, and his role in a Shakespearean play, was born in 100 B.C. He rose through the ranks of Roman politics and maneuvered himself into a consulship and later membership in the first triumvirate. The Roman authorities, fearful of Caesar's growing power, gave him the province of Gaul, hoping he would cross the Alps, hit a snowdrift, and find it difficult to return. But Caesar spent seven years building camps, taking over the barbarian cities, strengthening his army, and annexing much of western Europe to the Roman State. While he was gone, Pompey also built up an army and was threatening to take over Rome. More than a little miffed, Caesar crossed the Rubicon with his army, thus breaking the law against entering Rome accompanied by thousands of troops.

With those immortal words, *Alea iacta est* ("The die is cast"), he proceeded to take over the known world, fix up the calendar by adding a month with his name, July, and give a dinner for 22,000 people. Now that's a lot of salad.

The *Commentarii de Bello Gallico* was written while Caesar was in Gaul. It was intended as a report to the Roman people that Caesar, though far away across the Alps, was alive and well and conquering up a storm. It also happens to be the first written history of western Europe.

This selection, VI, 26–27, describes the remarkable animals found in the Hercynian forest in Germany.

Julius Caesar's prose has been read by Latin students for centuries, because it is clear and fairly simple. You have already translated the first line of his *de Bello Gallico*. With the help of a few notes, you should read this selection with ease.

Latin	Form	Meaning
cornu	nominative, singular, neuter	horn
his	ablative, plural, neuter	modifies cornibus
quo	ablative, singular	(after si) if any
quarum	genitive, plural, feminine	of these
consuerint	third person, plural, perfect, subjunctive	were accustomed

Est bos cervi figura cuius a media fronte inter aures unum cornu exsistit excelsius magisque derectum his quae nobis nota sunt cornibus; ab eius summo sic ut palmae ramique late diffunduntur. Eadem est feminae marisque natura, eadem forma magnitudoque cornuum.

Sunt item quae appellantur alces. Harum est consimilis capris figura et varietas pellium; sed magnitudine paulo antecedunt mutilaque sunt cornus et crura sine nodis articulisque habent; neque quietis causa procumbunt neque, si quo afflictae casu conciderunt, erigere sese ac sublevare possunt. His sunt arbores pro cubilibus; ad eas se applicant atque ita paulum modo reclinatae quietem capiunt. Quarum ex vestigiis cum est animadversum a venatoribus quo se recipere consuerint, omnes eo loco aut ab radicibus subruunt aut accidunt arbores, tantum ut summa species earum stantium relinquatur. Huc cum se consuetudine reclinaverunt, infirmas arbores pondere affligunt atque una ipsae concidunt.

Hysteria's Herstory

Less well known to us but certainly known to the Romans of Cicero's day was Clodia, a woman of noble lineage. In 61 B.C. she was 33 years old and a widow. Catullus, age 27, fell madly in love with her and wrote many blistering love poems to his *Lesbia*. After three years, Clodia dropped him like a hot potato for an even younger man, Caelius. Unfortunately, he then dropped her after two years and the vengeful Clodia brought trumped-up murder charges against him. Cicero successfully defended him in court and Clodia disappeared from history forever.

Vita Ciceronis (The Life of Cicero)

Marcus Tullius Cicero was a consul, senator, provincial governor, and lawyer. Through his voluminous writings, he gives us an intimate glimpse of life with Caesar, Pompey, Antony, and many of the movers and shakers during the fall of the republic. We can almost hear him wonder, "Whom shall I support? What's Brutus up to? How should I treat Caesar when I see him for dinner?"

Cicero is especially interesting because he was born into a middle-class family and became a self-made man. Although born at Arpinum, 60 miles southeast of Rome, and considered a country bumpkin, his father brought him to Rome for his later education. At age 25 he began his career in the law courts. After a trip to Greece to rest his voice and gain weight (baklava, anyone?), he returned to politics in Rome. In 76 B.C. he was selected to be *quaestor* in Sicily, which gave him automatic membership in the senate. His honest and attentive administrative skills were appreciated by the Sicilians, and in 70 B.C. Cicero was asked by the Sicilians to prosecute a corrupt governor, Verres. The successful prosecution led to more pleadings in the courts. In 66 B.C. Cicero supported the Manilian law that gave Pompey military authority in Asia Minor.

In 63 B.C. Cicero was elected consul, the highest office in Rome. He defeated Catiline, who did not take defeat lightly and plotted to assassinate Cicero and take over the city.

Cicero called an emergency meeting of the senate in the temple of Jupiter Stator on the Capitoline hill. There he delivered an address that includes the line, *O tempora, o mores* (Oh the times, oh the ways), bewailing the lawlessness of the times and pointing to the brooding Catiline, who sat apart from the crowd (at least according to the picture in my high school Latin classroom).

Catiline eventually left the city. His co-conspirators were apprehended and Cicero asked for the death penalty. They were hastily executed without trial.

The senate declared a thanksgiving in Cicero's name and called him *pater patriae,* "father of his country." It was a high point of his life, and it was all downhill from there.

All his life, Cicero tried to promote a *concordia ordinum* (a harmony of the orders), a first-century rainbow coalition between the nobles and the equestrians, but with no success. Nice thought, though.

When the first triumvirate of Pompey, Crassus, and Caesar were formed, Cicero was left out. Worse, Clodius, his sworn enemy, got himself elected tribune and promptly passed a law that condemned to exile anyone who put a citizen to death without a trial. Oops! Guess who that would be?

So Cicero hightailed it to Greece, where he fretted and fumed for a year until Pompey revoked the law.

In 56 B.C. Cicero retreated to the country to write and read philosophy. Five years later he was sent to Cilicia in Asia Minor as the provincial administrator and commander of the army. He didn't really command the army, however; like the president of the United States, he had the professional military do that.

When he returned to Rome, Crassus had died, Caesar had crossed the Rubicon, and all Hades had broken out. Cicero was courted by both Caesar and Pompey, but in the end sided with Pompey. It turned out to be a bad idea, since Pompey was defeated. Cicero retired again.

At this time Cicero decided to dump his wife of 20 years because she was spending a lot of money and to marry his young ward, Publilia, who had a lot of money. This unfortunate union lasted only a few months—a mother-in-law is sometimes credited with the break-up—and Cicero was left poorer than ever. His daughter Tullia died in 45 B.C., and he tried to work through his grief by more study and philosophical reading.

But Cicero was quickly back on his feet when Caesar was assassinated in 44 B.C. He returned to Rome to deliver a series of stinging speeches berating tyrants, dictators, and Marc Antony.

Unfortunately, Octavian and Antony had joined forces and, along with Lepidus, formed the second triumvirate. To stabilize their positions, they made lists of proscriptions—men to be eliminated, no medicines to be taken. Of the 200 names, Cicero's topped the list. Cicero attempted to escape to the sea in a curtained litter but was overrun by Antony's men. As he stuck his head out to see what was happening, he lost it.

Did You Know?

Clodius was the rogue who dressed as a woman and infiltrated the Bona Dea mystery rites that were being held at the home of Julius Caesar. Pompeia, Caesar's wife, was the hostess and it was her responsibility to see that no men were in the house during the ceremonies. To have a man sneaking around dressed as a flute player was a disgrace and Caesar promptly divorced her with that famous line, "Caesar's wife must be above suspicion." Gag.

Dining Room Scene

The following selection is from the *Epistulae ad Familiares, VII*, written in 46 B.C. from Cicero's villa in Tusculum. He had been corresponding with Gallus, a friend, but had to desist all work while recovering from a severe case of diarrhea. He probably didn't actually write anything himself, but rather dictated all his letters to his faithful slave, Tiro.

Don't let Cicero's word order confuse you. Sometimes the subject will be in the verb's place.

Word	Form	Meaning
mirere	second person, present passive	you wonder
litoteta	nominative, singular, feminine	simplicity
nata	neuter, plural, participle	things born from
deceptus sum	first person, singular, present perfect passive	I was taken down

At tamen, ne mirere, unde hoc acciderit, et quomodo commiserim. Lex sumptuaria, quae videtur litoteta attulisse, ea mihi fraudi fuit. Nam volunt isti lauti terra nata, quae lege excepta sunt, in honorem adducere. Fungos, heluellas, herbas omnes ita condiunt, ut nihil possit esse suavius. Cum incidissem in cena apud Lentulum, tanta me diarroia arripuit, ut hodie primum videatur consistere. Ita ego, qui me ostreis et muraenes facile abstinebam, a beta et a malva deceptus sum. Post hac igitur erimus cautiores.

My Sister-in-Law!

Cicero wrote many letters to his friend Atticus, spanning from 68 to 43 B.C. T. Pomponius Atticus was well known for his writings on Greek literature and culture. He wrote commentaries on Greek poets and translated many Greek plays into Latin. His surname was given to him because of his love and devotion to Greece.

The following letter was written in 51 B.C. Cicero was going from friend's villa to friend's villa, wending his way to Brundisium, from where he would sail to Cilicia for his year of governing. Cicero spent several weeks tying up loose ends, so to speak—paying debts, establishing political friendships, and basically dallying around before his big trip.

In this letter he speaks of having dinner with his brother, Quintus, who is married to Atticus's sister.

Letters can reveal how the Romans actually spoke. It is probable that the *nosti* ("you know") of his conversation was as used and overused as it is today.

Word	Form	Meaning
quae	relative, feminine, singular, nominative	this
se habet	third person, singular, present	is how it is
mite	accusative, nominative, singular	gentle, modifies nihil
dies	nominative, singular, masculine	festival day
nosti	second person, singular, present	you know
quo	relative, ablative, singular	there
lenius	comparative, masculine, singular	more kind
ducenda	gerund, ablative, singular	leading to marriage

Nunc venio ad transversum illum extremae epistulae tuae versiculum in quo me admones de sorore. Quae res se sic habet. ... Nihil tam vidi mite, nihil tam placatum quam tum meus frater erat in sororem tuam .... Postridie ex Arpinati profecti sumus. Ut in Arcano Quintus maneret, dies fecit, ego Aquini, sed prandimus in Arcano. Nosti hunc fundum. "Quo ut venimus, humanissime Quintus," Pomponia inquit, "tu invita mulieres, ego arcivero viros." Nihil potuit, mihi quidem ut visum est, dulcius idque cum verbis tum etiam animo ac vultu. At illa audientibus nobis "Ego ipsa sum" inquit hic hospita, quod antecesserat Statius, ut prandium nobis videret. Tum Quintus, "En" inquit mihi "haec ego patior cotidie." Dices: "Quid, quaeso, istuc erat?" Magnum; itaque me ipsum commoverat; sic absurde et aspere verbis vultuque responderat. Dissimulavi dolens. Discubuimus omnes praeter illam, cui tamen Quintus mensam misit. Illa reiecit. Quid multa? Nihil meo fratre lenius, nihil asperius tua sorore mihi visum est; et multa praetereo .... Quintus in Arcano remansit et Aquinum ad me postridie mane venit mihique narravit nec secum illam dormire voluisse.

In a later letter (*Ad Att.*, XIV.13.5), after Pomponia and Quintus had divorced, Cicero states:

> Abhorret a ducenda autem uxore "nihil iucundius libero lecto est."

My House!

While Cicero was in exile, Clodius seized his house on the Palatine hill, burned it to the ground, and offered Cicero's belongings for sale. He then had the property dedicated to a goddess, Liberty, so that the spot was sanctified and no private person could ever buy it. Clodius's brother-in-law, recently returned from a lucrative visit to Greece, performed the ceremony and evidently added a statue to the loot.

Here Cicero is pleading that the rites that were performed were illegal and, therefore, he should have the right to buy back his house.

In the end, of course, after Clodius was murdered, Cicero did recover his property. This selection is from *De Domo Sua, XLIII.*

Latin	Form	Meaning
meretrix	nominative, singular	prostitute, woman of the street
simulacrum	nominative, singular	statue
sepulcro	ablative, singular	tomb
sacerdote	ablative, singular	priest
aedilitatis	genitive, singular	of his aedilship
cogitarat	third person, singular, perfect	he thought
muneris	genitive, singular	of his gift
fanis	ablative, plural	shrines

"At unde est inventa ista (statua) Libertas?" quaesivi enim diligenter. Tanagraea quaedam meretrix fuisse dicitur. Eius non longe a Tanagra simulacrum e marmore in sepulcro positum fuit. Hoc quidam homo nobilis (Appius Clodius, frater Publi Clodi) non alienus ab hoc religioso Libertatis sacerdote, ad ornatum aedilitatis suae deportavit. Etenim cogitarat omnes superiores muneris splendore superare. Itaque omnia signa, tabulas, ornamentorum quod superfuit in fanis et communibus locis, tota e Graecia atque insulis omnibus honoris populi Romani causa sane frugaliter domum suam deportavit.

The Least You Need to Know

➤ Terence wrote plays that were performed out on the street.

➤ Caesar wrote a description of the Gallic Wars in which he comes out looking pretty good.

➤ Cicero wrote 900 letters with the help of a word processor named Tiro.

➤ Cicero got his house back.

Chapter 18

Selections from Vitruvius *et al.*

As Augustus continued his reign through the year 0 and attempted to establish a "pax Augusta," the peaceful times enabled poets, writers, and essayists to produce at a prodigious rate. Generous patronage continued and writers became more independent of their Greek predecessors. National consciousness was high, as seen in Vergil's and Livius's works, but then it slowly ebbed away to a more individual outlook. Histories, literary criticism, technical writing, and compilations were only part of the empire's contributions to Latin literature.

Vita Vitruivi

Marcus Pollio Vitruvius was a celebrated architect and engineer. About his personal life we know only that he lived in the first century B.C. His treatise on his profession, dedicated to Augustus, is the only book surviving from ancient times on architecture. Topics include building a city, covering everything from walls to bricks to entire buildings; creating colors; the physics of water; and a series of descriptions of ancient machines such as the water organ, water wheels, catapults, seige machines, and a water pump.

In the following passage from the preface to his book, Vitruvius describes a law regarding bids and contractors.

Latin	Form	Meaning
civitate	ablative, singular	in the city
constitua esse	perfect, infinitive	to have been instituted (with dicitur)
dura condicione	ablative, singular	with a hard condition
cum		when
tradita aestimatione	ablative, absolute	estimate having been handed over
bona	nominative, plural	goods

Nobili Graecorum et ampla civitate Ephesi lex vetusta dicitur a maioribus dura condicione sed iure non iniquo constituta esse. Nam architectus cum publicum opus curandum recipit, pollicetur, quanto sumptui futurum sit. Tradita aestimatione magistratui bona eius obligantur, donec opus perfectum sit. Absoluto autem, cum ad dictum inpensa respondit, decretis et honoribus ornatur. Item si non amplius quam quarta in opere consumitur, ad aestimationem est adicienda et de publico praestatur, neque ulla poena tenetur. Cum vero amplius quam quarta in opere consumitur, ex eius bonis ad perficiendum pecunia exigitur.

Utinam dii immortales fecissent, ea lex etiam Populo Romano non modo publicis sed etiam privatis aedificiis constitutua esset.

Vitruvius gives us directions on how to make an odometer. The Latin version and English translation follow.

Note the word *denticulum,* "a little tooth," and the author's frequent use of the subjunctive.

Transfertur nunc cogitatio scripturae ad rationem non inutilem sed summa sollertia a maioribus traditam, qua in via raeda sedentes vel mari navigantes scire possimus, quot milia numero itineris fecerimus. Hoc autem erit sic. Rotae, quae erunt in raeda, sint latae per medium diametrum pedum quaternum ut cum finitum locum habeat in se rota ab eoque incipiat progrediens in solo viae facere versationem, perveniendo ad eam finitionem, a qua coeperit versari, certum modum spatii habeat peractum pedes XII s.

Our next subject of writing is a useful machine which we owe to the great skill of our ancestors. Whether sitting in a carriage or sailing on the sea, we are able to know how many miles we have traveled. And here is how. The wheels, which will be on the carriage, are to be four feet in diameter and on one wheel a point is to be noted. When the wheel begins to move forward from this point and re-volves on the road, it will have completed a distance of $12^{1}/_{2}$ feet on arriving at the point from which it began its revolution.

His ita praeparatis tunc in rotae modiolo ad partem interiorem tympanum stabiliter includitur havens extra frontem suae rutundationis extantem denticulum unum. Insuper autem ad capsum raedae loculamentum firmiter figatur habens tympanum versatile in cultro conlocatum et in axiculo conclusum, in cuius tympani frontem denticuli perficiantur aequaliter divisi numero quadringenti convenientes denticulos tympani inferioris. Praeterea superiori tympano ad latus figatur alter denticulus prominens extra dentes.

Having prepared in such a way, then let a drum be secured to the inner side of the hub of the wheel with one tooth projecting from its exterior circumference. Above that, in the carriage, let a box be securely fixed with a drum revolving perpendicularly, and fastened to an axle. On the outside edge of the drum 400 teeth are to be set at equal intervals so as to meet the teeth on the lower drum. Further, at the side of the upper drum there is to be fixed a second tooth projecting beyond the other teeth.

Super autem planum eadem ratione dentatum inclusum in alterum loculamentum conlocetur, convenientibus dentibus denticulo, qui in secundi tempani latere fuerit fixus, in eoque tympano foramina fiant, quantum diurni itineris miliariorum numero cum raeda possit exire. Minus plusve rem nihil impedit. Et in his foraminibus omnibus calculi rotundi conlocentur, inque eius tympani theca, sive id loculamentum est, fiat foramen unum habens canaliculum, qua calculi, qui in eo tympano inpositi fuerint, cum ad eum locum venerint, in raedae capsum et vas aeneum, quod erit supposityum, singuli cadere possint. Ita cum rota progrediens secum agat tympanum imum et denticulum eisu singulis versationibus tympani superioris denticulos inpulsu cogat praeterire, efficiet ut cum CCCC imum versatum fuerit, superius tympanum semel circumagatur et denticulus, qui est ad latus eius fiexus, unum denticuluim tympani plani producat. Cum ergo CCCC versationibus imi tympani semel superius versabitur, progressus efficiet spatia pedum milia quinque, id est passus mille. Ex eo quot calculi deciderint, sonando singula milia exisse monebunt. Numerus vero calculorum ex imo collectus summa diurni itineris miliariorum numerum indicabit.

Moreover, above, there is to be placed a horizontal wheel toothed in the same manner, and enclosed in a similar case, with teeth which fit upon the single tooth which projects on the side of the second drum. In this drum openings are to be made equal in number to the miles which can be covered with the carriage in a day: whether the miles are more or less makes no difficulty. In all these openings, round stones are to be placed, and in the lining of the drum there is to be one opening attached to a small channel, where the stones placed in the drum when they come to the corresponding place can fall one by one into the carriage and a bronze vessel which is placed below. Thus when the wheel moves

183

forward and carries with it the lowest drum, in a single revolution, the wheel causes its one tooth to strike in passing the teeth in the upper drum. The effect will be that when the lower drum has revolved 400 times, the upper drum will revolve once; and the tooth fixed on the side of the upper drum moves one tooth of the horizontal drum. Since, therefore, in 400 revolutions of the lower drum, the upper drum will revolve once, as it moves it will record a distance of 5,000 feet, that is, of one mile. Hence when a stone falls, it will announce by its sound the traveling of a single mile, and the number of the stones collected from below will indicate, by their total, the number of miles for the day's journey.

Vita Titi Livi

Titus Livius lived from 59 B.C. to A.D. 17, spending his whole life either in Padua, his birthplace, or Rome. He wrote a monumental opus, *Ab Urbe Condita* (*From the Founding of the City*), a readable history of Rome in 142 books, only 35 of which exist today.

His work and reputation brought him to the attention of Octavian, later known as Augustus, who hired him to help his young nephew Claudius with his writing.

This selection from Book 2 relates an incident from 494 B.C. The plebeians of Rome, determined to escape the tyranny of the patricians, withdrew from the city. Tired of paying taxes to and dying for a city that did not even grant them basic civil rights, they marched to a field about three miles from Rome. The patricians, wondering who would defend Rome if an enemy were to attack, sent Menenius Agrippa to convince the plebeians to return. Livius repeats the words of Menenius and the outcome.

Latin	Form	Meaning
egit	third person, singular, perfect	did
Meneni Agrippae	genitive, singular	of Menenius Agrippa
consulum	genitive, plural	of the consuls (they were the highest political officers)

Corpus humanum multa membra habet inter quae manus, os, dentes, venter sunt. Olim reliquae partes corporis iratae erant, quod venter omnia accepit sed nihil sibi egit. Tum inter se hoc consilium ceperunt. Dentes nullum cibum mandere statuerunt; os, nullum cibum accipere, manus nullum cibum ad os ferre. Itaque venter ali non poterat, et totum corpus e vita excessit. Nolite, O cives, propter discordiam vestram patriam eodem modo delere.

Necesse erat corpus humanum omnes partes habere; necesse erat patriam et patres et plebem habere. Plebs fabulam Meneni Agrippae intellexit et condiciones pacis accepit. Novi magistratus creati sunt quorum erat officium contra violentiam consulum plebi auxilium semper dare.

Did You Know?

Did you know that the word *candidate* comes from the Latin *candidatus,* which means "dressed in white." Men seeking public office in republican days wore the *toga candida,* a plain white toga which was sometimes made even whiter by the use of chalk. Let's hope they were more candid than our candidates today, who can't hold a candle to the ancient politicians' candor.

Livius is also famous for some one-liners:

Hoc illud est praecipue in cognitione rerum salubre ac frugiferum, omnis te exempli documenta in inlustri posita monumento intueri. *Ab Urbe Condita,* praefatio, 10.

This especially makes history useful and desirable; it unfolds before our eyes a glorious record of exemplary actions.

Multitudo omnis sicut natura maris per se immobilia est; at venti et aurae cient. *Ibid.,* XXVIII, 27.

Every crowd is in itself motionless, just as the nature of the sea; but winds and breezes ruffle it.

Nullum scelus rationem habet. *Ibid.,* XXVIII, 28.

No crime is rational.

Maximae cuique fortunae minime credendum est. *Ibid.,* XXVIII, 30.

The greatest good fortune is the least to be trusted.

Nihil tam incertum nec tam inaestimabile est quam animus multitudinis. *Ibid.,* XXXI, 34.

Nothing is so uncertain and so incalculable as the mind of a crowd.

185

Vita Plini Secundi

Caius Plinius Secundus was born in A.D. 23 in Verona to a noble family. He held the office of augur and was governor of Spain, although he probably delegated the office work to an educated slave so he could spend his whole life making lists. He was known to have servants read to him while he ate so he could continue to take notes. He always appeared in Rome with his secretary. Pliny was courted and admired by two emperors, Titus and Vespasian.

Pliny was the commander of the fleet at Misenum when Vesuvius erupted in A.D. 79. He set sail in a small vessel to investigate the phenomenon and landed on the coast. He stayed overnight with a friend, intending to return the next day. But an earthquake and contrary winds kept him on shore, where he was finally overcome by smoke and ashes and died.

Of all his voluminous note-taking and list-making, only 37 books remain. Treatises on stars, heavens, wind, rain, hail, minerals, trees, flowers, plants, all living beasts, a geographical description of every place known to man, a history of every art and science, commerce, and navigation are just a small part of his work. His lists of sources and titles make up one book. He consulted 160 sources, 362 Greek authors, and 146 Roman authors.

Book 8, for example, covers mammals, both wild and domesticated; snakes, crocodiles, and lizards; and the appearance, behavior, history, and habitats of these animals. Book 9 describes aquatic species, including Nereids (they exist?), Tritons, sea-serpents, the use of fish as food, pearls, dyes obtained from fish, and the physiology of aquatic animals.

How to Catch an Elephant

The first selection is adapted from *Natural History,* VIII.viii.26.

Latin	Form	Meaning
novissimo	ablative, singular	last
spectato	ablative, singular, absolute	having been seen
totius	genitive, singular	of the whole
praeacuta bipenni	ablative, singular	with a sharp knife
cuncta	accusitive, plural	all things

Trogodytae Aethiopiae, qui se hoc solo venatu alunt, propinquas conscendunt arbores, inde totius agminis novissimo spectato, extremas in clunes desiliunt; laeva adprehendunt caudam, pedes stipant in sinistro femine; ita pendens alterum poplitem dextra caedit praeacuta bipenni. Crure tardato, alterius poplitis nervos caedit, cuncta praeceleri pernicitate peragens.

The Sad Fate of Oysters

This adaptation is from Pliny's *Natural History*, IX.lv.

Latin	Form	Meaning
veluti	—	just as
duces mirae	nominative, plural	admirable leaders
sunt	third person, plural, present	they are
obruunt	third person, plural, present	they bury
rosa carne omni	ablative, absolute	all meat having been gnawed away

Ita, sicut apibus, alii e numero concharum, singuli magnitudine et praecipui vetustate sunt. Veluti duces mirae ad cavendum sollertiae sunt. Urinantes has cura magna petunt. Illis captis, facile ceteras palantes retibus includunt. Deinde, eas obruunt sale in vasis fictilibus; rosa carne omni, nuclei corporum qui margaritae sunt in ima decidunt.

Hysteria's Herstory

Pliny tells the story of Cleopatra and Antony and the mother of all banquets. Cleopatra boasted that she could create a banquet that would cost 10 million sesterces. Bets were taken and on the very next day Cleopatra presented her lover with a rather ordinary dinner. But for dessert she ordered a cup of vinegar, took one of her huge pearl earrings off, dropped it into the cup and when it was dissolved, drank it. Lucius Plancus, who was overseeing the event, placed his hand on the other pearl when the queen was preparing to destroy it in a similar way, and declared that Antony had lost the battle—an ominous remark that came true.

After Cleopatra's death, the other pearl was cut in half and brought to Rome to beautify the ears of a statue of Venus in the Pantheon.

Fishponds and Showers

This selection is from Pliny's *Natural History,* IX.lxxix and lxxxi.

Latin	Form	Meaning
Sergius Orata	nominataive	proper name
mutua appendit	third person, singular, perfect	loaned out
quidem	—	any
amor	nominative, singular, feminine	love
orator	nominative, singular, masculine	(subject of habuit)
qua	ablative, singular	(piscinam is antecedent)
dilexit	third persion, singular, perfect	loved
vivarium	nominative, neuter	fishpond

Primus omnium Sergius Orata ostrearum invenit. Et is qui primus pensiles balineas invenit, ita mangonicatas villas subinde vendendo.

C. Hurrius ante alios murenarum vivarium privatim excogitavit. Is cenis triumphalibus Caesaris Dictatoris sex milia in numero murenarum mutua appendit; nam permutare quidem pretio noluit aut alia merce. Invasit deinde singulorum piscium amor. Apud Baulos in parte Baiana piscinam habuit Hortensius orator in qua murenam adeo dilexit ut exanimatam flevisse credatur. In eadem villa Antonia, uxor Drusi, murenae quam ille diligebat, inaures addidit.

Here are some more Pliniisms:

Solum ut inter ista vel certum sit nihil esse certi nec quicquam miserius homine aut superbius. *History Naturalis,* II.25.

Among these things, one thing seems certain—that nothing certain exists and nothing is more pitiful or more presumptuous than man.

Miraque humani ingeni peste sanguinem et caedes condere annalibus iuvat, ut scelera hominum noscantur mundi ipsius ignaris. *Ibid.,* VI, 43.

Because of a curious disease of the human mind, it pleases us to enshrine in history records of bloodshed and slaughter, so that persons ignorant of the facts of the world may be acquainted with the crimes of mankind.

Natura vero nihil hominibus brevitate vitae praestitit melius. *Ibid.,* L, 168.

Nature has granted man no better gift than the brevity of life.

The Least You Need to Know

➤ Augustus was the first of a long line of emperors, all calling themselves Caesar.

➤ Vitruvius was an engineer and architect.

➤ Livy wrote a long history of Rome.

➤ Pliny wrote about everything.

➤ Cleopatra had excellent taste.

Chapter 19

Look, Ma! I'm Reading Latin!

In This Chapter

➤ Sentences you can read and a review of cases

➤ More sentences and review of verb syntax

➤ More sentences and hints for translating

➤ Stories to read in Latin

➤ Psalms to read in Latin

The old Latin textbooks, the ones without the pictures, were divided into phonology, morphology, and syntax. Phonology discussed the letters and pronunciation of Latin. Morphology described the forms of Latin words, and syntax prescribed the rules for using those words. Nowadays, we have forms and usage.

In this chapter, you will practice your vocabulary and forms while translating some more Latin sentences. In the process you can review the syntax and usage rules as well.

Sentences You Can Read and a Review of Cases

The ending on a noun, pronoun, or adjective tells the reader how the word is used in the sentence.

Hysteria's Herstory

Roman mothers did not enjoy the status and reverence bestowed on mothers today. Mothers are not mentioned much in literature. Many women died in childbirth. Divorce was simple, and men simply walked out of a marriage and took the kids with them. Fathers had complete control over the people in the household. No Mother's Day! No Mommy Dearest! No Mom and Apple Pie!

The subject of the sentence is in the nominative case. The subject sometimes has modifiers, appositives, adjectives, or a noun in the genitive. Here are some examples:

1. Romulus rex moritur.
2. Bonus rex lacrimavit.
3. Libri Sanctarum Scripturarum saepe leguntur.
4. Is est in tua provincia.

Tene Memoria

Remember that the demonstrative pronouns are also the third-person pronouns *he, she, it,* or *they.*

The accusative case is used for the direct object, the object of a preposition, the subject of an infinitive for indirect statement, and for time and extent of space and exclamations. For example:

5. Marius Italiam liberavit.
6. Trans flumen transivit.
7. Dicunt Platonem in Italiam venisse.
8. Romulus septem et triginta annos regnavit.
9. Me miserum!

The dative case is used for the indirect object, with verbs of *favor, help, please, trust, persuade,* and the like, and to show possession:

10. Signum militibus dedit.
11. Ego numquam mihi placui.
12. Facile Helvetiis persuasit.
13. Mihi nomen est Caesar.

The genitive case is used to show possession or a part of something:

14. Officium consulis est mandata darc.
15. Clunis elephanti magnus est.
16. Mille militum misit.
17. Horum omnium fortissimi Belgae sunt.

The ablative case is used for everything left over. It primarily, however, shows *from or by, in* or *at,* means, time, or use in an absolute. It is also used with comparisons without *quam.* Here are some examples:

18. Ex concha margarita venit.
19. Ab eis amatur.
20. Nihil est iucundius vita.
21. Cornibus alces se tutantur.
22. Venatu solo vivunt.
23. Anno ipso Ennius natus est.
24. Agro capto, partem militibus Caesar dedit.

Nouns and adjectives agree in number, gender, and case. If an infinitive is used as a noun, it is neuter singular, as in these examples:

25. Dolere malum est.
26. Errare humanum est.
27. Haec vasa aurea in mensa sunt.

More Sentences and Review of Verb Usage

Every sentence has a verb. The complications begin when the verb has attachments—adverbs, clauses, direct and indirect objects, or prepositional phrases.

Just remember that the verb will agree with the subject in person and number. Also, the verb is frequently at the end of its clause or sentence. Here are some examples:

1. Romulus urbem condidit.
2. Gloria saepe laborem sequitur.

Cave!

Don't confuse *condio, ire, ivi, itus,* "to season," with *condo, ere, didi, ditus,* "to found." Garlic may be the foundation of your soup, but you can't found a city with it.

3. Sapientes laete vivunt.

4. In urbe Epheso, rex Graecus cum regina remansit.

5. Ego ad te scribam.

Latin verbs appear in six tenses. The present, imperfect, and future are formed from the infinitive form, the perfect active tenses from the third principal part, and the perfect passive tenses from the perfect passive participle or the fourth principal part. So when you see the fourth principal part followed by some form of the verb *esse* ("to be"), you know you have a verb that will translate as "has/have/had been ----ed." Also, the participle will have an ending that agrees with the subject. To refresh your memory, take a look at these examples:

6. Castor et Pollux ex equis pugnare visi sunt.

7. Vir a puero ab aqua tractus erat.

8. Strepitus a turba auditus est.

The verb *esse* is often omitted, as in these examples:

9. Rara avis.

10. Quot homines, tot sententiae.

11. Ars longa, vita brevis.

12. Quid hoc ad me?

Did You Know?

The famous brothers, Castor and Pollux, who are represented by the constellation Gemini (the Twins), were actually only half brothers. Castor was the son of Leda and the king of Sparta, Tyndareus, while Pollux was the son of Leda and Zeus, who visited her in the form of a swan. The brothers were supposed to have fought in the battle of Lake Regillus and were famed for their horsemanship.

The imperative mood is used to give commands. Negative commands use *noli, nolite* with the infinitive. The subjunctive mood shows unreal conditions and commands of the first and third persons. The subjunctive is often used on clauses within clauses. Here are some examples:

13. Libera rem publicam metu.

14. Nolite id velle quod fieri non potest.

15. Vincat.

16. In mundo deus est qui regat, qui gubernet, qui cursus astrorum conservet.

Passive verb forms have *r, mini,* and perfect tense forms with two words. Deponent verbs are always passive but have active meanings, as shown in these examples:

17. A deo mundus aedificatus est.

18. Rex magnopere amatur.

19. Hoc mirabar.

20. Homines id quod volunt credunt.

21. Amicitiae nostrae memoriam spero sempiternam fore.

More Sentences and Hints for Translating

Here are some more hints that will help with your Latin skills:

1. **Read the whole sentence.** Put mental (or real) parentheses around relative clauses, result or purpose clauses, prepositional phrases, or any other groups.

2. **Find the verb.** The verb will also lead you to the subject. If the verb is in the first or second person, you already have a subject: *I, you,* or *we.* If the verb is in the third person, look for a noun in the nominative that is in the same number. If the verb is third-person plural, look for a plural nominative. If the verb is in the third-person singular, look for the nominative singular. Remember that sometimes a phrase or clause or infinitive can also be the subject.

3. **Determine word order.** The usual word order is subject (and its attachments), indirect object, object, adverb and prepositions, and verb. For example:

   a. Si vincimus, omnia tuta erunt.

   b. Fortuna fortes adiuvat. (The verb tells you which word is the subject.)

   c. Nihilne te nocturnum praesidium Palati, nihil urbis vigiliae, nihil timor populi, nihil concursus bonorum omnium, nihil hic munitissimus habendi senatus locus, nihil horum ora vultusque moverunt?

   The *nihil* has the force of *non.* The subjects are all nicely in the nominative case, the verb is at the end, and the direct object is the second word.

4. **Think like a Roman.** The way *not* to translate is to write all the English meanings on pieces of paper and try to arrange them to make sense. This will not work and will lead to hours of frustration, not to mention an incorrect translation.

Stories to Read in Latin

Here's a translation hint: Often a Latin word will look like the English one. Here are some words you have not seen:

altus, a, um	high, deep
caelum, i, n.	sky
defessus, a, um	tired
diarroia, ae, f.	diarrhea
dis, ditis	rich
flumen, fluminis, n.	river
fluo, ere, fluxi, fluxus	flow
fortasse	perhaps
glaber, ra, rum	bald
harena, ae, f.	sands
lapis, lapidis, m.	stone
lavo, lavare, lavi, lautus (or lotus)	wash
litoteta, ae, f.	the rich life
maris, maris, n.	sea
navis, navis, f.	ship
nosti	you know
nimbus, i, m.	cloud, rain cloud
oculus, i, m.	eye
ossum, i, n.	bone
paro, parare, avi, atus	prepare
pluit, pluere, pluit	it rains
scelus, sceleris, n.	crime
somnus, i, m.	sleep
stupeo, ere, stupui	be silent
tergum, i, n.	back

tristis, is, e	sad
turpis, is, e	ugly, nasty, disgraceful
ubique	everywhere
unda, ae, f.	wave
velo, are, avi, atus	veil, wrap, put on
verto, ere, verti, versus	turn
vix	scarcely

Pyrrha et Deucalion

This classic Greek tale tells the story of the flood and how the people recovered.

Olim in omnibus locis terrae malum et scelus erant. Numquam homines tam turpes erant. Itaque Iuppiter terribilem poenam parabat. Ex omni caelo densos nimbos convocabat et multo pluebat. Neptunus quoque fratrem adiuvabat. Ubique flumina agros inundabant. Iam altum mare etiam summos montes inundabant. Parnasus solus ex undis exsistebat. Hic pius Duecalion cum femina Pyrrha parva nave manebat. Non iam ira deorum manet.

Statim Neptunus nimbos diffundebat et flumina mariaque revocabat. Sed ex omnibus mortalibus modo duo supererant. Tristes Deucalion et Pyrrha in templo a dea auxilium petebant. Inde Themis sic responsum dedit: "Velate capita, et post tergum ossa magnae parentis iacite." Diu stupebant. Duecalion tandem sic dicit: "Terra est magna parens omnium. Fortasse lapides sunt ossa magnae parentis." Inde a templo exeunt, capita velant, et saxa post tergum mittunt. Mox respiciunt. Iam saxa sunt viri et feminae. Sic dei terrae homines restituerunt.

Midas

This famous tale begins when Silenus, the drunken old man who accompanies Bacchus, god of wine, wanders into Midas's rose garden. Midas leads him back to where he belongs and is duly rewarded.

Olim Bacchus Midae, regi Phrygiae, donum dedit. "Quid vis, tibi dabo," dixit. Midas sic respondit: "Quicquid meo corpore contigero, id aurum sit." Cui deus dixit, "Ita sit." Midas laetus domum redivit. Vix bonae fortunae credens, portas tangit, quae in aurum vertuntur. Deinde domum percurrit, lectos, mensis, sellas, manu tangens. Brevi tempore omnia sunt aurea. Tum vero quicquid cibi rex ore contingit, id statim in aurum vertitur. Etiam vinum in aureum flumen vertitur. Midas attonitus dites effugere temptat sed frustra. Sic tandem secum dicit: "Tam stultus fui! Et ditissimus et pauperrimus mortalium sum!"

197

Inde Midas Bacchum diem noctemque quaerebat. Tandem defessus Midas deum invenit.

Tum dixit, "Quaeso, ab hoc crudeli fato me eripe." Cui deus respondet: "Vade ad flumen Pactolum et se lava in aqua." Rex Midas ad flumen succedit atque in aquam se mergit. Statim, mirabile dictu, aurum de eius corpore in flumen cedit. Usque ad hoc tempus Pactolus aureis harenis fluere dicitur.

Psalmus Davidis XXIII

The Bible has been translated into many languages, but the Latin version has a certain quality that recalls the age when Christianity began. Be sure to read these two familiar Psalms (Psalms 23 and 100) aloud and imagine yourself in a monastery high in the mountains of Italy, reading the daily devotionals and dedicating your life to God.

Jehova pastor meus est, non possum egere.

In caulis herbidis facit ut recubem, secundum aquas lenes deducit me.

Animam meam quietam efficit: ducit me per orbitas iustitiae, propter nomen suum.

Etiam cum ambularem per vallem lethalis umbrae, non timerem malum quia tu mecum es: virga tua et pedum tuum, ipsa consolantur me.

Instruis coram me mensam e regione hostium meorum: delibutum reddis unguento caput meum, poculum meum exuberans.

Nihil nisi bonum et benignitas prosequentur me omnibus diebus vitae meae: et quietus ero in domo Jehovae, quamdiu longa erunt tempora.

Psalmus pro gratiarum actione C

Clangite Jehovae, omnes incolae terrae.

Colite Jehovam cum laetitia, venit in conspectum eius cum cantu.

Agnoscite Jehovam esse Deum, ipsum effecisse nos (non autem nos ipsos) populum suum et gregem pastus sui.

Ingredimini portas eius cum gratiarum actione, atria eius cum laude: gratias agite ei, benedicite nomini eius.

Nam bonus est Jehova, in seculum est benignitas eius: et usque ad generationem quamque fides eius.

The Least You Need to Know

➤ Every sentence in the world has a subject and a predicate.

➤ Case endings indicate how the word is used in the sentence.

➤ Verb endings indicate who, when, and what mood the verb is in.

➤ Sorting all the words in a sentence alphabetically will not get you a translation.

➤ King Midas is not one noted for his wisdom.

Part 5

Coping with Latin in the Modern World

If you drive through upstate New York, you will pass through Rome, Greece, Syracuse, Utica, Ithaca, Troy, and Ilion. Latin survives all around you in quotations, mottoes, and classical references. Latin is in legal documents, names of botanical and zoological species, prescriptive medicine, and almost every part of your life except McDonald's. In this part, I'll show you how to cope with Latin in your everyday life.

Chapter 20

Legal Latin

In This Chapter

➤ Words to learn or learn again

➤ Legal terms and meanings

➤ Latin in your law school papers

➤ Sayings and quotations about the law

➤ Ancient Roman law

When a lawyer stands before the jury to present his case, he's not going to spout Latin. But when conversing with other lawyers or the judge, or when reading law books, he will need some Latin. You will find many terms in documents and legal writings in Latin. You will hear Latin when you watch *Court TV*—or, heaven forbid, you are in court yourself.

The following are the more frequently used terms in the courts or in legal papers. Remember that these terms have, for the most part, become English, and, therefore, the English pronunciation will be found in any dictionary.

Words to Learn or Learn Again

Lawyers themselves will say that pronunciation of the following Latin terms differs from place to place. The Latin pronunciation is never wrong, but since many of the terms have become part of the English language, the Anglicized version is correct also. Meanwhile, here are the original Latin words with their etymological information:

Latin	Forms	Meaning	Derivative
amicus	amici, m.	friend	amicable
bonus	bona, bonum	good	bonus
caveo	cavere, cavi	take care, beware	cautus
corpus	corporis, n.	body	corpse
curia	curiae, f.	senate house	court
delictum	delicti, n.	fault, misdeed	delict
dies	diei, m.	day	day
facies	faciei, f.	face, appearance	face
factum	facti, n.	deed	fact
flagrans	flagrantis	flaming	flagrant
forma	formae, f.	form	form
fructus	fructus, m.	fruit	fructify
habeo	habere, habui, habitus	have	habit
hic	haec, hoc	this	this
ius	iuris, n.	right, justice	jury
matrimonium	matrimoni, i, n.	marriage	matrimony
par	paris	equal	parity
operor	ari, atus sum	work hard	operator
pando	pandere, passus	spread out	expand
poena	poenae, f.	penalty	penal
primus	prima, primum	first	prime
tempus	temporis, n.	time	temporal
usus	usus, m.	use	usage
vinculum	vinculi, n.	chain	invincible

Legal Latin Terms and What They Mean

Here is a list of legal Latin terms you may have come across at some point in your life:

➤ *Ad hoc* (**"to this"**). The preposition *ad* takes the accusative case, and in this instance, the neuter accusative singular. This expression designates a specific purpose: the ad hoc committee, for example, for abolishing homework.

➤ *Amicus curiae* (**"friend of the court"**). *Curiae* is in the genitive singular, first declension. An *amicus curiae* is a person who is neutral to specific action and gives advice on matters not before the court. Often this is done when the case may be setting legal precedent.

➤ *A vinculo matrimoni* (**"from the chain of marriage"**). The preposition *a/ab* takes the ablative case. *Matrimoni* is in the genitive. Harsh term! This is the legal term for a permanent decree of divorce.

Hysteria's Herstory

In Republican times there were no divorce courts and a wife could not take her husband to court for adultery. However, if she was caught with the milkman, *in flagrante delicto*, she could be legally killed, beaten, or mutilated by her husband. The milkman, too, could be legally killed by the husband. After Augustus's law concerning divorce in late first century, it was not just *Res tuas tibi habeto*—"Take your things and go." There had to be witnesses, contracts, restoration of dowry, and other considerations that only lawyers think of.

➤ *Caveat* ("let him beware!"). This is in the subjunctive mood, a third-person command. A *caveat* is a formal warning to an officer or a court not to do a specified act—not to probate a will, for example—until the person can be heard in opposition.

➤ *Corpus delicti* ("the body of the crime"). *Corpus* is in the nominative case, *delicti* in the genitive. The *corpus delicti* is the object upon which a crime has been committed, but, of course, it doesn't have to be a body, in spite of the Latin. It could be your car.

➤ *De facto* ("concerning the deed"). A *de facto* situation is one that actually exists, whether it is legal or not.

➤ *De iure* ("concerning the law"). A *de iure* situation is one that is formally backed by law.

➤ *Habeas corpus* ("may you have a body"). Note that this is the subjunctive in a command sense. It's not that you have a body. That would be indicative, *habes*. Instead, the subjunctive indicates that it is not actual but is definitely desired. A writ of *habeas corpus* is an order by a judge to have a prisoner brought to trial to determine the legality of his imprisonment.

RETINEO

Grammar Guru

Ius, iuris, was a word heavily used by the legal-minded Romans. It was used for law, legality, the legal system or code, a rule, the binding decision of a magistrate, an oath, anything that is right, obligations from a relationship, one's due, or jurisdiction. Many of our legal terms come from this little, powerful word.

➤ *In flagrante delicto* (**"while the crime is still burning"**). Caught in the act! *Flagrante* is an adjective of the third declension and in the ablative case after *in*.

➤ *J.D.* (*iuris doctor*). This is a law degree.

➤ *Modus operandi* (**"the way of working"**). This is the gerund form of the verb, translated as *ing*. We are all creatures of habit, and a criminal's modus operandi will often give the police a lead.

➤ *Nolo contendere* (**"I do not wish to contest"**). Used primarily in criminal cases, the defendant declines to refute the evidence. In most situations, this response has the same effect as pleading guilty.

➤ *Prima facie* (**"on first appearance"**). At first glance or on the face of it, if you mail a letter, the person will get it. *Facies* is one of those rare fifth-declension nouns and appears here in the ablative case.

➤ *Pro bono publico* (**"for the public good"**). A lawyer takes a pro bono case and does not receive payment. The preposition *pro* can have several meanings: before, in front of, in the presence of, on behalf of, in favor of, in the service of, instead of, the same as, and for.

➤ *Pro forma* (**"for the form"**). Something is done as a matter of form, not because it is essential.

➤ *Pro tempore* (**"for the time being"**). This legalese term simply translates as "temporarily."

➤ *Sine die* (**"without a day"**). *Dies* is a fifth-declension noun; the ablative case is *die*. A judge will adjourn *sine die*, without a day set for a future meeting, in essence dismissing the case.

➤ *Subpoena* (**"under penalty"**). In Latin this is really two words, *poena* being in the ablative case after *sub*. A *subpoena* is an order of the court that requires a person to be present at a certain time and place or suffer a penalty.

➤ *Usufruct* (**"the fruit by use"**). Both these nouns, *usus* and *fructus,* are fourth-declension nouns, and the first is in the ablative case. *Usufruct* is the right to enjoy all the advantages of another's property, provided it is not destroyed or damaged.

Did You Know?

One of the greatest contributions to the field of law was the Roman concept of *ius gentium,* "the law of nations." This provided for all those within the Roman empire who were not citizens. It came to be seen as a universal law and proper for all peoples. In fact, the Roman citizens themselves preferred that their cases be tried by it rather than their own civil law. Here is how it read:

> Ius gentium, autem, omni humano genere commune est; nam, usu exigente, et humanis necessitatibus, gentes humanae iura quaedam sibi constituerunt. Bella etenim orta sunt, et captivitates sequtae, et servitutes, quae sunt naturali iuri contrariae.

> The law of nations is the law common to all mankind: for nations have settled certain things for themselves as occasion and necessities of human life required. For instance, wars arose, and then followed captivity and slavery, which are contrary to the law of nature.

> Corpus Iuris Civilis, *Institutiones,* II, 1, 2 (circa A.D. 588)

Latin in Your Law School Papers

Any kind of research paper, whether high school, college, or beyond, requires some use of Latin. Whether you are writing or just reading a scholarly paper, knowledge of the following abbreviations will surely be helpful:

➤ *ca., circa* ("about, approximately"). These are often used with dates when the exact date is unknown.

➤ *e.g., exempli gratia* ("for the sake of example"). Try to use this abbreviation correctly. It is easy to misuse *e.g.* and *i.e.* ("that is"). For example:

> Romance languages, e.g., French, Spanish, Italian

> Romance languages, i.e., languages from Latin of the Roman empire

➤ *et al., et alii* ("and others"). *Alii* is in the nominative plural masculine. Sorry, girls. When there is a mixed-gender group, the noun or adjective is used in the masculine gender. *Et al.* is often used to denote multiple authors.

➤ *et alia* (**"and other things"**). This is used when referring to anything other than people.

➤ *et seq., et sequens* (**"and the following"**). *Sequens* is the present participle of *sequor.*

➤ *etc., et cetera* (**"and so forth"**). *Cetera* is neuter plural, meaning "the other things, the remaining things, the rest."

➤ *fl., floruit* (**"flourished"**). These are used to denote the heyday of someone's life or a country's hegemony. *Fl.* is also useful if the exact dates are unknown.

➤ *ibid., ibidem* (**"in the same place"**). This is used in legal papers only.

➤ *i.e., id est* (**"that is"**). This is usually followed by an explanation or a synonym, not examples. See *e.g.* earlier in this list.

➤ *id., idem* (**"the same"**). This is used in footnotes and bibliographies to refer to persons except in law citations. According to Kate Turabian, author of *A Manual for Writers,* references following legal style employ *idem* in place of *ibid.* Legal style reserves *ibid* for references where there is no change in page or other part from the preceding reference.

➤ *passim* (**"here and there"**). This is from the Latin *pando, pandere, passus* ("to spread out").

➤ *q.v., quod vide* (**"see which"**). This is a command to "see which" and is used for cross-references.

➤ *sic* (**"thus"**). This is the only abbreviation that requires brackets, *sic* denotes that a wording has been written intentionally or quoted verbatim. For example, "She said, "I wander *[sic]* if this is correct."

➤ *supra* (**"above"**). This means not over your head, but recently mentioned.

➤ *s.v., sub verbo, sub voce* (**"under the word"**). Both *verbo* and *voce* are in the ablative following *sub. S.v.* is used in references to listings in encyclopedias and dictionaries.

➤ *viz., videlicet* (**"namely"**). This word is a combination of *videre,* "to see," and *licet,* "it is allowed, it is clear." In Latin, *videlicet* could mean "of course," "namely," "it is clear," or "evidently."

➤ *vs., versus* (**"against"**). This is often just *v.* in legal documents. For example: *Roe v. Wade* or the Cowboys vs. the Indians.

Sayings and Quotations About the Law

People have been commenting on the law since time began. Many Romans criticized the lawyers, as the *causidicii* were really trained to be persuaders, not champions of justice. Some of the ancient comments are still in use today, not as legal precedents but as maxims and words to live by. Here is a sampling of the more familiar ones:

Ius summum saepe summa est malitia. (Terence, second century B.C.E.)

Law at its most rigorous is often the worst evil.

Caveat emptor. Caveat vendor. Canem cave! (anon.)

Let the buyer beware. Let the seller beware. Beware the dog!

De minimis non curat lex. (anon.)

The law does not concern itself with trifles.

Iure naturae aequum est neminem cum alterius detrimento et iniuria fieri locupletiorem. (Publius Celsus, circa A.D. 77)

By the law of nature, it is only fair that no one should become richer through damages and injuries suffered by another.

Nemo est supra leges. (anon.)

No one is above the laws.

Publicum bonum privato est praeferendum. (anon.)

Public good should be preferred over private.

Lex est ratio summa insita in natura, quae iubet ea, quae facienda sunt, prohibetque contraria. (Cicero, *De legibus,* vi, 18)

Law is the highest reason situated in nature, which commands what ought to be done and forbids the opposite.

Qui tacet consentire videtur. (anon.)

He who is silent seems to consent.

Qui facit per alium, facit per se. (anon.)

He who acts through another, acts by himself.

Ut enim magistratibus leges, ita populo praesunt magistratus, vereque dici potest magistratum legem esse loquentem, legem autem mutum magistratum. (Cicero, *De legibus,* vi, 18)

RETINEO

Grammar Guru

Remember that the future passive participle, the *endum* form, denotes obligation when used with *est.*

As the laws govern the magistrates, so the magistrates govern the people, and it can truly be said that the magistrate is a speaking law, and the law a silent magistrate.

Ancient Roman Law

During the fifth century B.C.E., the Romans formed a committee to review their laws and customs and to get them written down. After a year of work, the committee, *mirabile dictu,* published the Twelve Tables of Laws. Written on 12 bronze tablets, they were set up in the Forum for all to see and obey. They served as the basis for Roman law for most of the Republican era. In Justinian's time, 528 C.E., the laws were organized again (there were lots more) and written into the *Corpus Iuris Civile,* a work still in use today.

Part of the whole text of the Twelve Tables has survived; here are some excerpts:

➤ Interest on a loan should not exceed one-twelfth part of the principal per year.

➤ Anyone will be punished who by enchantments causes another's crops to fail.

➤ Anyone committing a robbery by night may be lawfully killed by the owner of the premises.

➤ A father can imprison, beat, keep at hard labor, sell, or even slay his son.

➤ Useless and extravagant funerals are forbidden. No gold ornaments (except gold fillings in teeth), can be buried with the body. The buried or burned body cannot have more than three purple strips and no more than 10 flute players can attend the funeral.

➤ Anyone can go into another's property and pick up the fruit that has fallen from his own tree.

If a Roman noticed that his neighbor buried his uncle with four purple strips accompanied by 14 flute players, he could sue. The man would simply drag the other guy into court and ask for a day. When granted, the two would again appear and argue their own cases.

In the early days of the Republic, there were no lawyers. In fact, there were no lawyers at all before the Romans. Judges, priests, courts, and kings meted out justice and no one argued. In fifth-century B.C.E. Athens, the Greeks made oratory a part of the curriculum and thus began rhetoric and the art of persuasion.

During Roman times the orators and rhetoricians were *iuris prudentes,* "wise men of the law." Many were impartial interpreters of the law. The *iuris prudentes* were not like our lawyers today. They did not appear in court to plead cases. During the early days of Rome, private citizens were still pleading their own cases. But soon helpers appeared, *advocati,* literally "called to," who provided expert advice. Somewhere in the second century B.C.E. the *advocati,* also known as *causidicii,* were allowed to speak for their clients, and the rest is history.

Rules of evidence were a little looser than today. Lawyers were known to bring in weeping widows and hearsay evidence to persuade the court. While the *iuris prudentes* remained respected for their learning and impartiality, the *advocati* became famous for their theatrics and susceptibility to bribes.

The Least You Need to Know

➤ *Ius* means "law," "right," "justice," or "juice," all of which are necessary for a good life.

➤ If you have to write a paper, abbreviate—sparingly.

➤ Roman courts were high theater.

Chapter 21

Medical and Scientific Latin

> ### In This Chapter
>
> ➤ Rx for understanding your doctor
>
> ➤ Reading those prescriptions
>
> ➤ Reading those signs at the zoo
>
> ➤ The medical and scientific world of the Romans

There are many reasons why doctors use Latin. For one, they can stand at the foot of your hospital bed and pretend to be discussing the upcoming surgery, all the while saying things like, "Wow! She's really having a bad hair day."

Doctors like to use Latin because their patients won't question their authority. If your doctor said "You have a stuffy nose," you yourself might suggest a couple of aspirin. But if he diagnoses your condition as *chronic sinusitis,* you would probably nod your head miserably and get the prescription.

Seriously, one reason Latin is used in the sciences is that it is an unchanging, dead language. Scientists the world over can correspond and refer to anything with the same, reliable words. Another reason Latin is used is simply because the early medical and scientific writings were in Latin; why reinvent the wheel?

Rx for Understanding Your Doctor

The science of the structure of animals and plants, *anatomy,* is originally a Greek word meaning "to cut up." When the early anatomists cut up their specimens, they found that almost everything was connected: The ankle bone's connected to the shin bone, the shin bone's connected to the knee bone … well, you know the song. This accounts for the popularity of prepositional prefixes in anatomical terms, which show relationships. All those easy compound words reduce the number of original words doctors have to learn. So we have the nose—*nasal;* the back of the nose—*postnasal;* over the nose—*supranasal;* under the nose—*subnasal;* and *ad infinitum.*

Did You Know?

The *caduceus* originally meant "the staff of a herald." It had two snakes winding around it with two wings at the top. It is the staff of Mercury, the messenger of the gods, and of flower deliveries.

The *caduceus* has also become the symbol of a physician, probably because it is related to the staff of Aesculapius, a famous Greek doctor. Aesculapius was the son of the god Apollo and a mortal woman. He was so talented that he not only cured the sick but also brought the dead back to life. His staff had a snake curling around it because the snake is a symbol of renovation and rebirth. Unfortunately, Zeus was jealous of the power of Aesculapius and bonked him with a thunderbolt.

Here is a list of common prefixes, suffixes, and root words that will help you understand what your doctor is talking about:

➤ *ante* ("before"). Your pouting daughter can be referred to as having a prominent *antelabium. Anterior lingual gland* is the tip of the tongue. The *antebracchium* is your forearm.

➤ *arthro* ("joint"). An *arthropod* has jointed limbs and *arthritis* is the inflammation of joints.

➤ *ectomy* (the Greek *tome,* "to cut; ex, out"). This is a popular suffix: *hysterectomy, appendectomy, masectomy.*

➤ *femur* ("thigh"). The *femur* is the longest and largest bone, extending from the hip to the knee. And in case you are into anthropology, you can compare skeletons by their *femorotibial* index, the ratio of the length of the femur to the length of the tibia, or shin bone, times 100.

➤ *ferous* ("bearing"). If a fish bears baby fish live, it is *viviferous.* If it hatches eggs, then it is *oviferous.*

➤ *itis* ("**inflammation**"). *Mediastinitis,* for example, is the inflammation of the cavity that separates the lungs and contains the heart. *Appendicitis* is an inflamed appendix; *arthritis* is an inflamed joint.

➤ *med* ("**middle**"). The *mediastinium* is right in the middle of your body, and that famous middle finger is called the *medius.*

➤ *ocul* ("**eye**"). The *oculauditory* system includes sight and hearing.

➤ *musole, ule, le* ("**small**"). A muscle is from the Latin *mus* ("mouse"). Rippling muscles are reminiscent of a mouse under the skin.

➤ *osteo, oss* ("**bone**"). There are literally over 50 words with this prefix, most common *osteoporosis,* a disorder in which the bones become porous.

➤ *ovum* ("**egg**"). There is an *oviduct,* the *ovaries,* and an *ovule,* "a little egg."

➤ *palp* ("**feel, touch**"). There is a *palpus,* "a feeler," to *palpate, palpation,* and the *palpebra,* "the eyelid."

➤ *pedi* ("**foot**"). The spider has a *pedipalpus,* "a foot that palpates or feels." A *pedicoccus* is some kind of micrococcus that grows in beer and causes cloudiness and acid. Microbrewers!

➤ *post* ("**behind**"). Beyond *postnatal, postnasal,* and *postbracchium,* we have *postabdomen,* where the sting of the scorpion lies.

➤ *sub* ("**under**"). *Subcaudal* means "under the tail." *Submuscular* means "under the muscle." There are hundreds of compounds using this prefix, including *subungual,* "under the claw."

➤ *supra* ("**above**"). A *supranumerary* anything is extra, more than is usual. A supranumerary tooth causes many trips to the orthodontist. There is such a thing as a supranumerary placenta and supranumerary digit. This last would be a mother's nightmare; as soon as the newborn is brought to her hospital bed, she cautiously peeks under the blanket and starts counting fingers and toes ... 11? Supranumerary!

Cave!

Be careful not to confuse words that begin with the prefix *ped,* meaning "child" from the Greek *paedeia.* A *pedophile* is not someone who likes feet.

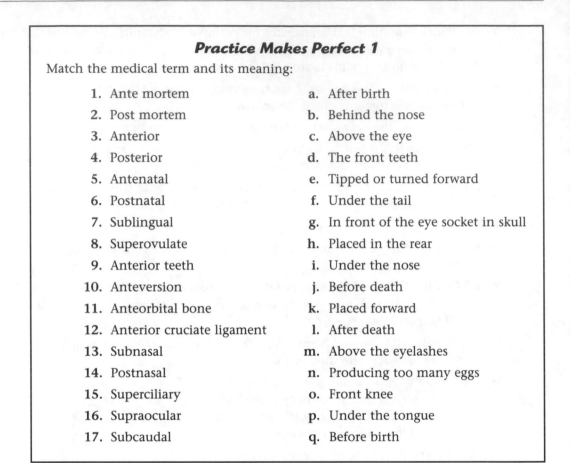

Practice Makes Perfect 1

Match the medical term and its meaning:

1. Ante mortem	a. After birth
2. Post mortem	b. Behind the nose
3. Anterior	c. Above the eye
4. Posterior	d. The front teeth
5. Antenatal	e. Tipped or turned forward
6. Postnatal	f. Under the tail
7. Sublingual	g. In front of the eye socket in skull
8. Superovulate	h. Placed in the rear
9. Anterior teeth	i. Under the nose
10. Anteversion	j. Before death
11. Anteorbital bone	k. Placed forward
12. Anterior cruciate ligament	l. After death
13. Subnasal	m. Above the eyelashes
14. Postnasal	n. Producing too many eggs
15. Superciliary	o. Front knee
16. Supraocular	p. Under the tongue
17. Subcaudal	q. Before birth

Reading Those Prescriptions

In ancient times there were no prescriptions. The doctor would just say "Drink a little wild boar's manure mixed with vinegar and call me in the morning."

Today we have that little piece of paper covered with chicken scratches. Your pharmacist can read it, and now you can, too. Here is your prescription key:

Abbreviation	Latin	Meaning
a.c.	ante cibos	before meals
p.c.	post cibos	after meals
c. (with long mark)	cum	with
s.	sine	without

Abbreviation	Latin	Meaning
i.d.	in die	a day
m.	mane	in the morning
n.	nocte	at night
b.	bis	twice
t.	ter	three times
q.	quater	four times
gtt.	guttae	drops
Rx	recipe	take
s.o.s.	si opus sit	if it is necessary
omn	omni	every
h.s.	hora somni	at the hour of sleep
ad lib.	ad libitum	freely
aq.	aqua	water
stat.	statim	immediately
p.o.	per os	by mouth

Hysteria's Herstory

Our friend Pliny mentions a method of contraception for women: You cut open the head of a hairy spider, retract two small worms, and tie them on a woman with a strip of deer-hide, and she will not get pregnant for one year. That's *your* story, Pliny.

There is another Latin word similar to *gutta* ("drop"). *Guttur, gutturis,* n., means "throat" and the English derivative is *guttural. Guttation* happens to your houseplants when they ooze drops of water.

Practice Makes Perfect 2

Write the following prescriptions in Latin and then translate into English:

1. Rx q.i.d. p.o.

   _____

2. o.n. 3 gtt. p.o.

   _____

3. c. aq. ad. lib.

   _____

4. a.c. s. aq.

   _____

5. h.s. 25 gtt.

   _____

Reading Those Signs at the Zoo—Flora and Fauna

It walks like a duck and it quacks like a duck, but the little sign at the zoo says *Anas platyrhnchos*. Here's Latin again, making things complicated. Actually, the Latin names for all plants (*flora*) and animals (*fauna*) make things less complicated. Scientists love to classify, sort, list, and categorize, and they have been trying to make the ultimate list since Aristotle. Finally, in the eighteenth century Linnaeus, using Latin, came up with the Mother of All Lists, dividing the world of living things into kingdoms, phylla, classes, orders, families, genera, and species.

Grammar Guru

Genus, generis, n., is a regular third-declension noun and, therefore, its plural is *genera*.

At the zoo, the signs will designate the genus with the capital letter and the species with a lowercase letter. The basic unit for all this classification is the species, a group of organisms that are more closely related than any other and capable of mating to produce offspring. The genus represents a group of species that are closely related, and so it goes.

Genus and species names are usually descriptive and often originate from a Latin or Greek source. Here are a few examples:

➤ *Arachnida* is a class of arthropods that includes scorpions, spiders, and mites. Arachne was a woman of Colophon, the daughter of Idmon, a dyer. A skillful weaver, she had the audacity to challenge Athena to a weaving contest. Of course, she lost and in disgrace, hanged herself. Athena changed her into a spider so she could go on spinning and weaving *ad infinitum*.

➤ *Bufo vulgaris,* the common toad, does not use inappropriate language, as his name suggests. *Vulgaris* is frequently used as a species name and refers to the common people.

➤ *Canidae* is the dog family. *Canis latrans,* the barking dog, is a coyote. *Canis lupus,* the wolf dog, is the gray wolf. *Canis familiaris* is the family dog.

➤ *Iris cristata,* the crested Iris, is named for the goddess of the rainbow, probably because of the multicolored flower. Iris led the souls of women to the Elysian Fields after they died, and Greeks put bouquets of iris on the graves. Iris actually means "eye of heaven," and, therefore, is an apt name for the center of the eye.

➤ *Lupinus perennis,* the wild lupine, is named for the lupus, the wolf, because the lupine robs the soil of its nutrients just as the wolf robs the shepherd of his sheep. Actually, it does just the opposite, but who's to contradict a good story?

➤ *Turdus migratorius,* the American robin, is actually a migratory thrush.

➤ *Spilogale putorius,* the skunk, sports a Greek name meaning "spotted weasel" and the Latin word for "smelly," appropriately beginning with the letters *P U!*

➤ *Nastursium officinale,* watercress, has the same name as the popular garden flower because they both have leaves that are bitter to the taste and will make your *nasus torquet,* or "nose twist."

The Medical World of the Romans

The most famous Greek doctor, Hippocrates (490 B.C.), enjoyed an excellent reputation, and, of course, left us his famous oath. In Roman times, medical practitioners were not so well esteemed. Many were Greeks of questionable education or Romans who simply followed another doctor around, picking up the art.

Martial, a first-century A.D. writer of epigrams, complains of being attended by a doctor who is accompanied by 100 medical students, all of whom have ice-cold hands. He writes the following:

> Languebam: sed tu comitatus protinus ad me venisti centum, Symmache, discipulis. Centum me tetigere manus Aquilone gelatae non habui febrem, Symmache, nunc habeo. (*Epigrams,* V.9)

> I was languishing. But you came to me, closely accompanied by 100 pupils, Symmachus. One hundred cold-as-ice hands touched me. I didn't have a fever, Symmachus, but now I do.

Often a Roman doctor's reputation was founded on how few of his patients died. Pliny the Elder reminds us that even though doctors' experiments on patients were often fatal, the medical profession protected them from prosecution.

> In hac artium sola evenit ut cuicumque medicum se professo statim credatur, cum sit periculum in nullo mendacio maius. Non tamen illud intuemur, adeo blanda est sperandi pro se cuique dulcedo. Nulla praeterea lex quae puniat inscitiam capitalem, nullum exemplum vindictae. Discunt periculis nostris et experimenta per mortes agunt, medicoque tantum hominem occidisse inpunitas summa est. Quin immo transit convicium et intemperantia culpatur ultroque qui periere arguuntur. (*Natural History,* 29.8, 16)

> This is the only profession where anyone is immediately believed who professes to be a doctor, when surely no untruth could be more dangerous. Nevertheless, we aren't bothered by that; each one of us is seduced by the sweet hope of being healed. And there is no law which punishes the ignorance which endangers us. They learn from our dangers, and their experiments lead to deaths; and only doctors can commit homicide with impunity. Indeed, the blame goes to the victim, who is chastised for intemperance and self-indulgence.

Many medical practices of Roman times reflect the lack of scientific knowledge that enhances our lives today. For fractures of the ribs, for example, Pliny recommends goat's manure mixed in wine. For jaundice, the ashes of a deer's antlers or the blood of an ass mixed with wine. Cure is guaranteed within three days. Onions were used for stomach trouble, snake sting, and dog bite. For ordinary bruises, crushed cabbage was applied.

On the other hand, Roman doctors used cures that have since been verified: burnt sponge for goiter (ashes of sponge contain iodine), a red-hot stone held against a wound (cauterization), chewing and swallowing of the berries of the castor oil plant as a purgative, and chewing sage for ulcers. The Romans thought that malaria came from bad night air, *malus aer,* not realizing that it was mosquitos that brought on the feverish disease.

Finally, the Roman doctors used the same psychology that modern doctors use today. They often used Greek, as we use Latin, to confound, confuse, and appear authoritative.

> Immo vero auctoritas aliter quam Graece eam tractantibus etiam apud inperitos expertesque linguae non est, ac minus credunt quae ad salutem suam pertinent, si intellegant. (*Natural History,* 29.8, 16–18)

> Truly medical treatises written in a language other than Greek have no prestige even among the unlearned men ignorant of Greek, and people tend to trust less any advice about their health if they understand the language.

The Least You Need to Know

➤ If you hear *ectomy,* it's probably not a good thing.

➤ If you hear *scopy,* it's better. The doctor's just looking.

➤ Prescriptions *can* be deciphered.

➤ There are a million and a half named species of plants and animals in the world. That's a lot of Latin!

Chapter 22

Late Latin and Church Latin

In This Chapter

➤ Words of the church fathers

➤ St. Augustine's *Confessions*

➤ Words of the church litany

➤ Church Latin

➤ Music, sacred and profane

There's no doubt that the Roman Empire fell around A.D. 500, which gradually lead to the Dark Ages. The reasons why such an empire would disintegrate range from too many undefended boundaries to lead poisoning from the drinking water. Nevertheless, just as Rome was being overrun by Goths and Visigoths, the Christian Church was beginning to come into its own. Cathedrals and monasteries were popping up all over Europe and were soon filled with holy brothers, all with not much to do but pray and copy manuscripts. Luckily for posterity, the monks occasionally copied a Latin manuscript from outside the church canon, thus preserving for us the works of Cicero, Vergil, Livy, and many others.

They also preserved Latin itself as a language; all the written works and church litany were written exclusively in Latin. The Latin of the Christian Church was basically the same language Cicero used, except new words were added or adapted to suit the needs of Christians. Medieval Latin differs slightly in spellings, forms, and syntax.

Hysteria's Herstory

According to St. Jerome, a noblewoman named Fabiola founded a large, free, public hospital at Ostia. She recruited other women to work as nurses and contribute funds. Jerome called her "the glory of the Church, the astonishment of the Gentiles, the mother of the poor, and the consolation of the saints." She was a saint.

Verba Sancta: Words of the Church Fathers

The Christian Church fathers were writers of Christian antiquity and thus the coiners of words that would eventually become medieval Latin. These were men who lived from New Testament times to the eighth century. To be an official church father, one had to be in constant communion with the Church, lead a holy life of exemplary conduct, achieve ecclesiastical approval, and be darned old. Among the most famous are St. Jerome, who wrote the first history of patristic literature; St. Ambrose, who helped transmit Eastern theology to the West; St. Augustine; and the last father, just getting in under the wire, St. Isidore of Seville.

St. Augustine (354–430) was born and educated in the Roman province of Africa. He went to Milan where he studied and wrote letters, essays, sermons, commentaries, and philosophical treatises. He was converted to Christianity in 387 and became bishop of Hippo in Africa. In the following adapted selection from *The Confessions,* St. Augustine describes his moment of conversion.

The following vocabulary list will help you read the selection from St. Augustine. Note that the forms are still very classical.

Latin	Form	Meaning	Derivative
aemulatio	onis, f.	rivalry	emulate
amarus	a, um	bitter	—
an	—	or	—
caelum	i, n.	sky	celestial
codex	codicis, m.	book	codicil
commessatio	onis, f.	drinking party	—
concitus	a, um	excited	—
confestim	—	immediately, suddenly	—

Latin	Form	Meaning	Derivative
crebro	adverb	frequently	—
crux	crucis, f.	cross	crucify
cubilis	e, n.	bed	—
diffugo	ere, fugi, fusus	flee; to be dispersed	diffuse
ebrietas	tatis, f.	drunkeness	inebriated
fleo	ere, flevi, fletus	weep	—
impetus	us, m.	impulse; attack	impetus
impudicitia	ae, f.	immodesty	impudence
infusus	a, um	diffused; permeating	infuse
mors	mortis, f.	death	mortify
ovum	ovi, n.	egg	ovary
pauper	eris	poor	pauper
tenebrae	arum, f. pl.	shades; night	tenebrism
thesaurus	i, m.	treasure	treasure
tollo	ere, sustuli, sublatus	raise	sublation
vado	ere, vasi	go; advance	invade
vendo	ere, vendidi, venditus	sell	vendor

Sublation is the act of taking away.

Tenebrism is a sixteenth-century school of art that uses a lot of dark background with the main subject illuminated by a streak of light.

St. Augustine's *Confessions*

St. Augustine is torn between worldly pleasures and a life of renunciation. He leaves his companion, Alypius, and goes out to the garden and weeps. He hears a voice that says, "Take, read." He does as told and is converted. Here's the story in the original:

> Dicebam haec et flebam, amarissima contritione cordis mei. Et ecce audio vocem de vicina domo cum cantu dicentis et crebro repetentis, quasi pueri and puellae, nescio: "Tolle, lege, tolle, lege." ... Repressoque impetu lacrimarum, surrexi ut aperirem codicem et legerem quod primum caput invenissem. Audieram enim de Antonio tamquam sibi diceretur quod legebatur: "Vade, vende omnia, quae habes, da pauperibus et habebis thesaurum in caelis: et veni sequere me," et tali oraculo confestim ad te esse conversum.

225

Itaque concitus redii in eim locum ubi sedebat Alpius: ibi enim posueram codicem apostoli, cum inde surrexeram. Arripui, aperui et legi in silentio capitulum, quo primum coniecti sunt oculi mei: "Non in commessationibus et ebrietatibus, non in cubilibus et impudicitiis, non in contentione et aemulatione, sed induite dominun Iesum Christum ...." Nec ultra volui legere, nec opus erat. Statim quippe cum fine huius sententiae, quasi luce securitatis infusa cordi meo, omnes dubitationis tenebrae diffugerunt.

I was saying these things and weeping, with the most bitter contrition in my heart. And behold, I hear a voice from a neighboring house of a person saying with a song and repeating over and over as if boys and girls, I do not know: "Take, read, take, read." ... After holding back my tears I got up in order to open the book and read what chapter I came upon first. For I had heard about Antony and what he is said to have read: "Go, sell everything that you have, give to the poor and you will have a treasure in heaven; and come, follow me" and with such a sign immediately he was converted to you.

And so I excitedly returned to that place where Alypius was sitting: for there I had put the book of the apostle when I had gotten up from there. I took it, opened it and read in silence the chapter where my eyes first glanced: "Not in parties and drunkeness, not in sin and lewdness, not in fighting and rivalry, but receive the Lord Jesus Christ ...." I wanted to read no further, nor was there need. Immediately, indeed, when I reached the end of this sentence, as if the light of security entered my heart, and all shades of doubt dispersed."

Verba Sancta: **Words of the Church**

When you hear Church Latin, you notice immediately some changes in pronunciation. The following guide to ecclesiastical pronunciation should help you speak or sing your Latin appropriately.

Letter	Example
a	father
e	met
e (at the end of syllable)	they
i	machine
o	note
oo	boot
y	machine

Letter	Example
Before ae, e, oe, i, y ...	
c	chain
cc	cat
sc	sheep
g	gentle
Otherwise ...	
c	candy
cc	accord
sc	Tabasco
g	good
v	very

The Roman Catholic Church used Latin in its liturgy from the second century to 1969, when the Vatican Council permitted vernacular languages among other reforms. The Mass is a celebration of the sacrament of the Eucharist, the ritual instituted by Jesus Christ at the Last Supper. The two parts of the Mass are the Liturgy of the Word and the Liturgy of the Eucharist. The first consists of readings and prayers. The second is the breaking of bread and communion.

The following table lists the most important terms of Church Latin:

Latin	Forms	Meaning	Derivative
adoro	are, avi, atus	worship (v.)	adore
aes	aeris, n.	bronze	—
agnus	i, m.	lamb	—
ardeo	ere, ardui	burn	ardent
benedico	ere, dixi, dictus	praise	benediction
benedictus	a, um	blessed	benediction
benignus	a, um	kind	benign
caritas	caritatis, f.	love, affection	charity
communicatio	onis, f.	fellowship	communication
ex parte	—	in part	—
facultas	facultatis, f.	goods	
glorifico	are, avi, tus	glorify	glorification
gratia	ae, f.	grace	grace

continues

continued

Latin	Forms	Meaning	Derivative
miseror	miserere	have pity	commiserate
pax	pacis, f.	peace	pacify
peccatum	i, n.	sin	peccadillo
perperam	—	incorrectly, wrongly	—
sanctus	a, um	holy	sanctify
sive ... sive	—	whether ... whether	—
spiritus	spiritus, m.	spirit	spirit
tinniens	entis	tinkling	tintinnabulation
unigenitus	—	the only son	—

The following is the Greeting:

Priest: In nomine Patris, et Filii, et Spiritus Sancti.

Congregation: Amen.

Priest: Gratia Domini nostri Jesu Christi, et caritas Dei, et communicatio Sancti Spiritus sit cum omnibus vobis.

Congregation: Et cum spiritu tuo.

Here is the Gloria (the translation can be found in Appendix D, "Answer Keys"):

Gloria in excelsis Deo
et in terra pax hominibus bonae voluntatis.
Laudamus te, benedicimus te,
adoramus te, glorificamus te
gratias agimus tibi propter
magnam gloriam tuam,
Domine Deus, Rex caelestis
Deus Pater omnipotens.
Domine Fili unigenite, Jesu Christe,
Domine Deus, Agnus Dei,
Filius Patris;
qui tollis peccata mundi
miserere nobis;
qui sedes ad dextram Patris,
miserere nobis.

Quoniam tu solus Sanctus,
Tu solus Dominus,
Tu solus Altissimus,
Jesu Christe,
cum Sancto spiritu
in gloria Dei Patris.
Amen.

Notice the vocative case when using direct address: *Christe, Domine, unigenite. Cum* is still followed by the ablative case, and the pronoun *te* is in the accusative case because it's the direct object.

The following excerpts are from the Bible, I Corinthians 13 (if you can't remember your Bible verses, the translation is provided in Appendix D):

1. Si linguis hominum loquar et angelorum, caritatem autem non habeam, factus sum velut aes sonans aut cymbalum tinniens.

2. Et si habuero prophetiam et noverim mysteria omnia et omnem scientiam et habuero omnem fidem ita ut montes transferam, caritatem autem non habuero, nihil sum.

3. Et si distribuero in cibos pauperum omnes facultates meas, et si tradidero corpus meum ut ardeam, caritatem autem non habuero, nihil mihi prodest.

4. Caritas patiens est, benigna est: caritas non aemulatur, non agit perperam, non inflatur.

5. Non est ambitiosa, non quaerit quae sua sunt, non irritatur, non cogitat malum.

6. Non gaudet super iniquitatem, congaudet autem veritati.

7. Omnia suffert, omnia credit, omnia sperat, omnia sustinet.

8. Caritas numquam excidit, sive prophetiae, evacuabuntur, sive linguae, cessabunt, sive scientia, destruetur.

9. Ex parte enim cognoscimus et ex parte prophetamus.

10. Cum autem venerit quod perfectum est, evacuabitur quod ex parte est.

11. Cum essem parvulus, loquebar ut parvulus, sapiebam ut parvulus, cogitabam ut parvulus. Quando factus sum vir evacuavi quae erant parvuli.

Grammar Guru

Medieval Latin writers were a little less particular about grammar. They often used the indicative mood when Classical Latin mandated the subjunctive. The present participle is used to indicate past tense—*profiscens* (having set out).

12. Videmus nunc per speculum in enigmate, nunc autem facie ad faciem. Nunc cognosco ex parte, tunc autem cognoscam sicut et cognitus sum.

13. Nunc autem manent fides, spes, caritas, tria haec: maior autem his est caritas.

Music, Sacred and Profane

The Mass was originally set to plainchant—a single melodic line sung by one person—but over the years the music has developed into an art form itself. Masses have been composed by musicians since the fifteenth century and include works by Hayden, Mozart, Beethoven, Berlioz, Dvorak, Verdi, Brahms, and Stravinsky.

Did You Know?

Did you know that *re, mi, fa, sol, la* come from Latin? Medieval singers used the first syllables of the first six half lines of the Latin hymn, "Ut Queant Laxis," because each begins on a higher note than the previous one, with a tone between each except the third and fourth where there is a semitone. Using *ut* instead of *do*, they could sing the scale on pitch:

UT queant laxis, REsonare fibris
MIra gestorum FAmuli tuorum
SOLve polluti LAbii reatum
Sancte Joannes.

So that your servants can sing with loosened throat
the wonders of your deeds,
free the guilt of unclean lips,
Holy John.

Many hymns and choral pieces for the Christian church are also sung in Latin, the words taken from the liturgy.

"Ave Maria" by Giuseppe Verdi

Ave Maria, gratia plena, Dominus tecum benedicta tu in mulieribus et benedictus fructus ventris tui, Iesus.

Sancta Maria, Mater Dei, ora pro nobis peccatoribus nunc et in hora mortis nostrae.

Classical Latin poetry and verse had a metrical system with its own rules: a quantitative system of long and short syllables. Medieval and Late Latin verse resembles the English meters, which are accentual. This came about thanks to a bunch of wandering young men, perhaps connected to the Church, called the Goliards. They traveled from town to town, spending as much time in taverns as in churches, and wrote drinking songs, satirical verses, and love songs. Collected in the thirteenth-century anthology *Carmina Burana,* these songs and verses are amusing and fairly easy to read. (For translations, turn to Appendix D.)

From "Amatoria, Potatoria, Lusoria," extr. 60

Bibit hera, bibit herus
bibit miles, bibit clerus
bibit ille, bibit illa
bibit servus, cum ancilla
bibit velox, bibit piger
bibit albus, bibit niger
bibit constans, bibit vagus
bibit rudis, bibit magus
Bibit pauper et aegrotus
bibit exsul et ignotus
bibit puer, bibit canus
bibit presul et decanus
bibit soror, bibit frater
bibit anus, bibit mater
bibit ista, bibit ille
bibunt centum, bibunt mille

Hera, herus are equal to *domina, dominus. Canus* is Late Latin for *senex,* "old man." *Presul* and *decanus* are "leader" and "deacon," respectively.

Note that the lines rhyme—something that classical Latin poetry did not do—and the accents form a regular meter.

From "Amatoria, Potatoria, Lusoria," extr. 43

Pulchra tibi facies
oculorum acies
capillorum series
o quam clara species!
Rosa rubicundior
lilio candidior
omnibus formosior
semper in te glorior!

> Your beautiful face,
> the look of your eyes,
> the braids of your hair,
> O how glorious you look!
> Redder than the rose,
> whiter than the lily,
> more beautiful than all the rest.
> I glory in you unceasingly!

Note the comparative form of the adjectives, *ior,* and the ablative of comparison, *lilio* and *rosa.*

Finally, Christmas Latin! It wouldn't be the holiday season without "Adeste Fideles," "In Dulci Iubilo," or "Pax in Terra." For all those carol fests and sing-a-longs, here are some Latin versions of more modern day songs.

"Tintinnabula"
("Jingle Bells")

Tinc, tinc, tonc, tinc, tinc, tonc
Tintinnabula!
Quam iucundum vehere in raeda festiva!
Tinc, tinc, tonc, tinc, tinc, tonc
Tintinnabula!
Quam iucundum vehere, Io Saturnalia!
Per nivem currimus
In raeda festiva
Per montes eximus
Ridens omnia
In equis sonora
In animis soles
In mundo omnia rident
Pro Tintinnabulis! Euge!

"Nicolaus Venit ad Nos"
("Santa Claus Is Coming to Town")

Attende ad te, noli flere
Noli plorare ausculta me
Nicolaus venit ad nos.
Te videt dormientem
Novit vigilantem.
Novit agentem ben et non
Igitur ne malus sis! Ergo!

"Rudolphus"
("Rudolph, the Red-Nosed Reindeer")

Rudolphus cervus nasum
rubicundum habebat
Quem si videre possis
elucere referas.
Lucificare cervi deridentes solebant
Neque sinebant eum comminus colludere.
Ecce dixit Nicholaus pride festum
"O, Rudolphe, nocte hac
visne Traham ducere?"
Quam tunc iucundus fuit
cervis iubilantibus!
"Rudolphe," nunc dicebant,
"Notus eris posteris."

"Adeste Fideles"
("O Come All Ye Faithful")

Adeste Fideles
Laeti triumphantes
Venite, venite in Bethlehem
Natum videte
Regem angelorum
Venite adoremus, venite adoremus, venite adoremus,
Dominum.
En grege relicto
Humiles ad cunas
Vocati pastores approperant
Et nos ovanti
gradu festinemu.
Venite adoremus, venite adoremus, venite adoremus
Dominum.

"Volumus Hilarem Festum"
("We Wish You a Merry Christmas")

Volumus hilarem festum
Volumus hilarem festum
Volumus hilarem festum
Et Bonum Annum

The Least You Need to Know

➤ The Christian Church is a treasure house of Latin.

➤ St. Augustine heard voices.

➤ "Ave" in "Ave Maria" is pronounced *AH-vay*.

➤ Goliards were the party people of the Middle Ages.

➤ Rudolphus was a Roman reindeer.

Chapter 23

Live! From Ancient Rome!

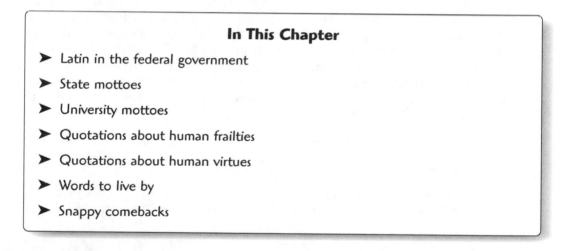

In This Chapter

➤ Latin in the federal government

➤ State mottoes

➤ University mottoes

➤ Quotations about human frailties

➤ Quotations about human virtues

➤ Words to live by

➤ Snappy comebacks

Romans quoted Romans. The Church fathers quoted Romans. The Renaissance writers quoted Romans. The Reformation writers and the Romantic writers quoted Romans. And so it went until we got books and books of Roman quotations. What are we to make of this?

We quote Roman writers for several reasons. First, what they said is often wise and useful. If we lived our lives according to all the precepts thought up by the Romans, we would all attain sainthood.

Second, we repeat what the Romans wrote because it reaffirms the frailty of mankind and makes us more sympathetic to our own failings. When we see that 2,000 years ago jealousy, greed, and insincerity were acknowledged as not good things, we can look upon today's society with a little more sympathy.

On the opposite side of the coin, when we read of men and women who value honesty, education, love, and family, isn't it heartening to think that we can still honor those ideals? If they've lasted 2,000 years, doesn't that give us hope that they will survive the next 2,000 as well?

Finally, we can use these quotes for your family, university, or doghouse seal. *Cave Canem!* would go very nicely over the doghouse door and will give Fido elevated status.

Latin in the Federal Government

Our Founding Fathers were steeped in Latin. The traditional education brought over from England required a working knowledge of the classics. The early patriots admired the Roman Republic and its venerable Senate. So it's no wonder that many of our federal seals contain Latin words.

The Great Seal of the United States features that eagle grasping a gravity-defying ribbon emblazoned with *E pluribus unum* ("Out of many, one"), meaning "one country from many states." Perhaps the Founding Fathers thought they were creating a country similar to one happy family with many members. The origins of this slogan are detailed in an article by Margaret A. Brucia in *The Classical Outlook* (fall 1997), which notes that the phrase was originally found in a Latin poem describing a poor farmer making a *moretum,* a pesto that combines the green garlic and white cheese into one color. This phrase is also on the presidential seal, the seal of the Senate, the State Department, and the Supreme Court.

The Air Force seal says *Coelum ad proelium elige* ("Choose the sky for battle"), while the Navy declares *Acta, non verba* ("Actions, not words"). The National Archive seal aptly says *Littera scripta manet* ("The written word remains").

Finally, on the lowly dollar bill, on the other side of the Great Seal, we find *Annuit coeptis* ("He nods approval of beginnings") and *Novus ordo seclorum* ("A new order of the ages").

State Mottoes

Most state mottoes are self-explanatory and can be found in any library reference section. Here's a brief list:

Arizona: *Diat Deus* ("God enriches"). Another word for Pluto, god of the Underworld, is Dis, the word meaning "rich" (presuming there is a connection with going underground and getting rich).

Arkansas: *Regnat populus* ("The people rule").

California: *Eureka!* ("I've found it!") Actually a Greek word, first-person present perfect indicative of *heuriskein* ("to find"), supposedly yelled by Archimedes when he perfected an experiment based on the principle of buoyancy that could test the purity of gold. So, too, yelled the Forty-Niners.

Colorado: *Nil sine numine.* ("Nothing without God.")

Connecticut: *Qui transtulit sustinet.* ("He who came across, holds up.")

District of Columbia: *Iustitia omnibus.* ("Justice for all.")

Idaho: *Esto perpetua.* ("Be always.")

Kansas: *Ad astra per aspera.* ("To the stars through difficulties.")

Maine: *Dirigo.* ("I direct.")

Massachusetts: *Ense petit placidam sub libertate.* ("With the sword he seeks peace under liberty.") Note the ablative of means, "by means of a sword."

Michigan: *Si quaeris peninsulam amoenam, circumspice.* ("If you are seeking a pleasant peninsula, look around.")

Mississippi: *Virtute et armis.* ("By courage and arms.")

Missouri: *Salus populi suprema lex est.* ("The welfare of the people is the supreme law.")

New Mexico: *Crescit eundo.* ("It grows as it goes.") *Eundo* is a gerund form of the verb *eo*, ablative of means, "by means of going."

New York: *Excelsior!* ("Higher!")

North Carolina: *Esse quam videri.* ("To be rather than to seem.")

Oklahoma: *Labor omnia vincit.* ("Work conquers all.")

Oregon: *Alis volat propriis.* ("He flies with his own wings.")

Puerto Rico: *Joannes est nomen eius.* ("John is his name.")

South Carolina: *Dum spiro, spero.* ("While I breathe, I hope.")

Virginia: *Sic semper tyrannis.* ("Thus always to tyrants.")

West Virginia: *Montani semper liberi.* ("Mountain men are always free.")

Wyoming: *Cedant arma togae.* ("Arms yield to the toga.")

Cave!

The *Montani semper liberi* motto belongs to West Virginia, not Montana, which happens to mean "mountainous."

University Mottoes

More than you'll ever want to know about the Latin mottoes and seal inscriptions used by institutions of higher education can be found in *U.S. Colleges and Universities*, written by Harry J. Farnon and published in the February/March 1989 issue of *The Classical Journal*. Here are just a few:

Amherst College: *Terras irradient.* ("Let them illumine the earth.")

Brooklyn College: *Nil sine magno labore.* ("Nothing without great effort.")

Brown University: *In Deo speramus.* ("In God we trust.")

City College of New York: *Respice, adspice, prospice.* ("Look back, look to the present, look to the future.")

Columbia University: *In lumine tuo videbimus lumen.* ("In thy light we shall see light.")

Dartmouth College: *Vox clamantis in deserto.* ("A voice of one crying in the wilderness.")

Delaware College: *Scientia sol mentis.* ("Knowledge, the sun of the mind.")

Fordham University: *Sapientia et doctrina.* ("Wisdom and knowledge.")

Harvard University: *Veritas.* ("Truth.")

Hunter College: *Mihi cura futuri.* ("My anxiety is for the future.")

Johns Hopkins University: *Veritas vos liberabit.* ("Truth will free you.")

Miami University: *Prodesse quam conspici.* ("To be productive, rather than to be ornamental.")

New York University: *Perstare et praestare.* ("To preserve and to surpass.")

Trinity College: *Pro ecclesia et patria.* ("For church and country.")

Tulane University: *Non sibi, sed suis.* ("Not for herself, but for her own.")

University of Chicago: *Crescat scientia, vita excolatur.* ("Let the knowledge grow, let life be enriched.")

University of Florida: *Civium in moribus rei publicae salus.* ("In the character of its citizens lies the welfare of the state.")

University of Michigan: *Artes, scientia, veritas.* ("The arts, knowledge, truth.")

University of Mississippi: *Virtute et armis.* ("By valor and arms.")

University of Missouri: *Salus populi.* ("The welfare of the people.")

University of New Mexico: *Lux hominum vita.* ("Light is the life of men.")

University of Washington: *Lux sit!* ("Let there be light!")

Yale University: *Lux et veritas.* ("Light and truth.")

RETINEO

Grammar Guru

Remember that the English preposition sometimes must be provided with the ablative case.

Quotations on Human Failings

No one is perfect, and so it has been since Caesar. All the vices possible then—greed, hate, making false statements, and excessive spending—are still with us, perhaps even multiplied and enhanced by modern technology.

Nemo liber est qui corpori servit.

No one is free who is a slave to his body.

Parva leves capiunt animas.

Small things capture small (light) minds.

Pessimum genus inimicorum laudantes.

Flatterers are the worst kind of enemies.

Proprium humani ingenii est odisse quem laeseris.

It is human nature to hate a person whom you have injured.

Radix omnium malorum est cupiditas.

Greed is the root of all evils.

Mendacem memorem esse oportet.

It is fitting that a liar should be a man of good memory.

Stultorum calami carbones moenia chartae.

Chalk is the pen of fools; walls, their paper.

Sumptus censum ne superet.

Let not your spending exceed your income.

Quotations on Human Virtues

Luckily, all the virtues of mankind—goodness, wisdom, sympathy, and honor—are still with us. It's a wonderful testimony to mankind that these ideas have survived.

Amicus humani generis.

A friend of the human race.

Ars longa, vita brevis.

Art is long; life, short.

Cogito, ergo sum.

I think, therefore I am.

Curae leves loquuntur ingentes stupent.

Slight griefs talk, great ones are speechless.

Docendo discimus.

We learn by teaching.

Donec eris felix, multos numerabis amicos.

As long as you are fortunate, you will have many friends.

Fabas indulcet fames.

Hunger sweetens the beans.

Fortiter in re, suaviter in modo.

Resolutely in action, gently in manner.

Non est vivere sed valere vita est.

Life is not being alive, but being well.

Omnia mutantur nos et mutamur in illis.

All things change, and we change with them.

Potius mori quam foedari.

Rather to die than to be dishonored.

Praemonitus praemunitus.

Forewarned is forearmed.

Vincit qui se vincit.

He conquers who conquers himself.

Did You Know?

The U.S. standard railroad gauge, the distance between the rails, is 4 feet 8$\frac{1}{2}$ inches. This is because a rut is a rut; the Romans built their roads to accommodate the Roman war chariot, and the roads and ruts never changed. There is some speculation that 4 feet 8$\frac{1}{2}$ inches is just wide enough to accommodate the back ends of two Roman war horses.

Words to Live By

Following the tenets of the Romans, goodness and mercy will continue, and our children and grandchildren will inherit a better world.

Veritas vos liberabit.

The truth will set you free.

Si finis bonus est, totum bonum erit.

If the end is good, everything will be good.

Non semper erit aestas.

It will not always be summer.

Beneficium accipere libertatem est vendere.

To accept a favor is to sell one's freedom.

Bonum vinum laetificat cor hominis.

Good wine gladdens a man's heart.

Carpe diem.

Seize the day.

De duobus malis, minus est semper eligendum.

Of two evils, the lesser is always to be chosen.

Fortes fortuna iuvat.

Fortune helps the brave.

Adversus solem ne loquitur.

Don't speak against the sun.

Amor vincit omnia.

Love conquers all.

Aut viam inveniam aut faciam.

I will either find a way or make one.

Hysteria's Herstory

In the largest collection of quotations published, Sappho is the only woman quoted from all Greek and Roman times. We have precious few words direct from Roman women, although many are quoted by men, and we know that Sempronia, wife of the consul in 77 B.C., did publish poetry.

Snappy Comebacks

There's nothing more satisfying than a snappy comeback in Latin. For one, your audience won't have the foggiest idea what you've said. You will have to expose their ignorance—"Oh, that's Latin. Don't you know Latin?"—and further humiliate them by translating for them.

A snappy comeback in Latin will drop mouths, raise eyebrows, and favorably impress your superiors. Here are some scenarios with the appropriate remark:

➤ **When the Dow plunges:** *Sic transit gloria mundi* ("Thus passes the glory of the world"). This saying has been attributed to Thomas à Kempis in the fifteenth century and is used in the crowning of the pope.

➤ **To critics of your work space:** *Imperium in imperio* ("An empire within an empire"). This was the original motto of the state of Ohio.

➤ **On seeing the most pitiful comb-over ever:** *Calvo turpius est nihil comato* ("Worse than baldness is nothing with hair").

➤ **In defense of your own most pitiful comb-over:** *Etiam capillus unus habet umbram* ("Even one hair has a shadow").

➤ **On making a colossal mistake:** *Experientia docet* ("Experience teaches").

➤ **Behind your brother-in-law's back, pointing to his head:** *Supellex curta* ("Scanty furniture").

The Least You Need to Know

➤ Human nature hasn't changed in 2,000 years.

➤ There is a Latin saying for every occasion.

➤ Insults are safer in Latin.

Vocabulary List

Latin to English Vocabulary

Latin	English
a	by
abhorreo, ere, ui	to shrink back, abhor
absolutus, a, um	perfect, complete
abstineo, ere, stinui	to abstain
absum, abesse, abfui	to be absent
absurdus, a, um	absurd
accido, ere, cidi	to happen, fall
accido, ere, cidi, cisus	to cut down
accipio, accipere, accepi, acceptus	to accept
actus, us, m.	act
ad	to, toward, near
addo, addere, addidi, additus	to add
adduco, ere, duxi, ductus	to bring
adeo	to such a degree
adicio, ere, ieci, iectus	to add on
adiutrix, icis, f.	helper
adiuvo, are, avi, atus	to help, aid
admoneo, ere, monui, monitus	to admonish, warn
aedificium, i, n.	building
aestimatio, aestimationis, f.	estimate
affero, afferre, attuli, allatus	to bring toward

continues

continued

Latin	English
affligo, ere, flixi, flictus	to damage, knock down
ager, agri, m.	field, land
agmen, inis, n.	line
ago, agere, egi, actus	to do
agricola, ae, m.	farmer
alces, alcis, m./f.	elk
alienus, a, um	foreign
aliquis, aliquid	someone, anyone
alius, a, um	another, other
alo, alere	to feed
alter, era, erum	the one, the other
altus, a, um	high, deep
ambulo, are, avi, atus	to walk
amica, ae, f.	friend (female)
amicus, i, m.	friend (male)
amo, are, avi, atus	to love
amplus, a, um	large, ample
animadverto, ere, verti, versus	to notice
animus, i, m.	mind, soul, disposition
anser, anseris, m./f.	goose
ante	before
antecedo, ere, cessi, cessus	to surpass
antequam	before
apis, apis, f.	bee
appello, are, avi, atus	to call, name
appendo, ere, di, sus	to pay out, weigh out
applico, are, avi, atus	to apply, attach
apprehendo, ere, di, sus	to grab
apud	at the home of
aqua, ae, f.	water
arbor, arboris, f.	tree
architectus, i, m.	architect
Arpinas, Arpinatis, n.	villa at Arpinum
arripio, ere, ripi, raptus	to catch hold of
articulus, i, m.	joint

Latin	English
ascendo, ere, di, sus	to climb
asper, aspera, asperum	sharp, harsh
astrum, i, n.	star
at	but
audio, ire, audivi, auditus	to listen
auris, auris, f.	ear
aurum, i, n.	gold
aut … aut	either … or
autem	moreover
auxilium, i, n.	aid
balineum, balinei, n.	bath
bellum, i, n.	war
beta, ae, f.	beet
bipennis, is, f.	axe
bonus, a, um	good
bos, bovis, m./f.	ox, cow
brevis, breve	short
cado, cadere, cecidi, casus	to fall
caedo, ere, cecidi, caesus	to kill, cut
caelum, i, n.	sky
Caesar, Caesaris, m.	Caesar
calamitas, calamitatis, f.	calamity
calidus, a, um	warm
canis, canis, m./f.	dog
canto, are, avi, atus	to sing
caper, capri, m.	goat
capio, capere, cepi, captus	to capture, make (plan)
caput, capitis, n.	head
caro, caronis, f.	meat
casus, us, m.	chance, accident
cauda, ae, f.	tail
causa, ae, f.	cause, sake
cautus, a, um	cautious
caveo, ere, cavi, cautus	to beware

continues

continued

Latin	English
cedo, cedere, cessi, cessus	to move, yield
celer, eris, ere	swift
cena, ae, f.	dinner
centum	one hundred
cervus, i, m.	deer
ceterus, a, um	other, remaining, the rest
cibum, i, n.	food
civis, civis, m./f.	citizen
civitas, civitatis, f.	city, state
clamo, are, avi, atus	to shout
clamor, oris, m.	noise
clunis, clunis, m.	buttock
coepi, coepisse	I began
comes, comitis, m./f.	companion
committo, ere, misi, missus	begin
commoveo, ere, movi, motus	upset, bother
communis, e	common
concha, conchae, f.	shell
concido, ere, cidi	to fall, kill
condicio, onis, f.	condition
condio, condire, ivi, itus	to season
condo, ere, condidi, conditus	to found, built
consilium, consili, n.	plan, counsel
consisto, ere, stiti	to stop, become solid
conspicio, ere, spexi, spectus	to see, catch sight of
constituo, ere, tui, tutus	to decide, be made
consuetudo, inis, f.	custom
consul, consulis, m.	consul
consumo, ere, sumpsi, sumptus	to consume, use up
contra	against
conventus, us, m.	coming together
convivum, i, n.	party
convolo, are, avi, atus	to fly about
coquo, coquere, coxi, coctus	to cook
coquus, coqui, m.	cook

Latin	English
cornu, us, n.	horn
corpus, corporis, n.	body
cotidie	daily
credo, ere, credidi, creditus	to believe
credulus, a, um	gullible
creor, ari, atus, sum	to create
crus, cruris, n.	leg
crux, crucis, f.	cross
cubile, cubilis, n.	bed
culpa, ae, f.	blame
cum	when, since, although
cura, ae, f.	cure
curia, ae, f.	senate house, court
curo, are, avi, atus	to care for
de	down, about, concerning
dea, ae, f.	goddess
decem	ten
deceptus, a, um	taken down
decido, ere, cidi	to fall down, cut down
decretum, i, n.	decree
defessus, a, um	tired
deinde	then, next
deleo, ere, delevi, deletus	to destroy
delictum, i, n.	fault
delinquo, ere, deliqui, delictus	to be short of established standards
dens, dentis, m.	tooth
deporto, are, avi, atus	to deport
derectus, a, um	straight
desilio, ire, ui, itus	to jump down
deus, dei, m.	god
dexter, ra, rum	right (not left)
diarroia (Greek)	diarrhea
dico, ere, dixi, dictus	to say
dictator, dictatoris, m.	dictator

continues

continued

Latin	English
dictum, i, n.	contract
dies, diei, m.	day
diffundo, ere, fudi, fusus	to pour out, scatter
dis, ditis	rich
discordia, ae, f.	discord
dissimulo, are, avi, atus	to pretend
diu	for a long time
do, dare, dedi, datus	to give
doleo, ere, ui	to be sad
domus, us, f.	home, house
donec	until
dormio, ire, ivi, itus	to sleep
duco, ducere, duxi, ductum	to lead
dulcis, is, e	sweet
dum	while
duo	two
durus, a, um	hard, harsh
dux, ducis, m.	leader
e, ex	out of
ego	I
eius	his, her
elephantus, i, m.	elephant
eo, ire, ii, itus	to go
Ephesus, i, m.	Ephesus
epistula, ae, f.	letter
equus, equi, m.	horse
erigo, ere, rexi, rectus	to straighten out
esse	to be
est	is
et	and
et ... et	both ... and
etiam	even also
Europa, ae, f.	Europe
exanimo, are, avi, atus	to die

Latin	English
excelsus, a, um	high, lofty, tall
excipio, ere, cepi, ceptus	to make exceptions
excogito, are, avi, atus	to think up, devise
exeo, exire, exii, exitus	to go out
exigo, ere, exegi, exactus	to take out, demand
exsisto, ere, stiti, stitus	to stand out
exspectatio, onis, f.	anticipation
exterus, a, um	outer
extremus, a, um	hindmost, last
fabula, ae, f.	story
facies, ei, f.	face, appearance
facile	easily
facio, ere, feci, factus	to do, make
factum, i, n.	fact, deed
femina, ae, f.	woman
femur, feminis, n.	thigh
fero, ferre, tuli, latus	to bear, carry
ferrum, i, n.	iron
fictilis, e	clay, earthenware
figura, ae, f.	shape
filia, ae, f.	daughter
filius, fili, m.	son
fio, fieri, factus sum	to become
flagrans, flagrantis	flaming
fleo, flere, flevi, fletus	to weep
flumen, fluminis, n.	river
fluo, fluere, fluxi, fluxus	flow
foras	out
forma, ae, f.	form
fortasse	perhaps
fortis, forte	brave, strong
frater, ris, m.	brother
fraus, fraudis, f.	mischief
frigidus, a, um	cold
frons, frontis, f.	forehead, brow

continues

251

continued

Latin	English
fructus, us, m.	fruit
funambulus, i, m.	tightrope walker
fundus, i, m.	estate, farm
fungus, i, m.	mushroom
gaudeo, ere, gavisus sum	to rejoice
gero, ere, gessi, gestus	to wear, wage
glaber, glabra, glabrum	bald
gladiator, oris, m.	gladiator
gloria, ae, f.	glory
Graecus, i, m.	Greek
habeo, ere, habui, habitus	to have
habito, are, avi, atus	to live
harena, ae, f.	sand
hecyra, ae, f.	mother-in-law
helvella, ae, f.	herbs, greens
herba, ae, f.	greens, grass
herbosus, a, um	grassy
hic	here
hic, haec, hoc	this, these
hippopotamus, i, m.	hippopotamus
hodie	today
homo, hominis, m.	man
honor, oris, m.	honor
hora, ae, f.	hour
hortus, i, m.	garden
hospita, ae, f.	guest
humanus, a, um	kind, gentle, humane
humilis, e	humble
iacio, ere, ieci, iactus	to throw, hurl
iam	now
idem, eadem	the same
igitur	therefore

Latin	English
ille, illa, illus	that, that one
immortalis, e	immortal
impensa, ae, f.	cost
imus, a, um	deepest
in	in, on
inaures, inaurium, f., pl.	earrings
incido, ere, cidi, cissus	to cut into
includo, ere, si, sus	to include
industria, ae, f.	work
inferior, inferius	inferior, lower
inferus, a, um	lower
infirmus, a, um	weakened
iniquus, a, um	unfair
inquit	he/she said
insula, ae, f.	island
intellegentia, ae, f.	knowledge
intellego, ere, intellexi, intellectus	to know
inter	between, among
interea	meanwhile
invado, ere, vadi, vasus	to attack, invade
invenio, invenire, inveni, inventus	to invent
invito, are, avi, atus	to invite
ipse, ipsa, ipsum	self
ipse, ipsa, ipsum	self, very
iratus, a, um	angry
is, ea, id	he, she, it
istuc	there, to that place
ita	in such a way
Italia, ae, f.	Italy
itaque	and so
item	in the same way, likewise
iter, itineris, n.	way, journey
iubeo, ere, iussi, iussus	to order
iucundus, a, um	pleasant
ius, iuris, n.	right, just

continues

continued

Latin	English
laboro, are, avi, atus	to work
lacrimo, are, avi, atus	to cry
laetus, a, um	happy
lana, ae, f.	wool
lapis, lapidis, m.	stone
latus, a, um	wide
lautus, lauti, m.	gourmet, gentleman
lavo, lavare, lavi, lautus	to wash
lectus, i, m.	bed, couch
lego, ere, legi, lectus	read, choose
lenis, is, e	gentle, kind
lex, legis, f.	law
liber, era, erum	free (adj.)
liber, libri, m.	book
libero, are, avi, atus	to free
licuit	it was allowed
litoteta (Greek)	simple life
locus, i, m.	place
longus, a, um	long
loquor, loqui, locutus sum	to speak
ludo, ere, lusi, lusus	to play
ludus, i, m.	school, game
luna, ae, f.	moon
lupus, i, m.	wolf
magis	more
magister, tri, m.	teacher
magistratus, us, m.	magistrate
magnitudo, magnitudinis, m.	size
magnopere	greatly
magnus, a, um	great
maiores, maiorum, m., pl.	ancestors, forefathers
malus, a, um	bad
malva, ae, f.	marrow
mando, are, avi, atus	demand, command

Latin	English
mane	in the morning
maneo, ere, mansi, mansus	to remain
mangonico, mangonicare, avi, atus	to improve appearance for a sale
manus, manus, f.	hand, band
margarita, ae, f.	pearl
maris, maris, n.	sea
mas, maris, m.	a male
mater, matris, f.	mother
matrimonium, i, n.	marriage
medius, a, um	middle of
membrum, membri, n.	member
mensa, ae, f.	table
merx, mercis, f.	merchandise
metus, us, m.	fear
meus, mea, meus	my
mihi	to me
miles, militis, m.	soldier
milia	thousands
miror, mirari, miratus	wonder
mirus, a, um	wonderful
miser, misera, miserum	wretched, miserable
mitis, mitis, mite	sweet, gentle, kind
mitto, ere, misi, missus	to send
modus, i, m.	way
moneo, ere, ui, monitus	to warn
morior, moriri, mortuus sum	to die
mors, mortis, m.	death
moveo, ere, movi, motus	to move
mox	soon
mulier, eris, f.	woman
multus, a, um	much, many
mundus, i, m.	world
muraena, ae, f.	moray eel
mutilus, a, um	broken
mutuus, mutua, mutuum	borrowed

continues

255

continued

Latin	English
nam	for
narro, are, avi, atus	to tell, narrate
nasus, i, m.	nose
nasutus, a, um	long-nosed
natus, a, um	born
navis, navis, f.	ship
necesse	necessary
nemo	no one
nervus, nervi, m.	nerve
nihil	nothing
nimbus, i, m.	cloud
nobilis, e	noble
nodus, i, m.	knot
nodus, i, m.	knot, node
noli, nolite	don't (plus inf.)
nolo, nolere, nolui	to not want
nomen, inis, n.	name
non	not
non modo	not only
noster, ra, rum	our
nosti	you know
notus, a, um	known
novem	nine
novissimus, a, um	last, latest
novus, a, um	new
nox, noctis, f.	night
nucleus, nuclei, m.	kernel
nullus, a, um	none
numquam	never
nunc	now
obligo, are, avi, atus	to obligate, earmark
obruo, ere, i, itus	to bury, hide
octo	eight
oculus, i, m.	eye

Latin	English
officium, i, n.	duty, office
olim	once upon a time
omnis, e	every, all
onus, oneris, n.	load, burden
opprimo, ere, pressi, pressus	to put down, press, crush
opus, operis, n.	work
orator, oratoris, m.	orator
orbis, orbis, m.	circle
orno, are, avi, atus	to decorate
os, oris, n.	mouth
ossum, i, n.	bone
ostrea, ostreae, f.	oyster
otiosus, a, um	at leisure
otium, i, n.	leisure
ovum, i, n.	egg
palla, ae, f.	stole
palma, ae, f.	palm
palor, palari, palatus	to wander
par, paris	equal
paro, are, avi, atus	to prepare
pars, partis, f.	part
parvus, a, um	small
pater, patris, m.	father
patior, pati, passus sum	suffer
patria, ae, f.	fatherland
paulo	a little
pax, pacis, f.	peace
pecunia, ae, f.	money
pellis, is, f.	skin, hide
pendo, pendere, di, sus	hang
pensilis, pensile	hanging
per	through
perficio, ere, feci, fectus	finish
permuto, are, avi, atus	exchange
perna, ae, f.	ham, thigh

continues

continued

Latin	English
pernicitas, atis, f.	agility
pes, pedis, m.	foot
peto, ere, ivi itus t	seek, attack
pisces, piscis, m./f.	fish
piscina, ae, f.	fishpond
plàcatus, a, um	pleasant
placeo, ere, placui, placitus	to please
plebs, plebis, f.	common people
pluit, pluere, pluit	to rain
poena, ae, f.	penalty
polliceor, eri, pollicitus	to promise
pondus, eris, n.	weight
pono, ere, posui, positus	to put, place
poples, poplitis, m.	behind the knee
populus, i, m.	people
porto, are, avi, atus	to carry
possum, posse, potui	to be able
post	after, behind
postquam	after
praeacutus, a, um	sharp
praeceler, celeris, e	very swift
praecipuus, a, um	special
praesto, are, steti, status	to take charge of
praeter	except
praetereo, ire, ii, itus	to omit, pass over
prandeo, ere, prandi, pransus	to eat, dine
prandium, i, n.	dinner
pretium, i, n.	price
primum	for the first time
primus, a, um	first
privatim	privately, at home
privatus, a, um	private
pro	for, on behalf of, in place of
procumbo, ere, cubui, cubitus	to fall down
proficiscor, proficisci, profectus sum	to leave

Latin	English
prope	near (adv.)
propinquus, a, um	near (adj.)
propter	on account of
publicus, a, um	public
puella, ae, f.	girl
puer, eri, m.	boy
pugil, pugilis, m.	boxer
pugno, are, avi, atus	to fight
pullus, i, m.	chicken
quaero, ere, quaesivi, quaesitus	to ask
qualis	what kind of
quam	than
quamquam	although
quando	when
quantus, a, um	how much
quartus, a, um	fourth
quattuor	four
que (enclitic)	and
qui, quae, quod	who, which
quidam, quaedam, quiddam	a certain
quies, quietis, f.	quiet, rest
quinam, quidnam	who, pray? what?
quinque	five
quis	who?
quisque	each, every
quisquis	whoever
quisvis	whomever you want
quo modo	how?
quoque	also
quot	how many?
radix, radicis, f.	root
ramus, i, m.	branch
recipio, ere, cepi, ceptus	to take on
recipio, ere, cepi, ceptus (se)	to retreat

continues

continued

Latin	English
reclino, are, avi, atus	to recline
refero, ferre, tuli, latus	to bring back
regina, ae, f.	queen
reicio, ere, ieci, iectus	reject
relinquo, ere, liqui, ictus	to leave behind
reliquus, reliqua, reliquum	the rest of
remaneo, ere, mansi, mansus	to remain
res, rei, f.	thing, matter
respondeo, ere, di, sus	to respond
rete, retis, n.	net
rex, regis, m.	king
rideo, ere, risi, risus	to laugh
rodo, ere, rosi, rosus	to gnaw at
Roma, ae, f.	Rome
Romanus, a, um	Roman
rumor, oris, m.	rumor
sacerdos, dotis, m.	priest
saepe	often
sal, salis, m./n.	salt
salio, ire, salui or salii, salitus	to jump
salveo, ere	to be well
sapiens, sapientis	wise
scelus, sceleris, n.	crime
scio, ire, scivi, scitus	to know
scribo, ere, scripsi, scriptus	to write
se	self (third-person reflexive pronoun)
sed	but
sed etiam	but also
sedeo, ere, sede, sessus	to sit
sedo, are, avi, atus	to soothe, refresh
sella, ae, f.	chair
semper	always
senator, senatoris, m.	senator
senatus, us, m.	senate

Latin	English
septem	seven
sequor, sequi, secutus sum	to follow
servus, i, m.	slave (male)
serva, ae, f.	slave (female)
sex	six
si	if
sic	thus
sicut	as just as
silentium, silenti, n.	silence
similis, e	similar
simul	at the same time
sine (used with abl.)	without
singulus, a, um	single
sinister, sinistra, sinistrum	left (not right)
soleo, ere, solui, solitus	to be accustomed to
sollertius, a, um	skilled
solus, a, um	alone
somnus, i, m.	sleep
soror, sororis, f.	sister
species, ei, f.	sight, appearance
specto, are, avi, atus	to look at
spero, are, avi, atus	to hope
statim	immediately
statuo, statuere, statui, statutus	to decide
stipo, are, avi, atus	to plant, press
sto, stare, steti, status	to stand
stola, ae, f.	dress
strepitus, us, m.	noise
stupeo, ere, stupui, stupitus	to be stupified
suavis, suave	delicious, pleasing
sub	under
subinde	immediately afterward
subito	suddenly
sublevo, are, avi, atus	to get up
subruo, ere, rui, rutus	uproot
sum	I am

continues

continued

Latin	English
sum, esse, fui, futurus	to be
summus, a, um	top of
sumptuarius, a, um	sumptuary, having to do with excessive spending
sumptus, us, m.	cost
sunt	they are
super/supra	above
superior, superius, superior	higher
supero, are, avi, atum	to surpass
suus, a, um	his/her/their own
taberna, ae, f.	shop, bar
taceo, ere, tacui, tacitus	to be quiet
tam	so
tamen	nevertheless
tantus, a, um	so great
tardo, are, avi, atus	slow down
tempus, temporis, n.	time
teneo, ere, ui, tentus	to hold
tergum, i, n.	back
terra, ae, f.	land
terreo, ere, ui, territus	to frighten
toga, ae, f.	toga
tot	so many
totus, a, um	whole
trado, ere, tradidi, traditus	to hand over
traho, ere, traxi, tractus	to draw, drag
trans (used with acc.)	across
transversus, a, um	lying crosswise
tristis, triste	sad
triumphalis, e	triumphal, of a triumph
trogodyta, ae, m./f.	cave man/woman
tu	you (s.)
tum	then
turba, ae, f.	crowd

Latin	English
turpis, turpe	disgusting, awful, base
tutor, ari	keep safe
tuus, tua, tuum	your (s.)
ubi	where, when
ubique	everywhere
ullus, a, um	any
umquam	ever
unda, ae, f.	wave
unde	from when, whence
unus, a, um	one
urbs, urbis, f.	city
urinator, is, m.	diver
urino, are, avi, atus	to dive
ursus, i, m.	bear (male)
ursa, ae, f.	bear (female)
usus, usus, m.	use
ut	in order that
utinam	would that!
uxor, uxoris, f.	wife
valeo, ere, valui, valiturus	to be strong, well
varietas, varietatis, f.	variety
vasum, i, n.	vase
velo, are, avi, atus	to cover, wear a veil
veluti	as, just as
venatus, us, m.	hunting
vendo, vendere, vendidi, venditus	to sell
venio, ire, veni, ventus	come
venter, ventris, m.	stomach
verbosus, a, um	wordy
verbum, i, n.	word
vereor, eri, veritus sum	to fear
vero	truly
versiculus, i, m.	a single line
verto, ere, verti, versus	to turn

continues

continued

Latin	English
vester, vestra, vestrum	your (pl.)
vestigium, i, n.	track
vetustas, vetustatis, f.	old age
vetustus, a, um	old
via, ae, f.	road
victoria, ae, f.	victory
videtur	it seems
villa, villae, f.	house
vinco, ere, vici, victus	to conquer
vinculum, i, n.	chain
violentia, ae, f.	violence
vir, viri, m.	man
vita, vitae, f.	life
vivarium, vivarii, n.	fishpond
vivo, vivere, vixi, victus	to live
vix	scarcely
volo, volere, velle, volui	to want
vos	you (pl.)
vox, vocis, f.	voice
vultus, us, m.	countenance, face

English to Latin

English	Latin
abhor	abhorreo
about	de
above	super, supra
abstain	abstineo
absurd (adj.)	absurdus
accept	accipio
across	trans
act (n.)	actus
add	addo
add on	addicio
after	post, postquam
against	contra
agility	pernicitas
aid (n.)	auxilium
all	omnis
allow	licuit
alone	solus
(even) also	etiam
also	quoque
although, since, when	cum
although	quamquam
always	semper
ancestors	maiores
and	et
and (enclitic)	que
and so	itaque
angry	iratus
another	alius
anticipation	exspectatio
any	ullus
anyone	aliquis
apply	applico
as, just as	veluti
ask	quaero
at the home of	apud

continues

continued

English	Latin
at the same time, together	simul
at the same time, likewise	item
attach	applico
attack	invado
axe	bipennis
back	tergum
bad	malus
bald	glaber
band	manus
bath	balineum
be	esse
be able	possum
be absent	absum
be accustomed	soleo
be derelict	delinquo
be dumbfounded	stupeo
be quiet	taceo
be sad	doleo
be upset	commoveo
be well, be healthy	salveo
be well, be strong	valeo
bear (n.)	ursus
bear, carry	fero
bed	cubile
bee	apis
beet	beta
before	ante
began	coepi
begin	committo
behind the knee	poples
believe	credo
between	inter
beware	caveo
blame (n.)	culpa

English	Latin
body	corpus
bone	ossum
book	liber
born	natus
borrowed	mutuus
boxer	pugilis
boy	puer
branch	ramus
brave	fortis
breathe	spiro
bring back	refero
bring to	adduco
bring toward	affero
broken	mutilus
brother	frater
building	aedificium
bury	obruo
but	at
but	sed
buttock	clunis
by	a, ab
calamity	calamitas
call (v.)	appello
capture (v.)	capio
care (n.)	cura
care for	curo
carry	porto
carry away	deporto
catch hold of	arripio
cause (n.)	causa
cautious	cautus
cave man/woman	trogodyta
certain	quidam
chair	sella
chance	casus

continues

continued

English	Latin
chicken	pullus
choose	lego
circle (n.)	orbis
citizen	civis
city	urbs
clay	fictilis
climb up	ascendo
cloud	nimbus
cold	frigidus
come	venio
come upon, invent	invenio
coming together (n.)	conventus
common	communis
common people	plebs
companion	comes
complete (adj.)	absolutus
concerning	de
condition	condicio
conquer	vinco
consume	consumo
contract (n.)	dictum
cook (v.)	coquo
cook (n.)	coquus
cost	impensa
cost	sumptus
couch	lectus
countenance, face	vultus
cow	bos
create	creor
crime	scelus
cross (n.)	crux
crowd	turba
cry (v.)	lacrimo
custom	consuetudo
cut (v.)	caedo

English	Latin
cut down	accido
cut into	incido
daily	cotidie
daughter	filia
day	dies
death	mors
decide, be made	constituo
decide	statuo
decorate	orno
decree	decretum
deep	altus
deepest	imus
deer	cervus
delicious, pleasing	suavis
demand (v.)	exigo
demand, command (v.)	mando
destroy	deleo
diarrhea	diarroia (Greek)
die	exanimo
die	morior
dinner	cena
breakfast, lunch	prandium
discord	discordia
disgusting	turpis
dive	urino
diver	urinator
do	ago
do, make	facio
do not	noli
dog	canis
down from	de
draw, drag	traho
dress (n.)	stola
duty	officium

continues

continued

English	Latin
each, every	quisque
ear	auris
earrings	inaures
easy	facilis
eat, dine	prandeo
egg	ovum
eight	octo
either ... or	aut ... aut
elk	alces
equal	par
estate	fundus
estimate	aestimatio
even	etiam
ever	umquam
everywhere	ubique
except	praeter
except, make exception	excipio
exchange (v.)	permuto
eye	oculus
fall, happen (v.)	accido
fall (v.)	cado
fall, kill (v.)	concido
fall down, cut down	decido
fall down	procumbo
farmer	agricola
father	pater
fatherland	patria
fear	metus
fear (v.)	vereor
feed	alo
field	ager
fight (v.)	pugno
finish (v.)	perficio
first	primus

English	Latin
fish	pisces
fishpond	piscina
fishpond	vivarium
five	quinque
flow (v.)	fluo
fly about	convolo
follow	sequor
food	cibum
foot	pes
for	nam
for a long time	diu
for, on behalf of	pro
forehead	frons
foreign	alienus
form (n.)	forma
found	condo
four	quattuor
fourth	quartus
free	liber
free (v.)	libero
friend	amicus
frighten	terreo
garden	hortus
gentle	lenis
get up	sublevo
girl	puella
give	do
gnaw at, wear away	rodo
go	eo
go out	exeo
goat	caper
god	deus
goddess	dea
gold (n.)	aurum
good (adj.)	bonus

continues

continued

English	Latin
goose	anser
gentleman	lautus
grab	apprehendo
grass, greens	herba
grassy	herbosus
great	magnus
greatly	magnopere
guest	hospita
ham, thigh	perna
hand (n.)	manus
hand over	trado
hang	pendo
hanging	pensilis
happen	accido
happy	laetus
hard	durus
have	habeo
he, she, it	is, ea, id
head	caput
hear	audio
help	adiuvo
helper	adiutrix
herbs, greens	helvella
here	hic
high, deep	altus
high, lofty, tall	excelsus
higher	superior
his, her	eius
hold	teneo
hope	spero
horn	cornu
horse	equus
hour	hora
house, home	domus

English	Latin
house	villa
how	quo modo
how many	quot
how much	quantus
humble	humilis
hundred	centum
hunting	venatus
I	ego
if	si
immediately	statim
immediately afterward	subinde
improve appearance	mangonico
in order that	ut
in such a way	ita
in, on	in
include	includo
invite	invito
iron (n.)	ferrum
island	insula
joint	articulus
jump	salio
jump down	desilio
just as, as	sicut
keep safe	tutor
kernel	nucleus
kill, cut	caedo
kill, fall	concido
kind, humane	humanus
king	rex
knock down	affligo
knot	nodus
know	intellego
know	scio
knowledge	intellegentia
known	notus

continues

continued

English	Latin
land (n.)	terra
large	amplus
last (adj.)	extremus
laugh (v.)	rideo
law	lex
lead (v.)	duco
leader	dux
leave behind	relinquo
leave, set out	proficiscor
left (not right; direction)	sinister
leg	crus
leisure	otium
letter	epistula
life	vita
line (n.)	agmen
listen	audio
little	paulo
live, dwell	habito
live	vivo
load, burden	onus
long	longus
long-nosed	nasutus
look at	specto
love	amo
lower	inferior
lying across	transversus
make	facio
make a plan	capio consilium
male	mas
man	homo
man	vir
marrow	malva
meanwhile	interea
meat	caro

English	Latin
member	membrum
merchandise	merx
middle of	medius
mind (n.)	animus
mischief	fraus
money	pecunia
moon	luna
moray eel	muraena
more	magis
moreover	autem
morning	mane
mother	mater
mother-in-law	hecyra
mouth	os
move, yield	cedo
move	moveo
much, many	multus
mushroom	fungus
my, mine	meus
name (v.)	appello
name (n.)	nomen
near (adv.)	ad
near (adj.)	prope
necessary	necesse
nerve	nervus
net	rete
never	numquam
nevertheless	tamen
new	novus
next to	propinquus
night	nox
nine	novem
no one	nemo
noble	nobilis
noise	clamor

continues

275

continued

English	Latin
noise	strepitus
none	nullus
nose	nasus
not	non
not want	nolo
nothing	nihil
notice	animadverto
now, already	iam
now	nunc
obligate	obligo
often	saepe
old	vetustus
old age	vetustas
omit, pass over	praetereo
on account of	propter
once upon a time	olim
one	unus
only	modo
order	iubeo
other	ceterus
our	noster
out of	e, ex
outer	exterus
outside	foras
own	suus
ox	bos
oyster	ostrea
palm	palma
part (n.)	pars
party (n.)	convivum
pay out	appendo
peace	pax
pearl	margarita

English	Latin
penalty	poena
people	populus
perhaps	fortasse
place (n.)	locus
plan (n.)	consilium
plant, press	stipo
play (v.)	ludo
pleasant	iucundus
please (v.)	placeo
pleasing	placatus
pour out	diffundo
prepare	paro
pretend	dissimulo
price	pretium
priest	sacerdos
private	privatus
privately	privatim
promise	polliceor
public	publicus
put down	opprimo
put, place	pono
queen	regina
quiet	quies
(it) rains	pluit
read	lego
recline	reclino
reject	reicio
rejoice	gaudeo
remain	maneo
remain	remaneo
respond	respondeo
(the) rest of	reliquus
retreat (n.)	se recipio
rich	dis

continues

continued

English	Latin
right (not left)	dexter
right, just	ius
river	flumen
road	via
root (n.)	radix
rumor	rumor
sad	tristis
said	inquit
salt	sal
same	idem
sand	harena
say	dico
scarcely	vix
school, game	ludus
sea	mare
season	condio
see	conspicio
seek, beg, attack	peto
seems	videtur
self	ipse
self (third-person reflexive pronoun)	se
sell	vendo
send	mitto
seven	septem
shape (n.)	figura
sharp, harsh	asper
sharp	praeacutus
shell	concha
ship	navis
shop, bar	taberna
short	brevis
shout	clamo
shrink back	abhorreo
sight, appearance	species

English	Latin
silence	silentium
similar	similis
simple life	litoteta (Greek)
since	cum
sing	canto
single	singulus
single line	versiculus
sister	soror
sit	sedeo
six	sex
size	magnitudo
skilled	sollertius
skin, hide (n.)	pellis
sky	caelum
slave	servus
sleep (v.)	dormio
sleep (n.)	somnus
slow down	tardo
small	parvus
so	tam
so great	tantus
soldier	miles
someone	aliquis
son	filius
soon	mox
soothe	sedo
soul	animus
speak	loquor
special	praecipuus
stand (v.)	sto
stand out	exsisto
star	astrum
state (n.)	civitas
stole, cloak	palla
stomach	venter
stone	lapis

continues

continued

English	Latin
stop (v.)	consisto
story	fabula
straight	derectus
straighten out	erigo
strong	fortis
suddenly	subito
suffer	patior
sumptuary; having to do with excessive spending	sumptuarius
surpass	antecedo
surpass	supero
sweet	dulcis
sweet, gentle	mitis
swift	celer
(very) swift	praeceler
table	mensa
tail	cauda
take charge of	praesto
take on	recipio
taken down	deceptus
teacher	magister
tell, narrate	narro
ten	decem
than	quam
that	ille
the other	alter
then, next	deinde
then	tum
therefore	igitur
thigh	femur
thing	res
think up	excogito
this	hic, haec, hoc
thousand	mille

English	Latin
through	per
throw	iacio
thus	sic
tightrope walker	funambulus
time	tempus
tired	defessus
to me	mihi
to such a degree	adeo
to that place	istuc
today	hodie
tooth	dens
so many	tot
toward	ad
track (n)	vestigium
tree	arbor
truly	vero
turn (v.)	verto
two	duo
under	sub
unfair	iniquus
until	donec
uproot	subruo
variety	varietas
very	ipse
victory	victoria
violence	violentia
voice	vox
wage	gero
walk	ambulo
wander	palor
want	volo
war	bellum
warm	calidus

continues

continued

English	Latin
warn, admonish	admoneo
warn	moneo
wash	lavo
water	aqua
wave	unda
way	modus
way, journey	iter
weakened	infirmus
wear	gero
wear a veil	velo
weep	fleo
weigh out	appendo
weight	pondus
what kind of	qualis
when, since, although	cum
when	quando
when, where	ubi
whence	unde
where, when	ubi
while	dum
who, which	qui
who, pray?	quinam
who?	quis
whoever you want	quisvis
whole	totus
wide	latus
wife	uxor
wise	sapiens
without	sine
wolf	lupus
woman	femina
woman	mulier
wonder	miror
wonderful	mirus
wool	lana

English	Latin
word	verbum
wordy	verbosus
work (n.)	industria
work (v.)	laboro
work (n.)	opus
world	mundus
would that!	utinam
wretched, miserable	miser
write	scrībo
yield	cedo
you (pl.)	vos
you (s.)	tu
your (pl.)	vester
your (s.)	tuus

Grammar Summary

This appendix provides all the grammar forms you will encounter in translating Latin. The "A Brief Summary of Syntax" section shows you how to use those forms to form sentences.

Forms

When you see an unfamiliar form of a Latin word, you can refer to this section for the case and number of a noun, or person, or number, tense, voice, or mood of a verb.

Nouns—First Declension

Nouns of the first declension are feminine except nouns denoting men. Some dative and ablative plurals are *abus,* for example, *filiabus, deabus.*

aqua, ae, f. ("water")

Case	Singular	Plural
Nominative	aqua	aquae
Genitive	aquae	aquarum
Dative	aquae	aquis
Accusative	aquam	aquas
Ablative	aqua	aquis
Vocative	aqua	aquae

Nouns—Second Declension

Nouns of the second declension that end in *us, er,* or *r* are masculine. Those ending in *um* are neuter.

lectus, i, m. ("bed")

Case	Singular	Plural
Nominative	lectus	lecti
Genitive	lecti	lectorum
Dative	lecto	lectis
Accusative	lectum	lectos
Ablative	lecto	lectis
Vocative	lecte	lecti

filius, i, m. ("son")

Case	Singular	Plural
Nominative	filius	filii
Genitive	fili	filiorum
Dative	filio	filiis
Accusative	filium	filios
Ablative	filio	filiis
Vocative	fili	filii

Irregular

deus, i, m. ("god")

Case	Singular	Plural
Nominative	deus	dei, dii, di
Genitive	dei	deorum, deum
Dative	deo	deis, diis, dis
Accusative	deum	deos
Ablative	deo	deis, diis, dis

dictum, i, n. ("saying")

Case	Singular	Plural
Nominative	dictum	dicta
Genitive	dicti	dictorum

Case	Singular	Plural
Dative	dicto	dictis
Accusative	dictum	dicta
Ablative	dicto	dictis

After the first century, Latin has been using the double *i* for the genitive singular. Generally in the times before Cicero the genitive had one *i*.

The vocative of a noun ending in *ius* ends with *i*.

Nouns—Third Declension

Some third-declension nouns have an *i* before the genitive plural and some neuter endings. These are called i stems.

mater, matris, f. ("mother")

Case	Singular	Plural
Nominative	mater	matres
Genitive	matris	matrum
Dative	matri	matribus
Accusative	matrem	matres
Ablative	matre	matribus

corpus, corporis, n. ("body")

Case	Singular	Plural
Nominative	corpus	corpora
Genitive	corporis	corporum
Dative	corpori	corporibus
Accusative	corpus	corpora
Ablative	copore	corporibus

Note: The nominative and accusative neuter forms are always the same.

Third-Declension i Stems: Masculine and Feminine

urbs, urbis, f. ("city")

Case	Singular	Plural
Nominative	urbs	urbes
Genitive	urbis	urbium
Dative	urbi	urbibus
Accusative	urbem	urbes(is)
Ablative	urbe	urbibus

Third-Declension i Stems: Neuter

mare, maris, n. ("sea")

Case	Singular	Plural
Nominative	mare	maria
Genitive	maris	marium
Dative	mari	maribus
Accusative	mare	maria
Ablative	mari	maribus

Nouns—Fourth Declension

In the fourth declension, nouns ending in *us* are masculine and those ending in *u* are neuter—except for *manus* and *domus,* which are feminine.

senatus, us, m. ("senate")

Case	Singular	Plural
Nominative	senatus	senatus
Genitive	senatus	senatuum
Dative	senatui	senatibus
Accusative	senatum	senatus
Ablative	senatu	senatibus

cornu, cornus, n. ("horn")

Case	Singular	Plural
Nominative	cornu	cornua
Genitive	cornus	cornuum
Dative	cornu	cornibus
Accusative	cornu	cornua
Ablative	cornu	cornibus

Irregular

domus, us, f. ("house, home")

Case	Singular	Plural
Nominative	domus	domus
Genitive	domus (i)	domuum (orum)
Dative	domui (o)	domibus
Accusative	domum	domos (us)
Ablative	domo (u)	domibus

Nouns—Fifth Declension

Fifth-declension nouns are feminine—except *dies,* which is masculine.

res, rei, f. ("thing")

Case	Singular	Plural
Nominative	res	res
Genitive	rei	rerum
Dative	rei	rebus
Accusative	rem	res
Ablative	re	rebus

Adjectives—First and Second Declensions

These adjective endings are similar to the nouns of the first and second declensions.

altus, a, um ("high, deep")

Case	Singular Masc.	Fem.	Neut.	Plural Masc.	Fem.	Neut.
Nominative	altus	alta	altum	alti	altae	alta
Genitive	alti	altae	alti	altorum	altarum	altorum
Dative	alto	altae	alto	altis	altis	altis
Accusative	altum	altam	altum	altos	altas	alta
Ablative	alto	alta	alto	altis	altia	altis

Adjectives—Third Declension (Three Endings)

Third-declension adjectives are similar to the third-declension i-stem noun (exception: ablative singular).

acer, ris, re ("sharp")

Case	Singular Masc.	Fem.	Neut.	Plural Masc.	Fem.	Neut.
Nominative	acer	acris	acre	acres	acres	acria
Genitive	acris	acris	acris	acrium	acrium	acrium
Dative	acri	acri	acri	acribus	acribus	acribus
Accusative	acrem	acrem	acre	acres	acres	acria
Ablative	acri	acri	acri	acribus	acribus	acribus

Adjectives—Third Declension (Two Endings)

For these adjectives, the nominative and feminine singular have the same endings.

omnis, omne ("all")

Case	Singular Masc.	Fem.	Neut.	Plural Masc.	Fem.	Neut.
Nominative	omnis	omnis	omne	omnes	omnes	omnia
Genitive	omnis	omnis	omnis	omnium	omnium	omnium

Case	Singular Masc.	Fem.	Neut.	Plural Masc.	Fem.	Neut.
Dative	omni	omni	omni	omnibus	omnibus	omnibus
Accusative	omnem	omnem	omne	omnes	omnes	acria
Ablative	omni	omni	omni	omnibus	omnibus	omnibus

Adjectives—Third Declension (One Ending)

For these adjectives, there is only one nominative singular form.

potens, potentis ("powerful")

Case	Singular Masc.	Fem.	Neut.	Plural Masc.	Fem.	Neut.
Nominative	potens	potens	potens	potentes	potentes	potentia
Genitive	potentis	potentis	potentis	potentium	potentium	potentium
Dative	potenti	potenti	potentibus	potentibus	potentibus	potentibus
Accusative	potentem	potentem	potens	potentes	potentes	potentia
Ablative	potenti	potenti	potenti	potentibus	potentibus	potentibus

Note: The present participle is declined like *potens* but has the ablative singular *e*.

Irregular Adjectives

ullus, a, um ("any")

Case	Singular Masc.	Fem.	Neut.	Plural Masc.	Fem.	Neut.
Nominative	ullus	ulla	ullum	ulli	ullae	ulla
Genitive	ullius	ullius	ullius	ullorum	ullarum	ullorulm
Dative	ulli	ulli	ulli	ullis	ullis	ullis
Accusative	ullum	ullam	ullum	ullos	ullas	ulla
Ablative	ullo	ulla	ullo	ullis	ullis	ullis

Note: Other irregular adjectives similarly declined are *alius, alter, neuter, nullus, totu, uter,* and *uterque.*

Adjectives—Comparison of Adjectives

The comparative forms are declined like third-declension nouns. Superlative forms are declined like first- and second-declension adjectives.

Regular

Positive	Comparative	Superlative
altus, a, um	altior, altius	altissimus, a, um
turpis, e	turpior, turpius	turpissimus, a,um
miser, era, erum	miserior, miserius	miserrimus, a, um
acer, ris, re	acrior, acrius	acerrimus, a, um
facilis, e	facilior, facilius	facillimus, a, um

Note: Adjectives ending in *er* have the *errimus* ending in the superlative.

Five adjectives ending in *lis* have *limus* in the superlative: *facilis, difficilis, similis, dissimilis,* and *humilis.*

Irregular

Positive	Comparative	Superlative
bonus ("good")	melior ("better")	optimus ("best")
malus ("bad")	peior ("worse")	pessimus ("worst")
magnus ("great")	maior ("greater")	maximus ("greatest")
parvus ("small")	minor ("smaller")	minimus ("smallest")
multus ("many")	plus ("more")	plurimus ("most")

Declension of Comparatives

| | Singular | | Plural | |
	Masc. and Fem.	Neut.	Masc. and Fem.	Neut.
Nominative	peior ("worse")	peius	peiores	peiora
Genitive	peioris	peioris	peiorum	peiorum
Dative	peiori	peiori	peioribus	peioribus
Accusative	peiorem	peius	peiores	peiora
Ablative	peiore	peiore	peioribus	peioribus

Adverbs—Comparison of Adverbs

Positive	Comparative	Superlative
alte	altius	altissime
misere	miserius	miserrime
fortiter	fortius	fortissime
facile	facilius	facillime

Numerals

Only *unus, duo, tres,* and *mille* are declined. All other numbers have only one form.

Declension of Numerals

unus, a, um ("one")

Case	Masc.	Fem.	Neut.
Nominative	unus	una	unum
Genitive	unius	unius	unius
Dative	uni	uni	uni
Accusative	unum	unam	unum
Ablative	uno	una	uno

duo ("two")

Case	Masc.	Fem.	Neut.
Nominative	duo	duae	duo
Genitive	duorum	duarum	duorum
Dative	duobus	duabus	duobus
Accusative	duos,duo	duas	duo
Ablative	duobus	duabus	duobus

tres ("three")

Case	Masc.	Fem.	Neut.
Nominative	tres	tres	tria
Genitive	trium	trium	trium
Dative	tribus	tribus	tribus
Accusative	tres	tres	tria
Ablative	tribus	tribus	tribus

mille ("one thousand")

Case	Singular (adjective)	Plural (noun)
Nominative	mille	milia
Genitive	mille	milium
Dative	mille	milibus
Accusative	mille	milia
Ablative	mille	milibus

Personal Pronouns

Remember that pronouns do not modify. Personal pronouns take the place of a person.

Case	First-Person Singular	First-Person Plural
Nominative	ego ("I")	nos ("we")
Genitive	mei ("of me")	nostrum or nostri ("of us")
Dative	mihi ("to me")	nobis ("to us")
Accusative	me ("me")	nos ("us")
Ablative	me ("by me")	nobis ("by us")

Case	Second-Person Singular	Second-Person Plural
Nominative	tu	vos
Genitive	tui	vestrum, vestri
Dative	tibi	vobis
Accusative	te	vos
Ablative	te	vobis

Case	Third-Person Singular (Reflexive)	Third-Person Plural (Reflexive)
Nominative	—	—
Genitive	sui	sui
Dative	sibi	sibi
Accusative	se *or* sese	se *or* sese
Ablative	se *or* sese	se *or* sese

Demonstrative Pronouns/Adjectives

When a demonstrative word modifies another word, it is an adjective ("this"). When it stands alone, it is a pronoun ("he," "she," or "it").

hic, haec, hoc ("this")

| Case | Singular | | | Plural | | |
	Masc.	Fem.	Neut.	Masc.	Fem.	Neut.
Nominative	hic	haec	hoc	hi	hae	haec
Genitive	huius	huius	huius	horum	harum	horum
Dative	huic	huic	huic	his	his	his
Accusative	hunc	hanc	hoc	hos	has	haec
Ablative	hoc	hac	hoc	his	his	his

ille, illa, illu ("that")

| Case | Singular | | | Plural | | |
	Masc.	Fem.	Neut.	Masc.	Fem.	Neut.
Nominative	ille	illa	illud	illi	illae	illa
Genitive	illius	illius	illius	illorum	illarum	illorum
Dative	illi	illi	illi	illis	illis	illis
Accusative	illum	illam	illud	illos	illas	illa
Ablative	illo	illa	illo	illis	illis	illis

is, ea, id ("this, that")

Case	Singular Masc.	Fem.	Neut.	Plural Masc.	Fem.	Neut.
Nominative	is	ea	id	ei	eae	ea
Genitive	eius	eius	eius	eorum	earum	eorum
Dative	ei	ei	ei	eis	eis	eis
Accusative	eum	eam	id	eos	eas	ea
Ablative	eo	ea	eo	eis	eis	eis

Relative Pronouns

The interrogative adjective looks exactly like the relative pronoun. For example, *Qui deus?* ("What god?").

qui, quae, quod ("who, which, what")

Case	Singular Masc.	Fem.	Neut.	Plural Masc.	Fem.	Neut.
Nominative	qui	quae	quod	qui	quae	quae
Genitive	cuius	cuius	cuius	quorum	quarum	quorum
Dative	cui	cui	cui	quibus	quibus	quibus
Accusative	quem	quam	quod	quos	quas	quae
Ablative	quo	qua	quo	quibus	quibus	quibus

Interrogative Pronouns

The plural of the interrogative pronoun has the same endings as the plural of the relative pronoun.

quis, quid ("who, what")

Case	Singular Masc.	Fem.	Neut.	Plural Masc.	Fem.	Neut.
Nominative	quis	quis	quid	qui	quae	quae
Genitive	cuius	cuius	cuius	quorum	quarum	quorum

Case	Singular Masc.	Fem.	Neut.	Plural Masc.	Fem.	Neut.
Dative	cui	cui	cui	quibus	quibus	quibus
Accusative	quem	quem	quid	quos	quas	quae
Ablative	quo	quo	quo	quibus	quibus	quibus

Regular Verbs

First Conjugation

Principal parts: *amo, amare, amavi, amatus.*

Stems: *ama, amav, amat.*

Indicative

Tense	Active Voice Singular	Plural	Passive Voice Singular	Plural
Present	amo ("I love")	amamus	amor ("I am loved")	amamur
	amas	amatis	amaris	amamini
	amat	amant	amatur	amantur
Imperfect	amabam ("I was loving")	amabamus	amabar ("I was being loved")	amabamur
	amabas	amabatis	amabaris	amabamini
	amabat	amabant	amabatur	amabantur
Future	amabo ("I will love")	amabimus	amabor ("I will be loved")	amabimur
	amabis	amabitis	amaberis	amabimini
	amabit	amabunt	amabitur	amabuntur
Present Perfect	amavi ("I loved")	amavimus	amatus sum ("I have been loved")	amati sumus
	amavisti	amavistis	amatus es	amati estis
	amavit	amaverunt	amatus est	amati sunt
Past Perfect (Pluperfect)	amaveram ("I had loved")	amaveramus	amatus eram ("I had been loved")	amati eramus
	amaveras	amaveratis	amatus eras	amati eratis
	amaverat	amaverant	amatus erat	amati erant

continues

Indicative (continued)

Tense	Active Voice Singular	Active Voice Plural	Passive Voice Singular	Passive Voice Plural
Future Perfect	amavero ("I will have loved")	amaverimus	amatus ero ("I will have been loved")	amati erimus
	amaveris	amaveritis	amatus eris	amati eritis
	amaverit	amaverint	amatus erit	amati erunt

Note: The participle will agree with the subject in number and gender. Alternate endings are *i, ae, a, us, a,* and *um.*

Subjunctive

Tense	Active Voice Singular	Active Voice Plural	Passive Voice Singular	Passive Voice Plural
Present	amem	amemus	amer	amemur
	ames	ametis	ameris	amemini
	amet	ament	ametur	amentur
Imperfect	amarem	amaremus	amarer	amaremur
	amares	amaretis	amareris	amaremini
	amaret	amarent	amaretur	amarentur
Present Perfect	amaverim	amaverimus	amatus sim	amati simus
	amaveris	amaveritis	amatus sis	amati sitis
	amaverit	amaverint	amatus sit	amati sint
Past Perfect (Pluperfect)	amavissem	amavissemus	amatus essem	amati essemus
	amavisses	amavissetis	amatus esses	amati essetis
	amavisset	amavissent	amatus esset	amati essent

Imperative

Tense	Active Voice		Passive Voice	
	Singular	**Plural**	**Singular**	**Plural**
Present ("Love!" "Be loved!")	ama	amate	amare	amamini
Future	amato	amatote		

Infinitive

Tense	Active Voice	Passive Voice
Present	amare ("to love")	amari ("to be loved")
Perfect	amavisse ("to have loved")	amatus esse ("to have been loved")
Future	amaturus esse ("to be about to love")	amatus iri ("to be about to be loved")

Participles

Tense	Active Voice	Passive Voice
Present	amans ("loving")	—
Perfect	—	amatus ("having been loved")
Future	amaturus ("about to love")	amandus, a, um ("about to be loved")

Second Conjugation

Principal parts: *moneo, ere, monui, monitum* ("to warn").

Stems: *mone, monu, monit.*

Indicative

	Active Voice		Passive Voice	
Tense	Singular	Plural	Singular	Plural
Present	moneo	monemus	moneor	monemur
	mones	monetis	moneris	monemini
	monet	monent	monetur	monentur
Imperfect	monebam	monebamus	monebar	monebamur
	monebas	monebatis	monebaris	monebamini
	monebat	monebant	monebatur	monebantur
Future	monebo	monebimus	monebor	monebimur
	monebis	monebitis	moneberis	monebimini
	monebit	monebunt	monebitur	monebuntur
Present Perfect	monui	monuimus	monitus sum	moniti sumus
	monuisti	monuistis	monitus es	moniti estis
	monuit	monuerunt	monitus est	moniti sunt
Past Perfect (Pluperfect)	monueram	monueramus	monitus eram	moniti eramus
	monueras	monueratis	monitus eras	moniti eratis
	monuerat	monuerant	monitus erat	moniti erant
Future Perfect	monuero	monuerimus	monitus ero	monitus erimus
	monueris	monueritis	monitus eris	monitus eritis
	monuerit	monuerint	monitus erit	monitus erunt

Subjunctive

	Active Voice		Passive Voice	
Tense	Singular	Plural	Singular	Plural
Present	moneam	moneamus	monear	moneamur
	moneas	moneatis	monearis	moneamini
	moneat	moneant	moneatur	moneantur

Tense	Active Voice		Passive Voice	
	Singular	**Plural**	**Singular**	**Plural**
Imperfect	monerem	moneremus	monerer	moneremur
	moneres	moneretis	monereris	moneremini
	moneret	monerent	moneretur	monerentur
Present Perfect	monuerim	monuerimus	monitus sim	moniti simus
	monueris	monueritis	monitus sis	moniti sitis
	monuerit	monuerint	monitus sit	moniti sint
Past Perfect (Pluperfect)	monuissem	monuissemus	monitus esse	moniti essemus
	monuisses	monuissetis	monitus esses	moniti essetis
	monuisset	monuissent	monitus esse	moniti essent

Imperative

Tense	Active Voice		Passive Voice	
	Singular	**Plural**	**Singular**	**Plural**
Present	mone	monete	monere	monemini

Infinitive

Tense	Active Voice	Passive Voice
Present	monere	moneri
Perfect	monuisse	monitus esse
Future	moniturus esse	monitum iri

Participles

Tense	Active Voice	Passive Voice
Present	monens	—
Perfect	moniturus	monendus
Future	—	monitus

Third Conjugation

Principal parts: *mitto, mittere, misi, missus.*

Stems: *mitt, mis, miss.*

Indicative

Tense	Active Voice Singular	Plural	Passive Voice Singular	Plural
Present	mitto	mittimus	mittor	mittimur
	mittis	mittitis	mitteris	mittimini
	mittit	mittunt	mittitur	mittuntur
Imperfect	mittebam	mittebamus	mittebar	mittebamur
	mittebas	mittebatis	mittebaris	mittebamini
	mittebat	mittebant	mittebatur	mittebantur
Future	mittam	mittemus	mittar	mittemur
	mittes	mittetis	mitteris	mittemini
	mittet	mittent	mittetur	mittentur
Present Perfect	misi	misimus	missus sum	missi sumus
	misisti	misistis	missus es	missi estis
	misuit	miserunt	missus est	missi sunt
Past Perfect (Pluperfect)	miseram	miseramus	missus eram	missi eramus
	miseras	miseratis	missus eras	missi eratis
	miserat	miserant	missus erat	missi erant
Future Perfect	misero	miserimus	missus ero	missi erimus
	miseris	miseritis	missus eris	missi eritis
	miserit	miserint	missus erit	missi erunt

Subjunctive

Tense	Active Voice Singular	Plural	Passive Voice Singular	Plural
Present	mittam	mittamus	mittar	mittamur
	mittas	mittatis	mittaris	mittamini
	mittat	mittant	mittatur	mittantur

Tense	Active Voice		Passive Voice	
	Singular	**Plural**	**Singular**	**Plural**
Imperfect	mitterem	mitteremus	mitterer	mitteremur
	mitteres	mitteretis	mittereris	mitteremini
	mitteret	mitterent	mitteretur	mitterentur
Present Perfect	miserim	miserimus	missus sim	missi simus
	miseris	miseritis	missus sis	missi sitis
	miserit	miserint	missus sit	missi sint
Past Perfect (Pluperfect)	misissem	misissemus	missus esse	missi essemus
	misisses	misissetis	missus esses	missi essetis
	misiset	misissent	missus esse	missi essent

Imperative

Tense	Active Voice		Passive Voice	
	Singular	**Plural**	**Singular**	**Plural**
Present	mitte	mittete	mittere	mittemini

Infinitive

Tense	Active	Passive
Present	mittere	mitti
Perfect	misisse	missus esse
Future	missurus esse	missum iri

Participles

Tense	Active	Passive
Present	mittens	—
Perfect	missurus	missus
Future	—	mittendus

Third Conjugation io and Fourth Conjugation

Principal parts: *capio, capere, cepi, captus.*

Stems: *capi, cep, capt.*

Indicative

Tense	Active Voice		Passive Voice	
	Singular	**Plural**	**Singular**	**Plural**
Present	capio	capimus	capior	capimur
	capis	capitis	capieris	capimini
	capit	capiunt	capitur	capiuntur
Imperfect	capiebam	capiebamus	capiebar	capiebamur
	capiebas	capiebatis	capiebaris	capiebamini
	capiebat	capiebant	capiebatur	capiebantur
Future	capiam	capiemus	capiar	capiemur
	capies	capietis	capieris	capiemini
	capiet	capient	capietur	capientur
Present Perfect	cepi	cepimus	captus sum	capti sumus
	cepisti	cepistis	captus es	capti estis
	cepit	ceperunt	captus est	capti sunt
Past Perfect (Pluperfect)	ceperam	ceperamus	captus eram	capti eramus
	ceperas	ceperatis	captus eras	capti eratis
	ceperat	ceperant	captus erat	capti erant
Future Perfect	cepero	ceperimus	captus ero	capti erimus
	ceperis	ceperitis	captus eris	capti eritis
	ceperit	ceperint	captus erit	capti erunt

Subjunctive

Tense	Active Voice		Passive Voice	
	Singular	**Plural**	**Singular**	**Plural**
Present	capiam	capiamus	capiar	capiamur
	capias	capiatis	capiaris	capiamini
	capiat	capiant	capiatur	capiantur
Imperfect	caperem	caperemus	caperer	caperemur
	caperes	caperetis	capereris	caperemini
	caperet	caperent	caperetur	caperentur

Tense	Active Voice		Passive Voice	
	Singular	**Plural**	**Singular**	**Plural**
Present Perfect	ceperim	ceperimus	captus sim	capti simus
	ceperis	ceperitis	captus sis	capti sitis
	ceperit	ceperint	captus sit	capti sint
Past Perfect (Pluperfect)	cepissem	cepissemus	captus esse	capti essemus
	cepisses	cepissetis	captus esses	capti essetis
	cepisset	cepissent	captus esse	capti essent

Imperative

Tense	Active Voice		Passive Voice	
	Singular	**Plural**	**Singular**	**Plural**
Present	cape	capite	capieris	capiemini

Note: The fourth-conjugation present passive infinitive is *iri;* for example, *muniri* ("to be fortified").

Infinitive

Tense	Active Voice	Passive Voice
Present	capere	capi
Perfect	cepisse	captus esse
Future	capturus esse	captum iri

Irregular Verbs

Irregular verbs often have different endings in the present and imperfect tenses.

Principal parts: *sum, esse, fui, futurus* ("to be").

Indicative

Present		Imperfect		Future	
Singular	**Plural**	**Singular**	**Plural**	**Singular**	**Plural**
sum	sumus	eram	eramus	ero	erimus
es	estis	eras	eratis	eris	eritis
est	sunt	erat	erant	erit	erunt

Note: Other tenses are formed regularly. For example:

fui	fuimus
fuisti	fuistis
fuit	fuerunt

Subjunctive

Present	
Singular	**Plural**
sim	simus
sis	sitis
sit	sint

Note: All other tenses are formed regularly. For example:

essem	essemus
esses	essetis
esset	essent

Imperative

Present: *es, este.*

Future: *esto, estote.*

Principal parts: *possum, posse, potui* ("to be able").

Present Indicative		Present Subjunctive	
Singular	**Plural**	**Singular**	**Plural**
possum	possumus	possim	possimus
potes	potestis	possis	possitis
potest	possunt	possit	possint

Note: All other forms are regular.

Principal parts: *fero, ferre, tuli, latus* ("to carry").

Indicative

Present Tense

Active Voice		Passive Voice	
Singular	**Plural**	**Singular**	**Plural**
fero	ferimus	feror	ferimur
fers	fertis	ferris	ferimini
fert	ferunt	fertur	feruntur

Note: All other forms are regular.

Principal parts: *eo, ire, ivi* or *ii, iturus* ("to go").

Present Tense

Indicative		Subjunctive	
Singular	**Plural**	**Singular**	**Plural**
eo	imus	eam	eamus
is	itis	eas	eatis
it	eunt	eat	eant

Principal parts: *fio, fiere, factus sum* ("to be made").

Present Indicative (Active Voice)

Singular	**Plural**
fio	fimus
fis	fitis
fit	fiunt

Note: All other forms of this verb are regular.

Indicative (Active Voice)

Tense	Singular	Plural
Imperfect	ibam	ibamus
	ibas	ibatis
	ibat	ibant
Future	ibo	ibimus
	ibis	ibitis
	Ibit	ibunt

Volo

Principal parts: *volo, velle, volui* ("to wish, want").

Indicative

Tense	Singular	Plural
Present	volo	volumus
	vis	vultis
	vult	volunt

Subjunctive

Tense	Singular	Plural
Present	velim	velimus
	velis	velitis
	velint	velint

Note: All other forms are regular.

Nolo

Principal parts: *nolo, nelle, nolui* (" to be unwilling").

Indicative

Tense	Singular	Plural
Present	nolo	nolumus
	non vis	non vultis
	non vult	nolunt

Subjunctive

Tense	Singular	Plural
Present	nolim	nolimus
	nolis	nolitis
	nolit	nolint

Note: All other tenses are regular.

Malo

Principal parts: *malo, malle, malui* ("to prefer").

Indicative

Tense	Singular	Plural
Present	malo	malumus
	mavis	mavultis
	mavult	malunt

Subjunctive

Tense	Singular	Plural
Present	malim	malimus
	malis	malitis
	malit	malint

Note: All other tenses are regular.

A Brief Summary of Syntax

A full explanation of syntax and examples can be found in the chapters indicated in the next section.

Nouns

➤ An appositive is in the same case as the noun it describes. (Chapter 19)

➤ An adjective agrees with the noun it modifies in number, gender, and case. (Chapter 7)

➤ An adjective can be used as a noun. (Chapter 7)

➤ The relative pronoun agrees with its antecedent in number and gender, but takes its case depending on its use in its own clause. (Chapter 13)

➤ A relative pronoun can be used at the beginning of a sentence as a conjunction. (Chapter 13)

➤ The reflexive pronoun usually refers to the subject of the clause in which it appears. (Chapter 8)

➤ The subject of a verb is in the nominative case. (Chapter 3)

➤ A predicate noun or adjective is in the nominative case. (Chapter 3)

➤ The person or thing directly addressed is in the vocative case. (Chapter 19)

➤ The genitive case is used to show possession. (Chapter 3)

➤ The genitive case is translated using *of* or *'s*. (Chapter 3)

➤ The dative case is used for the indirect object. (Chapter 9)

➤ The dative case is used with verbs *favor, help, please, trust, believe, persuade, command, obey,* and the like. (Chapter 9)

➤ The dative case is used with *sum* to show possession and to emphasize personal interest, as in *Est mihi cura* ("It is a care of mine"). (Chapter 9)

➤ The accusative case is used for the direct object. (Chapter 7)

➤ The subject of the infinitive in an indirect statement is in the accusative case. (Chapter 16)

➤ The accusative case shows duration of time or extent of space. (Chapter 19)

➤ The accusative is used as the object of many prepositions. (Chapter 11)

➤ The accusative is used with prepositions *ad* and *in* to show motion toward. (Chapter 11)

➤ Exclamations use the accusative case. (Chapter 11)

➤ The ablative case is used to show from, with, when, or where. (Chapter 9)

➤ The ablative case is used with the passive voice and preposition *ab* to show personal agent. (Chapter 5)

➤ The ablative case without a preposition shows means or instrument by which something is done. (Chapter 19)

➤ The ablative is used to show cause. (Chapter 19)

➤ The ablative is used with many prepositions. (Chapter 11)

➤ The ablative absolute construction is in the ablative case (duh!). (Chapter 12)

➤ With Latin words for "town"—*domus* and *rus*—the locative case shows the location. This is the singular of the first- and second-declension genitive. (Chapter 9)

Verbs

➤ The present tense represents an action going on in the present. (Chapter 5)

➤ The imperfect tense denotes continued or repeated action in the past. (Chapter 10)

➤ The future tense represents an action in the future. (Chapter 10)

➤ The present perfect tense represents action that has been completed or is being completed at the time of speaking. (Chapter 10)

➤ The past perfect tense denotes an act completed in the past before another act was begun. (Chapter 10)

➤ The future perfect tense denotes action as completed by a certain moment in the future. (Chapter 10)

➤ The indicative mood is used to express a fact. (Chapter 14)

➤ The subjunctive mood can be used to represent an idea as willed. The present subjunctive is used, and the negative is *ne*. (Chapter 14)

➤ Purpose clauses introduced by *ut* take the subjunctive mood. The negative is *ne*. (Chapter 14)

➤ Verbs of fearing are followed by the subjunctive introduced by *ut* ("that, lest") or *ne* ("that not"). (Chapter 14)

➤ Result clauses introduced by *ut* take the subjunctive. The negative is *ut non*. (Chapter 14)

➤ *Cum* ("when, since, although") is followed by the subjunctive. (Chapter 14)

➤ Noun clauses in indirect statement, indirect questions, causal clauses, or conditional clauses are all in the subjunctive. (Chapter 16)

➤ The infinitive can be used as the subject of a verb. (Chapter 6)

➤ The infinitive is used after verbs like *say, know, think, tell,* and *perceive*. (Chapter 6)

311

➤ The imperative mood is used to give commands. (Chapter 10)

➤ A participle is a verbal adjective and must agree with the noun it modifies in number, gender, and case. (Chapters 6 and 10)

➤ The future passive participle and the verb *to be* are used to show obligation. (Chapter 6)

 # Test Your Skills—Latin Exams

This appendix provides a series of exams so you can test your knowledge of Latin.

Examen I (Chapters 1 and 2)

A. Choose the correct answers to fill in the blanks.

1. Latin is a/an _____ language.

   a. Dead

   b. Easy

   c. Useful

   d. All of the above

2. People use Latin today to _____ their listeners.

   a. Confuse

   b. Amuse

   c. Impress

   d. Bore

3. English pronunciation of *alumnae* rhymes with _____.

   a. *Bah*

   b. *Knee*

   c. *Eye*

   d. *Ayee*

4. Pliny's villa was similar to a modern _____.

   a. Luxury condo

   b. Farm

   c. Penthouse

   d. Tenement

5. The Greek word *hysteria* means _____.

    a. Wild

    b. Happy

    c. Past

    d. Womb

6. Latin comes from the _____ language.

    a. Chinese

    b. Proto-Indo-European

    c. German

    d. English

7. Julius Caesar wrote _____.

    a. *The Gallic Wars*

    b. *Julius Caesar*

    c. *Aeneid*

    d. *Odyssey*

8. Another Indo-European language is/are _____.

    a. French

    b. Italian

    c. Spanish

    d. All of the above

9. The founder of Rome was _____.

    a. Augustus

    b. Julius Caesar

    c. Aeneas

    d. Saturn

10. Sulpicia was a Roman _____.

    a. Singer

    b. Dancer

    c. Weaver

    d. Poet

B. Translate the following into English:

1. Esne senator?

_____

2. Calamitas discordia est.

_____

3. Est cura.

_____

4. Italia in Europa est.

_____

5. Forma humana est.

_____

6. Clamor non silentium est.

_____

7. Troglodyta superior est.

_____

8. Fungus inferior est.

_____

9. Roma in Italia est.

_____

10. Esne nobilis?

_____

Examen II (Chapters 3–6)

A. Choose the correct answers to fill in the blanks.

1. First-conjugation verbs are characterized by the letter _____.

   a. *a*

   b. *e*

   c. *i*

   d. *u*

2. Second-conjugation verbs end in _____.

   a. *io*

   b. *eo*

   c. *ao*

   d. *oo*

3. Third-conjugation verbs have _____ for the infinitive ending.

   a. *are*

   b. *ire*

   c. *ore*

   d. *ere*

4. The city that was the enemy of Rome during the Punic Wars was _____.

   a. Punia

   b. Carthage

   c. Athens

   d. Sparta

5. Passive periphrastic indicates _____.

   a. Must be

   b. Ought to be

   c. Should be

   d. All of the above

6. *Condiment* comes from the Latin word meaning _____.

   a. Build

   b. Buy

   c. Season

   d. Eat

7. The first king of Rome was _____.

    a. Romper

    b. Romulus

    c. Rhombus

    d. Rhonda

8. The woman who was a symbol of virtue and honor was _____.

    a. Monica

    b. Lucretia

    c. Tarquinia

    d. Musca

9. *Patria potestas* was the complete power in a family of _____.

    a. The wife

    b. The father

    c. The spoiled brat

    d. The family pet

10. Lucretia's father was _____.

    a. Brutus

    b. Collatinus

    c. Expialadotius

    d. Lucretius

B. Translate the following into English:

1. Volo superare.

    _____

2. Dormire bonum est.

    _____

3. Audientes laeti sunt.

    _____

4. Romulus rex appellatur.

    _____

5. Vultus patris nobilis est.

    _____

6. Murenae non mandunt.

    _____

7. Equus sublevat.

   _____

8. Vetustae arbores decidunt.

   _____

9. Turba mulierum convolat.

   _____

10. Betae coquuntur.

    _____

Examen III (Chapters 7–10)

A. Choose the correct answers to fill in the blanks.

1. Adjectives agree with the noun they modify in _____.

    a. Number

    b. Gender

    c. Case

    d. All of the above

2. A *teetotum* is a/an _____.

    a. Drink

    b. Top

    c. Pair of dice

    d. American Indian tribe

3. The comparative form of a Latin adjective often ends in _____.

    a. *are*

    b. *ior*

    c. *iar*

    d. *nt*

4. The direct object of a verb is in the _____ case.

    a. Accusative

    b. Genitive

    c. Nominative

    d. Ablative

5. Of the following, _____ is not a pronoun.

    a. *qui*

    b. *hic*

    c. *tu*

    d. *puer*

6. Adverbs in English often end in _____.

    a. *tion*

    b. *ous*

    c. *ly*

    d. *ent*

7. Romans dated years from _____.
   a. The fall of Troy
   b. The Marathon victory
   c. The founding of Rome
   d. The birth of Romulus and Remus

8. The imperfect tense sign is _____.
   a. *ba*
   b. *bi*
   c. *bo*
   d. *bu*

9. Aqueducts carry _____.
   a. Roads
   b. People
   c. Germs
   d. Water

10. The future tense sign is usually _____.
    a. *bi*
    b. *bo*
    c. *bu*
    d. All of the above

B. Translate the following into English:

1. Filius troglodytae dolet.

   _____

2. Ducam equum ad aquam.

   _____

3. Viri infirmi esse dissimulaverunt.

   _____

4. Lex insulae dura erat.

   _____

5. Quantam pecuniam habes?

   _____

6. Est nullum aureum pro nobis.

   _____

7. Duo Romani cenam deportaverant.

_____

8. Consilium Dei non notum est.

_____

9. Uxor murenam magnam dextra apprehendit.

_____

10. Non modo pax sed etiam silentium me placat.

_____

Examen IV (Chapters 11–14)

A. Choose the correct answers to fill in the blanks.

1. Some prepositions are used as _____.

    a. Propositions

    b. Suffixes

    c. Prefixes

    d. Conjunctions

2. Nice Roman women did not _____.

    a. Overeat

    b. Read

    c. Watch mimes

    d. Kiss

3. *Eheu* indicates _____.

    a. Happiness

    b. Boredom

    c. Hysteria

    d. Sadness

4. Deponent verbs are _____.

    a. Active in form, passive in meaning

    b. Passive in form, active in meaning

    c. Not all there

    d. All of the above

5. The ablative absolute often uses the phrase _____.

    a. Has been _____ed

    b. Had been _____ed

    c. Having been _____ed

    d. Out there

6. Relative clauses begin with a _____.

    a. Relative pronoun

    b. Indefinite pronoun

    c. Relative noun

    d. Personal pronoun

7. The verb in a purpose clause is always in _____.

    a. Trouble

    b. The indicative

    c. The subjunctive

    d. The infinitive

8. *Scholae* in Greek means _____.

    a. School

    b. Scold

    c. Leisure

    d. Work

9. The subjunctive may be translated _____.

    a. "If"

    b. "May"

    c. "Always"

    d. "Is"

10. The Romans used gods' names _____.

    a. For their own

    b. On backpacks

    c. As logos

    d. As interjections

B. Translate the following into English:

1. Propter reginam, sedere non poteramus.

    _____

2. Trans viam pullus ambulavit.

    _____

3. Ursus super montem ivit.

    _____

4. Ursus in tabernam ivit.

    _____

5. Ad te remaneo.

    _____

6. Bos super lunam saluit.

    _____

323

7. Cervus qui cornus habuit Bambi appellatus est.

   _____

8. Femina quae margaritas habuit erat Cornelia.

   _____

9. Puella ad tabernam ivit ut cantaret.

   _____

10. Bos tantus obesus erat ut non super lunam saltire posset.

   _____

Examen V (Chapters 15–18)

A. Choose the correct answer to fill in the blank.

1. An English derivative from *traho* is _____.
   a. Train
   b. Trace
   c. Trail
   d. Tractor

2. If you are *jocund*, you are _____.
   a. Happy
   b. Round
   c. Second best
   d. Daily

3. *Diu* is an _____.
   a. Adjective
   b. Adverb
   c. Noun
   d. Preposition

4. Which of the following is not an accusative ending: _____
   a. *as*
   b. *os*
   c. *a*
   d. *ae*

5. A predicate noun renames the _____.
   a. Direct object
   b. Subject
   c. Indirect object
   d. Verb

6. In indirect statement, the subject is in the _____ case.
   a. Nominative
   b. Genitive
   c. Accusative
   d. Dative

7. Julius Caesar wrote _____.

    a. Commentaries

    b. Counterrevolutionaries

    c. A Shakespeare play

    d. Comedies

8. Terence was born in _____.

    a. Asia

    b. Africa

    c. Rome

    d. Spain

9. Livy wrote a history called _____.

    a. *Ab Bello Gallico*

    b. *Ab Urbe Condita*

    c. *Ab Urbe Carthago*

    d. *Ab Urbe New York*

10. Pliny died in _____.

    a. A fishpond

    b. A volcanic eruption

    c. An elephant hunt

    d. An oyster bed

B. Translate the following into English:

1. Antonia murenae inaures addidit.

_____

2. Sergius pensiles balneas invenit.

_____

3. Urinantes has conchas cura magna petunt.

_____

4. Stipant pedes in sinistro femine.

_____

5. Corpus humanum multa membra habet.

_____

6. Boves helvellas et herbas edunt.

_____

7. Turba hominum erat.

_____

8. Alces similes capris sunt.

_____

9. Fiat lux!

_____

10. Volo fieri sicut pullus.

_____

Examen Ultimum (Chapters 19–23)

A. Choose the correct answers to fill in the blanks.

1. Cogito, ergo _____.
   a. Est
   b. Lux
   c. Cor
   d. Sum

2. Ars longa, vita _____.
   a. Brevis
   b. Vincit
   c. Ergo
   d. Volat

3. Ditat _____.
   a. Dum
   b. Sol
   c. Deus
   d. Angelus

4. Amicus _____.
   a. Amor
   b. Habet
   c. Curiae
   d. Caveat

5. Corpus _____.
   a. Panis
   b. Habeas
   c. Delicti
   d. Canis

6. Habeas _____.
   a. Corpus
   b. Habito
   c. Regnum
   d. Patriam

7. _____ familiaris.
   a. Fames
   b. Canis
   c. Felix
   d. Villa

8. Per _____.
   a. Se
   b. Diem
   c. Os
   d. All of the above

9. Gloria in Excelsis _____.
   a. Donec
   b. Deo
   c. Maria
   d. Angelo

10. Miserere _____.
    a. Nobis
    b. Te
    c. Se
    d. Vobis

B. Translate the following sentences:

1. Nun manent fides, spes, caritas, tria haec.

   _____

2. Tinc, tinc, tonc, tinc, tinc, tonc, Tintinnabula!

   _____

3. Bibit servus, bibit ancilla.

   _____

4. Rx. 4 gtt. p.o. b.i.d.

   _____

5. Bufo vulgaris non pulcher est.

   _____

6. Caveat emptor.

   _____

7. Qui tacet consentire videtur.

   _____

8. Regnat populus.

   _____

9. Sic semper tyrannis.

   _____

10. Docendo discimus.

    _____

Answer Keys

The answer keys include answers to all the "Practice Makes Perfect" questions, as well as any exercises and translations within the chapters. Note that all translations from the Latin go to my credit.

Chapter 2

Practice Makes Perfect

Ask questions to a friend or your boss:

1. Are you a consul?
2. Are you a hippopotamus?
3. Are you a cave woman?
4. Are you an orator?
5. Are you a senator?
6. Are you an architect?
7. Are you an elephant?
8. Are you a mushroom?

Chapter 3

Practice Makes Perfect 1

Translate from Latin into English:

1. Life of an oyster
2. Friend of the girl

3. Water of Rome

4. Dinner of grass

5. Daughter of a goddess

6. Glory of the cause

7. Industry of the island

Translate from English into Latin:

1. Herba Romae

2. Vita puellae

3. Mensa troglodytae

4. Margarita ostreae

5. Femina piscinae

Practice Makes Perfect 2

Translate from Latin into English:

1. The nerve of the tightrope walker

2. A man of silence

3. Nose of an elephant

4. Leisure of the people

5. Vase of iron

6. Way of the world

7. Place of the woman

8. Shell of a beet

9. Mother-in-law of an eel

10. Victory of the Greek

11. Son of violence

12. Intelligence of the soul

13. Dinner of ham

Translate from English into Latin:

1. Pretium terrae

2. Verbum poenae

3. Filius lauti

4. Versiculus epistulae

5. Hospita Graeci

6. Pretium togae

7. Verbum Dei

8. Villa auri

Practice Makes Perfect 3

Translate from Latin into English:

1. Knots of men

2. Nerves of steel

3. Kernels of oysters

4. The way of leisure

5. Fish of the baths

6. Tails of the hippos

7. Silence of Rome

8. Friend of god

9. Streets of Rome

10. Industry of the tightrope walker

Translate from English into Latin:

1. Vasa deae

2. Cenae virorum

3. Loci filiorum

4. Vita convivi

5. Lectus hospitae

6. Pecunia agricolae

7. Conchae ostrearum

8. Consilium dicti

Practice Makes Perfect 4

Translate from Latin into English:

1. Ham and eggs

2. Women and men

3. Public and private

4. Oysters but not elephants

5. Elephants but also hippos

6. Cook and tightrope walker

7. Palms and pearls

8. Either water or potherbs

9. The senate and the Roman people

10. Not only beets but also marrow

Chapter 4

Practice Makes Perfect 1

Translate from Latin into English:

1. Act/acts of the brother

2. Line of elephants

3. Calamity of the state

4. Old age of the dictator

5. Friend of the woman

6. Condition of peace

7. Work of an oyster

8. Leisure of men

9. Agility of a fish

10. Tooth of the mouth

Translate from English into Latin:

1. Adiutrices Spartaci

2. Aestimationes architecti

3. Tempus vitae

4. Arbores Romae

5. Clunes ferri

6. Poples viri

7. Bipennes uxorum

8. Res civitatis

9. Res ducis

10. Pretium carnis

Practice Makes Perfect 2

Fill in the correct endings:

| Declension | Nominative | | Genitive | |
	Singular	Plural	Singular	Plural
First	a	ae	ae	arum
Second	us	i	i	orum
Third	—	es	is	um
Fourth	us	us	us	uum
Fifth	—	es	ei	erum

Translate from Latin into English:

1. The thing of life

2. Feet of the boxers

3. Net of the gladiator

4. Vase of salt

5. Silence of the lambs

6. Cost of time

7. Crowd of divers

8. Wife of Caesar

9. Right of the ancestors

10. Price of the merchandise

Translate from English into Latin:

1. Feminae domus

2. Strepitum viarum

3. Conventus comitum

4. Crus agni

5. Duces mundi

6. Expectationes turbae

7. Femur feminae

8. Fraus fratris uxoris
9. Inaures murenae
10. Leges populi

Check the correct column:

| | Nominative | | Genitive | |
Latin Word	Singular	Plural	Singular	Plural
gloriae		X	X	
Caesaris			X	
alumni		X	X	
alumna	X			
ostreae		X	X	
pacis			X	
res	X	X		
rete	X			
uxor	X			
ferri			X	
strepitus	X	X	X	
sumptuum				X
comitium				X
viri		X	X	
silenti			X	
pacum				X

Chapter 5

Practice Makes Perfect 1

Translate from Latin into English:

1. They plant
2. I cook
3. The tightrope walkers surpass
4. The table falls
5. The brother leaves
6. They grab
7. They fly about

8. He stands out
9. I fight
10. They lie

Practice Makes Perfect 2

Fill in the blanks:

1. Graecus
2. Dux
3. Coquus
4. Muraenae
5. Dictatores
6. Trogodytae
7. Arbores
8. Apis
9. Funambulus
10. Ostreae

Write in Latin:

1. Peto
2. Venit
3. Concidunt
4. Volunt
5. Applicat
6. Obruunt
7. Concido
8. Refert
9. Condio
10. Praestant
11. Possumus

Practice Makes Perfect 3

Translate from Latin into English:

1. Mushrooms are scattered.
2. Caesar is called dictator.

3. He is left.

4. It is said.

5. Money obligates.

6. The nerve demands.

7. The house is decorated.

Translate from English into Latin:

1. Caro consumitur.

2. Labor.

3. Ostrea tenetur.

4. Pedes stipantur.

5. Aurum obruitur.

Chapter 6

Practice Makes Perfect 1

Translate from Latin into English:

1. To sleep

2. To bring, carry

3. To change

4. To do

5. To overcome

Translate these into Latin:

1. Ferre

2. Erigere

3. Esse

4. Mandare

5. Sublevare

And now some sentences:

1. He wants to sleep.

2. He seemed to do.

3. It is necessary to get up.

4. It is permitted to give.

5. To stop is to die.

Ready to translate into Latin?

1. Potest mandare.

2. Permutare.

3. Dormire est superare.

4. Videtur esse.

5. Necesse est erigere.

Practice Makes Perfect 2

Translate from Latin into English:

1. The diving boys

2. The grieving woman

3. Hanging garden

4. Acting

5. Listening

Translate from English into Latin:

1. Audientes

2. Peragens

3. Dolentes feminae

4. Urinans

5. Pendentes

Practice Makes Perfect 3

Translate Latin into English:

1. It must be changed

2. It must be added

3. It must be done

Now some gerunds:

1. Selling
2. Leading
3. Being careful
4. Getting up

Translate English into Latin:

1. Dolentis
2. Dormiendum
3. Tempus est peragendi
4. Permutat ad vendendo

And now a few longer combinations:

1. To be or not to be.
2. Carthage must be destroyed.
3. Way of working.
4. Hanging gardens of Babylon.
5. I want to get up and straighten out.

Reviewing Verbals

Gerund: vendendo, agendi, perficiendum

Passive periphrastic: curandum est, adicienda est

Infinitive: dormire, consistere, agere, dare

Present participle: stantium

Chapter 7

Practice Makes Perfect 1

Translate:

1. Noblewoman
2. Triumphal dinner
3. In the middle of the tail

4. Weak building

5. Roman people

Translate the English into Latin:

1. Terra communis

2. Lex sumptuaria

3. Singulus troglodyta

4. Sola ostrea

5. Elephantus iratus

The Most Agreeable Words

senatoris—nervosi

vasis—Graecis

coquus—bonus

prandium—superius

denti—longo

hospitam—suavem

hippopotamus—absurdus

Practice Makes Perfect 2

Translate the Latin into English:

1. More noble

2. Longer

3. Most angry

4. Weakest

5. More common

Translate the English into Latin:

1. Dextra

2. Iucundius sale

3. Maius quam vita

Match these words:

1. Poplites—mutili (g)
2. Dei—immortales (f)
3. Cibum—nullum (e)
4. Res—medias (a)
5. Aedificiis—publicis (b)
6. Cornu—praeacutum (c)
7. Corporis—alterius (d)

Choose the adjective that agrees with the noun in number, gender, case, and common sense:

1. Opus publicum
2. Lex tota
3. Homo alienus
4. Arbores propinquas
5. Balineas pensiles
6. Cura vetusta
7. Apes singuli
8. Graecia magna
9. Romani populi

Practice Makes Perfect 3

Translate the Latin into English:

1. I capture the flag.
2. I catch the goose.
3. I seize the elephant.
4. I uproot the trees.
5. The cook cooks dinner.
6. Work consumes time.
7. I look for Caesar.

Translate into the Latin:

1. Ostream condio.
2. Murenam ornat.
3. Gladiatores relinquimus.

Practice Makes Perfect 4

Turn the phrases into questions and translate:

1. Num vexillum capio? "Do I capture the flag?"
2. Apprehendone anserem? "Am I grabbing the goose?"
3. Elephantumne capio? "Am I capturing the elephant?"
4. Nonne arbores subruo? "I'm uprooting trees, aren't I?"
5. Coquusne cenam coquit? "Is the cook cooking?"
6. Laborne tempus consumit? "Does work take time?"
7. Caesaremne peto? "Am I attacking Caesar?"
8. Condione ostream? "Do I season the oyster?"
9. Murenamne ornat? "Does he decorate the eel?"
10. Gladiatoresne relinquimus? "Do we leave the gladiators behind?"

Chapter 8

Practice Makes Perfect 1

Translate from Latin into English:

1. Our father
2. Your sister
3. I am (a) dictator.
4. We the people
5. Your letter
6. My brother
7. I love you.
8. Call me Ishmael.
9. Don't call me, I'll call you.
10. I am a mother.

Practice Makes Perfect 2

Translate from Latin into English:

1. She says
2. He was

3. She lies down

4. They walk

5. Her/his house

6. They hang

7. Victory is theirs

8. In her place

9. I love her

10. She reclines

Practice Makes Perfect 3

Translate from Latin into English:

1. She grabs her brother.

2. He decorates his house.

3. This calamity

4. That thing

5. This net

6. He plants himself.

7. We hear ourselves.

8. You lead yourselves.

9. The elephant brings himself.

10. His/her goods

Practice Makes Perfect 4

Translate from Latin into English:

1. You are sad

2. You stop

3. You hear

4. You destroy

5. You add on

6. He goes out

7. They return

8. You omit

9. He goes in
10. You go

Chapter 9

Practice Makes Perfect 1

Match the faces with the adverbs:

humiliter

laete

sane

innocenter

suaviter

absurde

calide

misere

irate

frigide

Practice Makes Perfect 2

Translate:

1. Hodie, non mane
2. Numquam secunda hora
3. Irate
4. Olim

Now translate the Latin into English:

1. Two and two make four
2. Now or never
3. Then and now
4. Truly first
5. Again, I am certain
6. Always faithful

Chapter 10

It's an Imperfect World

Translate from Latin into English:

1. We were making
2. They were carrying
3. We were
4. He was giving
5. You were doing
6. He was able
7. I was throwing
8. You were seizing

What's in Your Future?

Translate these verbs from Latin into English:

1. You will say
2. We will be

3. I will love

4. You will be able

5. They will have

The Perfect Tenses (Active and Passive Voices)

Translate the following verbs in perfect tense from Latin into English:

1. I have asked

2. He has carried away

3. He did not want

4. He had surpassed

5. She had moved

6. It was/has been

7. They made

8. He has had

9. I cut into

10. I was able

The Imperative—a Commanding Lead

Try yelling these commands:

1. Eat!

2. Move!

3. Don't move!

4. Go!

5. Carry!

6. Speak!

Practice Makes Perfect

Identify the person, number, tense, voice, and then translate the verb:

1. **Fuimus:** first person, pl., present perf. act. "We have been"

2. **Misit:** third person, sing., present perf. act. "He has sent"

3. **Veni:** first person, sing., present perf. act. "I came"

4. **Veniebant:** third person, pl., imperfect, act. "They were coming"

5. **Potueram:** first person, sing., pluperfect act. "I had been able"

6. **Amavit:** third person, sing., pres. perf. act. "He has loved"

7. **Factum est:** third person, sing., pres. perf. pass. "It has been done"

8. **Data erant:** third person, pl., pluperf. pass. "They had been given"

9. **Steti:** first person, sing., pres. perf.act. "I stood"

10. **Ceperint:** third person, pl., future perf. act. "They will have taken"

11. **Respondit:** third person, sing., pres. perf. act. "He has answered"

12. **Prandimus:** first person, pl., pres. perf. act. "We have eaten"

13. **Petitus erat:** third person, sing., pluperf. pass. "He had been attacked"

14. **Praeterivi:** first person, sing., pres. perf. act. "I have omitted"

15. **Lati sunt:** third person, pl., pres. perf. pass. "They have been washed"

16. **Iecerunt:** third person, pl., pres. perf. act. "They have thrown"

17. **Voluit:** third person, sing., pres. perf. act. "He wanted"

18. **Tuleram:** first person, sing., pluperf. act. "I had brought"

19. **Invitavero:** first person, sing., future perf. act. "I will have invited"

20. **Visum est:** third person, sing., pres. perf. pass. "It has been seen"

Find the seven verbs in perfect tense and then translate them into Latin:

1. Vidi

2. Invitavero

3. Praeterivi

4. Deportavit

5. Quaesivi

6. Narravit

7. Exstetit

Translate from Latin into English:

1. I saw the consul.

2. I will have invited the men.

3. I myself am a guest.

4. I overlooked many things.

5. The man carried away the dog.

6. They season mushrooms and herbs.

7. I looked diligently.

8. The kernels are pearls.

9. The woman told a story.

10. One horn stood out.

Chapter 11

In the Blink of an Eye—Coming or Going?

Translate these prepositional phrases:

1. To the house

2. By the sister

3. From the number of shells

4. After dinner

5. By the priest

6. Against violence

7. For watching

8. Toward me

9. With you

10. From life

Prepositions as Prefixes—Preposterous!

Guess the meaning of these compounds:

1. He goes out

2. He goes in

3. I walk in

4. He arrives

5. He led away

6. They arrived

7. He puts down

8. He put on

9. We enter

10. We went across

Practice Makes Perfect

Choose the proper interjection:

1. Hei
2. Oh
3. Eheu
4. Oi
5. Io
6. Minime
7. Io
8. Ohe

Respond in Latin:

1. Are you an architect? (Reader's choice)
2. Do you love asparagus? (Reader's choice)
3. Does the elephant climb a tree? *Minime.*
4. Do you live in a fishpond? (Reader's choice)
5. Do you love to read? (Reader's choice)
6. Is the farmer a good man? *Certe.*
7. Does the Queen of Sheba live in your house? (Reader's choice)

Chapter 12

Practice Makes Perfect 1

Translate these sentence fragments:

1. When you see a star
2. Before I read a book
3. After the soldier walks across the road
4. At the same time as they sing
5. Although the road is long
6. Because he is dead
7. Because she is wearing a dress
8. When the decree is brought to the consul

9. When the boy laughs

10. Although the latest custom is to move the ears greatly

Practice Makes Perfect 2

Translate from Latin into English:

1. The dog having been fed, we made the trip.

2. The farmer having been pleased, the horses were led from the city.

3. When the toga was put on, the senator walked out of the house.

4. The Lord having been born, we sing in church.

5. The republic having been saved, Cicero was praised.

6. When Marius and Valerius were consuls, the Greek were not pleased.

7. When the tray was brought in, the party began.

8. These things having been said, Caesar left the rostrum.

9. With you as leader, I will carry my brother.

Translate from English into Latin:

1. Puero viso, pater risit.

2. Aqua recepta, Caesar tardavit.

3. Cibo consumpto, femina stolam gessit.

4. Die constituto, astra spectavimus.

5. Libro lecto, hecyra sapiens erat.

Practice Makes Perfect 3

Translate the following clauses:

1. He was born.

2. I speak.

3. They were going forth.

4. I suffered.

5. Are you wandering?

Now change the following into Latin:

1. Creamur

2. Patior

3. Locuti sunt

4. Sequerisne?

5. Polliceor meum optimum facere.

Chapter 13

Practice Makes Perfect 1

Fill in the correct relative pronoun:

1. Which

2. Whom

3. Who

4. Whom

5. Whose

6. That

7. Whom

8. Whom

9. Which

Whoosier Relative Pronoun?

Translate from English to Latin:

1. Corvus

2. Femina

3. Epistula

4. Vir or Caesar

5. Bos

6. Vir or Caesar

Practice Makes Perfect 2

Translate the following clauses:

1. The line in which you warn me

2. She to whom Quintus sent a table

3. I who abstained from oysters

4. The kernels which are pearls

5. He who first invented hanging baths

6. For the eel which he loved

7. The mother-in-law I was never allowed to be present in silence

8. Members, among which are the hands, mouth, teeth

9. The cow whose one horn stands out

10. There are those which are called elks

Practice Makes Perfect 3

Translate from Latin into English:

1. A certain deer has a red nose.

2. Which cow jumped over the moon?

3. Invite whoever you wish.

4. Caesar himself was in the baths.

Now swap the English for Latin:

1. Quisque servus aures lavat.

2. Casus victoriae magnus est.

A couple more Latin phrases to translate:

1. I am eating something.

2. Eat whatever.

Chapter 14

Words to Learn in Order to Be Educated

1. Expectatio ludi

2. Pellis cervi

3. Cibus canis

4. Forma frontis

5. Quies otii

6. Pondus officii

7. Species terrae

8. Radix arboris
9. Venter ostreae
10. Fabula civis

Clauses with a Purpose

1. Many praise some so that they may be praised by others.
2. Many were praising some so that they would be praised by others.
3. He sent slaves into the shop to seize the friend.

Clauses with a Result

1. He made such a noise that it was necessary to leave.
2. He loved the eel to such a degree that he sat in the fishpond.

Practice Makes Perfect

1. ... because he was special (d)
2. ... when there is nothing to do (e)
3. ... in order to capture the deer (c)
4. ... when we hear a story (b)
5. ... if my dog was away (a)

Translate from Latin into English:

1. When Caesar heard these things, he ordered the soldiers to retreat.
2. Since this is so, I will go to Rome.
3. I did these things, while it was permitted.
4. While these things were being done, the slaves left.
5. Stay at home until I return.
6. If he stays, he lives.

Chapter 15

Simple Sentences—I can learn Latin.

Translate from Latin into English:

1. I saw nothing.
2. I come to the line written across.
3. They grab the tail.
4. We left Arpinati.
5. He cut the nerves.
6. I myself am a guest.
7. I suffer daily.
8. I omit many things.
9. They fall themselves.
10. They have legs without joints.
11. Would that I would conquer the world.

Translate the following sentences:

1. The gourmets season mushrooms, boiled greens, and grasses.
2. The noble man carries away this statue.
3. Sergius Orata invented the fishpond.
4. The wife added earrings.
5. The cave men climb trees.
6. The human body has members.
7. The common people knew a story.

Be flexible with these translations:

1. I inquired diligently.
2. Some are single.
3. There is silence.
4. One horn stands out.
5. The kernels fall.
6. Horses are not cows.
7. Let us rejoice.

8. The rooms are cold.

9. I believe you.

10. We all believe.

Interrogative Sentences: Can I learn Latin?

Translate from Latin into English:

1. Will you invite men and clients?

2. Where will you put the body?

3. How many togas do you have?

4. Will you remember all the laws?

5. Have you been away from your house?

6. Is there a house far away?

Practice Makes Perfect

Translate the following sentences:

1. I come to the line written across in which you warn me.

2. The day made it happen that Quintus remained in Arcanum.

3. She said, "I myself am a guest," because Statius had gone ahead to see to dinner for us.

4. We all reclined except her, to whom Quintus sent a table.

5. The gourmets want to add among the honored those things born from the earth which have been excluded from the law.

6. They season mushrooms, potherbs, and grasses in such a way that nothing is able to be more pleasing.

7. I, who was abstaining from oysters and eels, was taken down by the beet and marrow.

8. All the meat having been eroded, the kernels of the bodies, which are pearls, fall to the bottom.

9. Antonia added earrings to the eel, which he loved.

10. The leg being slowed, he cuts the nerves of the other hamstring.

11. I bring to you *Hecyra,* which has never been permitted to me to be present in silence.

12. When rumor came about gladiators, I was not able to keep my place safe.

13. The human body has many members, among which are the hands, mouth, teeth, and stomach.

14. They cut down the trees so that only the top is left with the appearance of those standing.

15. I am angry because I am not well.

16. A woman is accustomed to wear a dress which is long.

17. The slave is accustomed to wear a tunic which is short.

Chapter 16

Compound Sentences

Translate the following compound sentences:

1. In the noble city of Ephesus, Greeks lived and it is said that an unfair law was enacted.

2. An architect receives a public job and sets his price.

3. The shape of an elk is similar to a goat but is a little bit bigger.

4. They lean themselves on trees and in such a way take a rest.

5. Either they uproot the trees by the roots or cut them down.

6. They knock the weakened trees down with their weight and they themselves fall.

7. Cave men of Ethiopia feed themselves by hunting alone and climb trees daily.

8. He plants his feet on the left thigh and cuts the hamstring with his right hand.

9. The elephant is slowed by his leg and in a short time is dead.

10. And so it had bothered me that she had spoken so sharply.

Compound-Complex Sentences

Translate the following gems:

1. If not more than a quarter of the cost is used up in the work, it is added to the estimate with no penalty.

2. They do not lie down to rest nor, if they fall down by accident, are they able to straighten out and get up.

Indirect Statements

Statements by ancient authors:

1. Quintus told me that she did not want to sleep with him. (Cicero)

2. They say that he is most wise who knows himself what the work is. (Cicero)

3. Gullible hope encourages life and says that tomorrow will always be better. (Tibullus)

4. For no one is so old as to think that he is not able to live for one more year. (Cicero)

Indirect Questions

Some examples of indirect questions:

1. Do not wonder when this happened and why I am suffering. (Cicero)

2. He promises to say how much the cost will be. (Vitruvius)

3. To not know what happened before you were born is to always remain a child. (Cicero)

4. Now I know what love is. (Vergil)

5. Many doubt what would be best. (Cicero)

Indirect Commands

Some examples of indirect commands:

1. Caesar urged his soldiers not to be afraid.

2. He warned the girls not to do this.

3. He persuaded them to do this.

Practice Makes Perfect

Translate from Latin into English:

1. Quintus remained in Arcanum and the next morning he came to me in Aquinum and told me that she did not want to sleep with him and, when she had left, she was of the same mood as I had seen.

2. All of Gaul is divided into three parts, one of which the Begians inhabit, another the Aquitani, and a third, which in their own language are called Celts, and in ours, Gauls.

Chapter 17

A Street Scene

Adapted from *Hecyra* by Terence, prologue 21–36.

> I bring to you *Hecyra,* which I have never been able to do in silence. Disaster has overwhelmed it (the production) in such a way.

> Your understanding will appease this calamity if there will be a sympathizer of our work. When first I began to produce it, the glory of boxers, the expectation of a tightrope walker, the gathering of friends, noise and the shouting of women made it so I had to leave before it was time.

> I bring it again. I get through the first act. Meanwhile rumor comes about gladiators, people fly around, they shout, they fight for a place; I am not able to keep a safe place.

> Now there is no crowd; there is peace and quiet. The time has come for me to present my play.

Woodland Scene

From Caesar, *de Bello Gallico,* VI, 26–27.

> There is an ox in the shape of a deer, from whose forehead between the ears one horn stands out, higher and more straight than those horns which are known to us. From the top of this horn it spreads out widely like palm branches. The same nature is for both male and female, the same shape and size of the horns.

> There are also those called elks. The figure of these is similar to goats and they have a variety of pelts. But they are a little bigger and have broken horns and legs without joints and nodes; neither do they lie down for the sake of rest, nor, if by some chance they are afflicted and fall down, are they able to stand themselves up. These use trees for beds; to which they lean and thus leaning, get a little rest. When it is known from the tracks of these by hunters where they are accustomed to rest, they root up all the trees in the place or cut the trees so that the exact appearance of standing trees remains. Here, when they lean according to their custom, they knock the trees over with their weight and fall down with them.

Dining Room Scene

Adapted from Cicero, *Epistulae ad Familiares, VII.*

Anyhow, lest you wonder when this happened and how I began—the sumptuary law which seemed to have brought simplicity, was a problem for me. For the gourmets want to honor food born from the earth that is exempted from the law. So they season mushrooms, boiled greens, all greens in such a way that nothing is able to be more tasty. When I fell into them at a dinner at the house of Lentulus, such great diarrhea attacked me that today is my first day well. And so I, who abstain easily from oysters and eels, was taken down by a beet and a marrow. Therefore, after this, I will be more cautious.

My Sister-in-Law!

Adapted from Cicero's *Letters to Atticus,* Book V.1.

Now I come to the little note written across the end of your letter, in which you warn me about your sister. This is how it is. ... I have seen nothing so gentle, nothing so pleasing as my brother at that time was to your sister .... On the next day we set out from Arpinum. A festival made Quintus remain in Arcanum, I in Aquinum, but we dined in Arcanum. You know that place. As we arrived there, Quintus said, "Pomponia, you invite the women, I will invite the men." Nothing was able, as indeed it seemed to me, to be sweeter with words as well as in intention and countenance. But she, while we were listening, said, "I am myself a guest here" ... because Statius, had gone ahead to prepare dinner for us. Then Quintus said to me "Oh, I suffer these things daily." You say, "What, if you please, was the problem?" Much; and so she upset me, too; so absurdly and harshly she had responded with words and countenance. Sadly, I pretended otherwise. We all reclined except her, to whom nevertheless Quintus sent a tray. She refused it. What more? Nothing seemed to me more kind than my brother, nothing more harsh than your sister; and I omit a lot .... Quintus remained in Arcanum and on the next morning came to me at Aquinum and told me that she refused to sleep with him.

He shies away from marrying again: "Nothing is more pleasant than an empty bed."

My House!

From Cicero, *De Domo Sua*, XLIII.

"But where was that Liberty found?" I asked around carefully. It seems that there was a certain woman of the streets at Tanagra. Not far from the city her

statue from marble had been placed on a tomb. A certain nobleman, not uncon-
nected to this religious priest of Liberty, carried it to decorate his aedilship. And
so he thought to surpass all his predecessors by the splendor of his gift. And so
all statues, pictures, furniture which was left over in the shrines and public
places in all of Greece and every island, for the sake of the honor of the Roman
people, wisely and frugally he brought to his own home.

Chapter 18

Vita Vitruivi

From Vitruvius, *On Architecture, Book X*, preface.

In the noble and large city of Ephesus of the Greeks, an old law is said to have
been instituted by the forefathers, with a hard condition, but not unfair. For the
architect, when he receives a public work to be done, he promises how much
the cost will be. The estimate is handed over and his goods are earmarked to the
magistrate until the work is finished. At completion, moreover, when the cost
responds to the contract, he is decorated with decrees and honors. Likewise, if it
is no more than a quarter more than the estimate, it must be added to the estimate and paid for by the public. Nor is any penalty paid. But when it is more
than a quarter over, the money is exacted from his own goods for finishing.

Would that the immortal gods would make it that this law be instituted for the
Roman people, not only for public buildings, but for private ones as well!

Vita Titi Livi

Adapted from Livy, *Ab Urbe Condita*, II.

The human body has many members, among which are the hands, mouth,
teeth, stomach. Once the rest of the parts of the body were angry because the
stomach received everything but did nothing for himself. Then they made this
plan together. The teeth decided not to chew the food; the mouth not to receive
food, the hands not to bring food to the mouth. And so the stomach was not
able to be fed and the whole body died. Do not, o citizens, on account of your
discord, destroy your country in the same way.

It was necessary that the human body have all parts. It was necessary that the
country have both patricians and plebeians. The plebians understood the story
of Menenius Agrippa and accepted the conditions of peace. New magistrates
were created whose duty was to always give aid to the plebians against the violence of the consuls.

How to Catch an Elephant

From Pliny, *Natural History,* VIII.viii.26.

> The cave men of Ethiopia, who feed themselves by hunting alone, climb the nearest trees, and from there, having seen the last of the whole line of elephants, jump down on the last hindquarters; they grasp the tail with their left hand, plant their feet on the left thigh; hanging in such a way, he cuts one of the hamstrings with his right hand with a very sharp two-edged knife. When the elephant is slowed down by his leg, he cuts the nerves of the other knee, doing it all with amazing speed.

The Sad Fate of Oysters

From Pliny, *Natural History,* IX.lv.

> Thus, as with bees, some of the shells are singular in size and unusual in old age. Just as admirable leaders they are skillful in evading capture. Divers look for these with great care. These having been captured, the divers easily catch the rest who are wandering with nets. Then they bury them in salt in clay vases. All the meat is gnawed away and the kernels of the bodies, which are pearls, fall to the bottom.

Fishponds and Showers

From Pliny, *Natural History,* IX.lxxix and lxxxi.

> First of all, Sergius Orata invented the fish hatcheries. And it is he who first invented hanging baths (showers) and in such a way improved the appearance of houses for immediate sale.

> C. Hurrius before others thought up the private fishpond for eels. He loaned out for the triumphal dinners of Caesar the Dictator 6,000 eels, for he did not want to exchange them for a price or any other merchandise. Next love of single fish came into vogue. At Baulos, in a part of Baiana, Hortensius the orator had a fishpond in which he loved an eel to such an extent that he is believed to have wept when it died. In the same house, Antonia, wife of Drusus, put earrings on an eel which he was fond of.

Chapter 19

Sentences You Can Read and a Review of Cases

1. Romulus, the king, died.
2. The good king cried.
3. The Books of the Holy Scripture are read often.
4. He is in your province.
5. Marius freed Italy.
6. He went across the river.
7. They say that Plato came to Italy.
8. Romulus reigned for 37 years.
9. Oh, poor me!
10. He gave the signal to the soldiers.
11. I have never pleased myself.
12. He persuaded the Helvetians easily.
13. My name is Caesar.
14. The duty of the consul is to give commands.
15. The thigh of an elephant is large.
16. He sent a thousand soldiers.
17. The bravest of all these are the Belgians.
18. A pearl comes out of the shell.
19. He is loved by them.
20. Nothing is more pleasing than life.
21. Elks are protected by horns.
22. They live by hunting alone.
23. In that same year, Ennius was born.
24. The land captured, Caesar gave part to the soldiers.
25. It is bad to be sad.
26. To err is human.
27. These golden vases are on the table.

More Sentences and a Review of Verb Usage

1. Romulus founded a city.
2. Glory often follows work.
3. Wise men live happily.
4. In the city of Ephesus, a Greek king remained with the queen.
5. I was writing to you.
6. Castor and Pollux were seen fighting from their horses.
7. A man had been dragged by a boy from the water.
8. The noise was heard by the crowd.
9. It is a rare bird.
10. As many men there are, there are as many opinions.
11. Art is long, life, short.
12. What is this to me?
13. Free the republic from fear.
14. Do not wish what cannot be done.
15. Let him conquer.
16. In the world, God is he who reigns, who governs, who watches over the courses of the stars.
17. By God the world was built.
18. The king is loved greatly.
19. I was wondering at this.
20. Men believe what they want.
21. I hope that the memory of our friendship will be eternal.

More Sentences and Hints for Translating

Even more sentences you can read:

a. If we conquer, all will be safe.
b. Fortune favors the brave.
c. Do not the nightly guard on the Palatine, the watches of the city, the fear of the people, the meeting of all good men, the fortification of the senate's meeting place, the faces and expressions of these men move you?

Pyrrha et Deucalion

Once upon a time there was evil and crime all over the land. Men had never been so base. And so Jupiter prepared a terrible punishment. From the sky he pulled together dense clouds and it rained a lot. Neptune also helped his brother. All over rivers flooded the lands. The sea was so deep that even the tops of the mountains were covered. Mt. Parnasus alone stood out from the waves. Here pious Deucalion with his wife Pyrrha remained in a small boat. Not now does the wrath of the gods remain.

Immediately Neptune scattered the clouds and called back the rivers and seas. But from all the mortals, only two survived. Sadly, Deucalion and Pyrrha asked for help from a goddess in a temple. From there Themis gave an answer: "Cover your heads and throw behind your back the bones of the great parent." For a long time they were quietly puzzled. Finally Deucalion said: "The land is the great parent of all. Perhaps stones are the bones of the great parent." They left the temple, covered their heads, and threw stones over their backs. Soon they looked back. Now the stones are men and women. Thus the gods restored men to the earth.

Midas

Once upon a time Bacchus gave a gift to Midas, king of Phrygia. "What you want, I will give you," he said. Midas answered, "Whatever I touch with my body, let it become gold." The god said, "So be it." Midas happily returned home. Scarcely believing his good fortune, he touched the doors, which turned into gold. Then he ran through the house, touching with his hand beds, tables, chairs. In a short time everything was gold. Then whatever food the king brought to his mouth, it, too, turned to gold. Even wine turned into a river of gold. The astonished Midas tried to escape the riches, but in vain. Then finally he said to himself, "I was so foolish. I am both the richest and poorest of mortals." From there Midas sought Bacchus day and night. Finally, exhausted, Midas found the god.

Then he said, "Please, take me from the cruel fate." The god responded, "Go to the river Pactolus and wash yourself in the water." King Midas went to the river and immersed himself in the water. Immediately, miraculous to say, the gold fell from his body into the river. And up to this time, the Pactolus is said to flow with golden sands.

Psalmus Davidis XXIII

1. The Lord is my shepherd; I shall not want.

2. He makes me lie down in green pastures; He leads me beside still waters.

3. He restores my soul; He guides me in the paths of righteousness for his name's sake.

4. Even though I walk through the valley of the shadow of death, I fear no evil: for Thou art with me; Thy rod and Thy staff, they comfort me.

5. Thou dost prepare a table before me in the presence of my enemies: Thou hast anointed my head with oil; My cup overflows.

6. Surely goodness and mercy will follow me all the days of my life, and I will dwell in the house of the Lord forever.

Psalmus pro gratiarum actione C

1. Shout joyfully to the Lord, all the earth.

2. Serve the Lord with gladness; Come before Him with joyful singing.

3. Know that the Lord Himself is God; it is He who has made us, and not we ourselves; we are His people and the sheep of His pasture.

4. Enter His gates with thanksgiving and His courts with praise. Give thanks to Him, bless His name.

5. For the Lord is good; His loving kindness is everlasting and His faithfulness to all generations.

Chapter 21

Practice Makes Perfect 1

Match the medical term and its meaning:

1. j
2. l
3. k
4. h
5. q
6. a
7. p
8. n
9. d
10. e
11. g
12. o

13. i
14. b
15. m
16. c
17. f

Practice Makes Perfect 2

Write the following prescriptions in Latin and then translate:

1. Take four times a day by mouth.
2. At night, three drops by mouth.
3. With water, freely.
4. Before meals, without water.
5. At bedtime, 25 drops.

Chapter 22

The Gloria

Glory to God in the highest,
and peace to his people on earth.
Lord God, heavenly King,
almighty God and Father,
we worship you, we give you thanks
we praise you for your glory,
Lord Jesus Christ,
only son of the Father,
Lord God, Lamb of God,
you take away the sin of the world,
have mercy on us;
you are seated at the right
hand of the Father;
receive our prayer.
For you alone are the Holy One,
you alone are the Lord,
you alone are the Most High,
Jesus Christ,
with the Holy spirit,
in the glory of God the Father.
Amen.

I Corinthians 13

1 If I speak with the tongues of men and of angels, but do not have love, I have become a noisy gong or a clanging cymbal.

2 And if I have the gift of prophecy, and know all mysteries and all knowledge; and if I have all faith, so as to remove mountains, but do not have love, I am nothing.

3 And if I give all my possessions to feed the poor, and if I deliver my body to be burned, but do not have love, it profits me nothing.

4 Love is patient, love is kind, and is not jealous; love does not brag and is not arrogant.

5 It is not ambitious; it does not seek its own, is not provoked, it does not take into account a wrong suffered.

6 It does not rejoice in unrighteousness, but rejoices with the truth.

7 Love bears all things, believes all things, hopes all things, endures all things.

8 Love never fails; but if there are gifts of prophecy, they will be given away; if there are tongues, they will cease; if there is knowledge, it will be given away.

9 For we know in part, and we prophesy in part.

10 But when the perfect comes, the partial will be done away.

11 When I was a child, I used to speak as a child, think as a child, reason as a child; when I became a man, I did away with childish things.

12 For now we see in a class darkly, but then face to face; now I know in part, but then I shall know fully just as I also have been fully known.

13 But now abide faith, hope, love, these three; but the greatest of these is love.

From the Carmina Burana

The mistress drinks, the master drinks,
the soldier drinks, the cleric drinks,
this man drinks, that woman drinks,
the servant drinks with the maid,
the active man drinks, the lazy man drinks,
the white man drinks, the black man drinks,
the settled man drinks, the wanderer drinks,
the ignorant man drinks, the scholar drinks.

The poor man and the sick man drink,
the unknown man and the exile drink,
the boy drinks, the old man drinks,
the leader and the deacon drink,

the sister drinks, the brother drinks,
the old woman drinks, the mother drinks,
this woman drinks, that man drinks,
hundreds drink, thousands drink

Appendix C

Examen I

A.

1. d
2. c
3. b
4. a
5. d
6. b
7. a
8. d
9. c
10. d

B.

1. Are you a senator?
2. A calamity is discord.
3. There is a cure.
4. Italy is in Europe.
5. The form is human.
6. The noise is not silence.
7. A cave man is superior.
8. A mushroom is inferior.
9. Rome is in Italy.
10. Are you noble?

Examen II

A.

1. a
2. b
3. d
4. b
5. d
6. c
7. b
8. b
9. b
10. d

B.

1. I want to surpass.
2. It is good to sleep.
3. Listeners are happy.
4. Romulus was named king.
5. The face of the father is noble.
6. Eels do not command.
7. The horse rises up.
8. Old trees fall down.
9. The crowd of women fly about.
10. Beets are cooked.

Examen III

A.

1. d
2. b
3. b
4. a
5. d

6. c

7. c

8. a

9. d

10. d

B.

1. The son of the cave man is sad.

2. I will lead the horse to water.

3. Men pretended to be weak.

4. The law of the island was harsh.

5. How much money do you have?

6. There is no gold for us.

7. Two Romans carried out dinner.

8. The plan of God is not known.

9. The wife grabbed the large eel, with her right hand.

10. Not only peace but also silence pleases me.

Examen IV

A.

1. c

2. c

3. d

4. b

5. c

6. a

7. c

8. c

9. b

10. d

B.

1. On account of the queen, we were not able to sit.

2. The chicken walked across the road.

3. The bear went over the mountain.

4. The bear went into the shop.

5. I remain near you.

6. The cow jumped over the moon.

7. The deer who had horns was called Bambi.

8. The woman who had pearls was Cornelia.

9. The girl went into the shop to sing.

10. The cow was so fat that it could not jump over the moon.

Examen V

A.

1. d

2. a

3. b

4. d

5. b

6. c

7. a

8. b

9. b

10. b

B.

1. Antonia added earrings to an eel.

2. Sergius invented hanging baths (showers).

3. Divers look for these shells with great care.

4. They plant their feet on the left thigh.

5. The human body has many members.

6. Cows eat potherbs and grass.

7. There was a crowd of men.

8. Elks are similar to goats.

9. Let there be light!

10. I want to be like a chicken.

Examen Ultimum

A.

1. d
2. a
3. c
4. c
5. c
6. a
7. b
8. d
9. b
10. a

B.

1. Now there remains faith, hope, love, these three.
2. Jingle bells
3. The slave drinks, the handmaiden drinks.
4. Take four drops by mouth, twice a day.
5. The common owl is not pretty.
6. Let the buyer beware.
7. He who is silent appears to give consent.
8. Let the people rule.
9. Thus always to tyrants.
10. We learn by teaching.

Index

W–Z